ALCOHOL
AND THE
ADDICTIVE BRAIN

ALCOHOL AND THE ADDICTIVE BRAIN

New Hope for Alcoholics from Biogenetic Research

Kenneth Blum, Ph.D.
in collaboration with
James E. Payne

THE FREE PRESS
A Division of Macmillan, Inc.
NEW YORK

Maxwell Macmillan Canada
TORONTO

Maxwell Macmillan International
NEW YORK   OXFORD   SINGAPORE   SYDNEY

The Free Press
A Division of Macmillan, Inc.
866 Third Avenue, New York, N.Y. 10022

Maxwell Macmillan Canada, Inc.
1200 Eglinton Avenue East
Suite 200
Don Mills, Ontario M3C 3N1

Macmillan, Inc. is part of the Maxwell Communication Group of
Companies.

Printed in the United States of America

printing number
3   4   5   6   7   8   9   10

Library of Congress Cataloging-in-Publication Data

Blum, Kenneth.
  Alcohol and the addictive brain : new hope for alcoholics from
biogenetic research / Kenneth Blum : in collaboration with James E.
Payne.
      p.   cm.
  Includes index.
  ISBN 0-02-903701-8
    1. Alcoholism—Genetic aspects.   2. Brain—Effect of drugs on.
3. Alcohol—Physiological effect.   4. Alcoholism—Treatment.
5. Alcoholism—Prevention.   I. Payne, James E.   II. Title.
  [DNLM: 1. Alcohol, Ethyl—adverse effects.   2. Alcohol, Ethyl
—pharmacology.   3. Alcoholism—genetics.   4. Brain—drug effects.
5. Alcoholism—therapy.   6. Alcoholism—prevention & control. WM
274 B6592a]
RC565.B553   1991
616.86'1042—dc20
DNLM/DLC
for Library of Congress   90–14144
                                                                  CIP

We dedicate this book to the people who have died prematurely from alcoholism, and to those members of our families whose encouragement and patience have sustained us in our work:
to Arlene, Jeffrey, and Seth Blum;
to Marjorie, Sherry, and Robert Payne

Contents

List of Illustrations

Preface and Acknowledgments

We have written this book for two audiences. The first is alcoholics, their families, and those who are involved with alcoholics as physicians, counselors, employers, co-workers, or friends. This group includes 25 percent of the American population. The second is all those who seek to understand the complex interactions of the brain and behavior in compulsive disorders.

Our first goal is to illuminate the nature of alcoholism, which still is a subject of intense controversy, and to explore its human costs. Our second goal is to report on scientific advances that have provided new insight into the causes of alcoholism, and on research pathways that offer real promise of eventual prevention or cure.

After twenty-five years of studying alcoholism, I find profound satisfaction in knowing that productive research on addiction is accelerating in many allied disciplines, and that every month brings new insights of potential value to the clinician and the public. (The "I" in the book is Kenneth Blum, the scientist, but the work has been a collaboration, in the finest sense of the word, between James Payne and me.)

I recognize the importance of *psychological* research; for example, advances in learning theory and conditioning, and new understandings of group interaction which have brought powerful new tools to the psychiatrist and counselor.

I recognize also the importance of *sociological* concepts: For example, the view of alcoholism as a way of life which, in itself, colors the alcoholic's judgments and decisions, leading to a rejection of cultural norms and values.

But the growing weight of laboratory and clinical findings leaves no doubt in my mind that alcoholism is a *physiological disease process*, largely genetic in origin, that can be triggered or complicated by psychological or sociological influences. Consequently, although I will briefly discuss psychological and sociological views, my main focus will be on the pioneering neurophysiological, pharmacological, and biogenetic investigations that have been carried out in the past five decades.

The book is divided into two sections: *The Problem,* and *The Search for the Solution.* It presents the research findings that, in my judgment, have contributed most to our current understanding of the causes and progression of the disease of alcoholism. This is the first time that such a comprehensive effort has been made, and James Payne and I have found it an enormously exciting and gratifying adventure.

For a closer look at the work under way in this rapidly changing field, Payne and I traveled ten thousand miles and visited 26 laboratories and 9 treatment centers throughout the United States. In addition, I visited colleagues in Canada, England, France, Italy, Germany, the Orient, and Russia. After we returned, Payne went through Family Week at a local treatment center as a participant, and attended some two hundred meetings of Alcoholics Anonymous, Al-Anon, and CODA, an organization similar to Al-Anon. At the end of this period we began a two-year writing program, working together at the computer to translate the science into language understandable to a general audience.

To those colleagues who were so generous with their time when we visited their laboratories or clinics, or who through interviews—quoted throughout the book—shared their ideas and unpublished research, we express our sincerest thanks:

Michael Aldrich, Fritz-Ludlow Library, San Francisco; Zalman Amit, Department of Psychiatry, Concordia University, Montreal; William Banks, Tulane University, New Orleans; Henri Begleiter, Department of Psychiatry, State University of New York; Gerald Cohen, Department of Neurology, Mt. Sinai School of Medicine, New York; Michael Collins, Department of Biochemistry, Stritch School of Medicine, Loyola University, Chicago; Tommie Dahlmann, Certified Counselor, San Antonio; Virginia Davis, Veterans Administration Hospital, Houston; Ivan Diamond, Department of Neurology, University of California at San Franciso; Clyde Elliott, Glenwood Regional Medical Center, West Monroe; B. A. Faraj, Emory University School of Medicine, Atlanta; Gian Gessa, Instituto di Farmacologia, Universita Cagliari, Cagliari; Christina Gianoulakis, Department of Psychiatry, McGill University, Montreal; Donald Goodwin, Department of Psychiatry, University of Kansas Medical Center, Kansas City; Enoch Gordis, National Institute on Alcohol Abuse and Alcoholism (NIAAA), Rockville; Alessandro Guidotti, Fidia-

Georgetown Institute for the Neurosciences, Washington; Albert Herz, Max Planck Institute, Munich; Paula Hoffman, NIAAA, Rockville; Norman Hoffmann, CATOR, St. Paul; Daryl Inaba, Haight-Ashbury Free Medical Clinic, San Francisco; Yedy Israel, Addiction Research Foundation, Toronto; E. Roy John, Brain Research Laboratory, New York University Medical Center, New York; Harold Kalant, Department of Pharmacology, University of Toronto, Toronto; Philip Knowles, Republic Health Systems, Dallas; Wayne Kritzberg, Certified Counselor, Austin; Frederick Lemere, Schick Shadel Hospitals, Seattle; Horace Loh, Department of Pharmacology, University of California at San Francisco; Earl Marsh, Addictionologist, San Francisco; Robert Maslansky, Department of Psychiatry, Bellevue Hospital, New York University Medical Center, New York; Gerald McClearn, Pennsylvania State University, University Park; Robert D. Myers, Department of Pharmacology and Psychiatry, East North Carolina University, Greenville; Claudio Naranjo, Department of Psychiatry, University of Toronto, Toronto; Ernest Noble, Department of Psychiatry, University of California at Los Angeles; Charles O'Brien, Department of Psychiatry, University of Pennsylvania, Philadelphia; Nicholas Pace, Pace Health Services, New York; Meg Patterson, Addictionologist, London; Stephen Paul, National Institute of Mental Health, Rockville; David Ross, Department of Pharmacology, University of Texas Health Science Center, San Antonio; Kenneth Roy, Woodland Hills Hospital, New Orleans; Marc Schuckit, Department of Psychiatry, University of California at San Diego; Peter Sheridan, University of Texas Health Science Center, San Antonio; Eric Simon, Department of Psychiatry, New York University Medical Center, New York; David Smith, Youth Projects, San Francisco; James Smith, Schick Shadel Hospitals, Seattle; Solomon Snyder, Department of Pharmacology, Johns Hopkins University Medical Center, Baltimore; John Stark, Woodland Hills Hospital, New Orleans; Larry Stein, Department of Pharmacology, University of California at Irvine; Paul Sze, Department of Pharmacology, Chicago Medical School, Chicago; Boris Tabakoff, NIAAA, Rockville; M. K. Ticku, Department of Pharmacology, University of Texas Health Science Center, San Antonio; Joseph R. Volpicelli, Department of Psychiatry, University of Pennsylvania, Philadelphia; John Wallace, Edgehill-Newport Hospital, Newport; E. Leong Way, Department of Pharmacology, University of California at San Francisco; Sharon Wegscheider-Cruse, Onsite Training and Consulting, Inc., Rapid City; Lawrence Wharton, Faulkner Treatment Center, Austin; George Woody, Department of Psychiatry, University of Pennsylvania, Philadelphia.

We also want to express our special gratitude to A. H. Briggs, Chairman, Department of Pharmacology, University of Texas Health Science Center, San Antonio; to the staff of the Health Science Center library; to Jeffrey Blum and Nicholas Montfort for their diligent assistance in literature searches; to Marjorie Payne for her painstaking and invaluable editorial assistance; to Cleo Murphy, Roberta Case, and David Smith of the Faulkner Center in Austin for their insight as counselors that helped us understand the treatment experience; and to Schick Shadel Hospital, Fidia Pharmaceutical Corporation, and NeuroGenesis, Inc., for their grant support.

Finally, we want to pay a heartfelt tribute to Laura Wolff for her original contribution to the conception of the book, and to our editor Susan Milmoe and her staff for their insight, patience, unfailing encouragement, and wise criticism at every stage of the project.

We are also grateful to Charles Whitehead at the University of Texas Health Science Center, San Antonio, for preparing the artwork.

SECTION
ONE

THE PROBLEM
AND EARLY
ATTEMPTS
TO DEFINE AND
COPE WITH IT

1

Introduction: From Stigma to Solutions

Alcoholism is one of the most disruptive problems in our society. The following careful estimates place it in perspective:

- In the United States, more than 15 million adults are believed to experience problems as a direct result of their own alcohol use. At least 9,171,000 are considered alcohol dependent, and another 5,929,000 are considered alcohol abusers.
- Nearly half of the violent deaths from accidents, suicide, and homicide are alcohol related.
- Approximately half of all automobile crash fatalities involve alcohol. It is estimated that the risk of a fatal crash, per mile driven, is at least eight times higher for a drunk driver than for a sober one.
- Alcohol abuse is associated with a wide range of diseases and disorders, including liver disease, cancer, and cardiovascular problems. Cirrhosis of the liver, alone, caused primarily by heavy drinking, was responsible for nearly 27,000 deaths in 1986.
- The estimated cost of health care in the United States for accidents and illnesses related to alcohol abuse in 1986 was $16.5 billion.
- The total cost to the country as a whole for alcohol abuse, including lost employment and reduced productivity, was an estimated $128.3 billion.[1]

The social effects are equally severe. In the United States, at least 40 million wives, husbands, children, and close relatives suffer from the alcoholic's destructive behavior. In the community, other millions of friends, teachers, employers, and co-workers are similarly, though less directly affected. It is no exaggeration to call alcoholism a social plague.

3

Against this background the figures on research spending take on stark significance. According to information provided by the National Institute on Drug and Alcohol Abuse Clearing House, the National Institute of Heart and Lung Disease, and the National Cancer Institute, estimated spending in the United States for 1989 was:

- Cancer research: $1,186,320,000
- Heart and vascular research: $929,981,000
- Alcoholism research: $69,560,000

These figures reflect a deep-seated social and personal conflict about alcohol. We rhapsodize about the taste and bouquet of fine wines, and have built a cultural mystique around the tavern and bar. We use alcohol as a personal reward after hard work or to relax after a trying day, and as a social lubricant during the business lunch, cocktail hour, and holiday dinner.

On the other hand we recognize, in a general way, the dangers of alcohol; for example, drunk driving and violence. We attach a powerful stigma to those individuals, particularly women, who habitually drink too much; and, as shown in chapter 2, periodically we rise up and write laws to limit the sale of alcohol or actually prohibit its use—yet we provide only minimal support for research into the causes and treatment of alcoholism.

Positive and negative attitudes toward alcohol have alternated at intervals in most Western societies throughout history. Complicating this conflict have been two blind spots. First, as described in chapters 2 and 3, as long as we can, we refuse to face the fact of alcoholism in ourselves, our families, our neighbors, and among our fellow workers. When we think of the "alcoholic" we tend to think of the Bowery bum, the wife beater, or the party clown who passes out under the table. We try to ignore the self-destruction going on in those alcoholics we love or with whom we are associated. If the individuals are relatives, friends, or co-workers, we are likely to do serious harm by covering up for them, literally enabling them to develop and maintain their habit.

Second, despite a hundred years of accumulating scientific and clinical evidence that has often been reported in the press and in popular books, many people—including some physicians and psychiatrists—still resist the idea that alcoholism is a disease, or a serious physiological disorder. Somehow, we prefer to believe that "those people who drink too much" are simply weak-willed or morally deficient, and could change their behavior if they wanted to—an attitude that was reflected in the recent ruling by the U.S. Supreme Court in which alcoholism was characterized as willful misconduct.[2]

This attitude enables us to regard alcoholism as an embarrassment, and not a national medical problem—at a level with cancer and heart disease—that must be solved.

Because of this attitude, too, most nonalcoholics, and many members of alcoholic families in the past have shied away from learning the truth about alcoholism, and consequently have remained uninformed about its causes and profoundly ignorant of the disastrous effects that alcohol addiction has on the individual, the family, and the society. This lack of knowledge and insight further lowers the social priority of research and treatment.

For the alcoholic, however, the biopsychic nature of the disease is all too real. There may be denial, but as the addiction develops, life becomes a nightmarish progression of periods of short-term release and euphoria, followed by anxiety, guilt, anger, or depression; growing physical disability; loss of competence, self-esteem, love, and friendship; increasing alienation growing out of self-distrust and self-disgust; and—if untreated—death.

In the family, as shown in chapter 2, the alcoholic individual and the other family members interact to make home life unpleasant or unbearable. The alcoholic defends his or her habit angrily and stubbornly, denying the addiction and seeking to shift the blame. The family members try to control the drinking by pleading, getting angry, making accusations, and bargaining, knowing that the effort will fail, but feeling compelled to try. And in the midst of arguments, abuse, or outright physical cruelty, they all cooperate in an effort to hide the drinking and its consequences from friends, neighbors, and employers. The operative words are *concealment* and *silence*.

Add to this tragic drama the high probability that the children in the family are genetically at risk of becoming alcoholics in their turn, and the seriousness and scope of the problem become apparent. Even if they do not develop a drinking habit, some or all of the children are likely to exhibit various types of irrational anxiety, anger, and depression characteristic of the alcoholic, helping to make the family even more dysfunctional.

Members of the alcoholic family generally are driven by the need to control destructive behavior and suppress or hide feelings of guilt and shame. More importantly, perhaps, the children have no satisfactory role model.

Development of effective treatment for alcoholism has long been hindered by the failure to understand its nature. There were occasional speculations that alcoholism might be approached as a medical problem, but not until late in the eighteenth century did this viewpoint begin to be respectable. In 1785, a Philadelphia physician named Benjamin Rush published a temperance tract entitled *An inquiry into the Effects of Ardent Spirits upon the Human Mind and Body* in which he made the blunt statement that alcoholism is a disease. In that same year, a British physician named Thomas Trotter published a tract in which he also advanced this point of view.[3]

This disease concept stimulated the development of a wide variety of new treatment methods during the nineteenth and early twentieth centuries. The better ones combined medical treatment for the direct physiological effects of alcoholism with some form of psychological counseling to cope with associated behavioral problems.

Beginning in 1935, a new, nonprofessional movement called Alcoholics Anonymous (AA) came into being. It was to develop side by side with professional treatment programs, and has become a major force in coping with alcoholism, as shown in chapter 3. AA members meet in small groups, provide encouragement and support for each other, strive for total abstinence, and follow a Twelve-Step program that encourages religious faith and self-honesty. AA subscribes to the disease concept of alcoholism. Two related groups called Al-Anon and Alateen were formed later. Al-Anon is primarily for spouses and children of alcoholics; Alateen is for teenage children of alcoholic families. Independent groups called Alatots have also been formed around the country to serve children from 4 to 12 years of age.

Not until the mid-twentieth century, however, was a serious effort made to develop a systematic description of alcoholism that reflected clinical observations. As explained in chapter 6, E. M. Jellinek, director of the Yale University Center of Alcohol Studies, advanced a theory of five types of alcoholism, beginning with psychological addiction and ending with binge drinking. He classed two of these types as belonging in the disease category, two as not belonging in it, and one as problematical. He saw the disease as a progression which, if unchecked, could kill directly or through secondary medical complications.[4]

The recognition that alcoholism was a problem that might respond to professional treatment, and that for many the self-help approach of AA could lead to sobriety, spurred a tremendous growth in the number of alcoholics seeking help with their problem. In the year ending on October 31, 1987, an estimated 1,430,000 clients were treated in 5,586 alcoholism treatment facilities in the United States. Eighty-five percent received outpatient care; 15 percent were treated in inpatient or residential settings.[5]

Membership in Alcoholics Anonymous was also expanding rapidly.

According to figures supplied by Alcoholics Anonymous, Inc., membership in the United States and Canada rose from an estimated 170,000 in 1968, to approximately 900,000 in 1989 (see chapter 3).[6]

These figures are encouraging, but if the estimated 1,430,000 undergoing professional treatment are added to the 900,000 in AA, this makes a total of only 2,330,000 million who are receiving significant help. Furthermore, the treatment figures and the AA figures overlap, for most patients in treatment centers are encouraged to join AA. This may bring the total number who are receiving assistance to well below the 2 million mark—probably no more than one in five of those who have a severe drinking problem.

A substantial percentage of individuals who do seek help eventually "backslide" and resume drinking. Some remain technically sober but continue to exhibit a high level of anxiety, anger, or other forms of disruptive behavior characteristic of the alcoholic. They also tend to abuse other substances ranging from food, coffee, sugar, and cigarettes to cocaine and heroin.

However, although statistics on the success of the Alcoholics Anonymous program, and of the various professional treatment programs, are not very dependable, there is no question that thousands of people are helped to achieve sobriety each year. Figures provided by the General Services Office of Alcoholics Anonymous in New York, for example, show that of those who attend meetings, a member with less than one year's sobriety has approximately a 40 percent chance of remaining sober another year; and a member with more than five years' sobriety has approximately a 90 percent chance of remaining sober another year. But these figures are based largely on self-reporting, and do not reflect the experiences of those who stop attending meetings at some stage in the recovery process.

An estimate of the effectiveness of professional treatment programs is provided by a study of 2,303 patients from 22 adult programs in 12 states carried out by CATOR, the Chemical Abuse/Addiction Treatment Outcome Registry of St. Paul, Minnesota. Two years after completion of treatment, 57 percent of those surveyed reported that they had remained completely abstinent. This is highly encouraging, but again, despite some degree of cross-checking with friends or relatives, the figures are derived largely from self-reporting.[7]

One problem in interpreting posttreatment statistics arises from the fact that abstinence is only one measure of recovery. How many succeeded in achieving a feeling of well-being and the joy of living? How many were still troubled by feelings of low self-esteem? How many remained abnormally self-centered? How many continued to be subject to periods of deep anxiety, or sudden attacks of explosive anger? How many substituted another abusable substance such as caffeine or sugar? How many committed suicide?

The situation has improved greatly in the last half century, but I feel that we have just begun. Until we achieve a deeper knowledge of the disease we cannot develop truly satisfactory methods of prevention and treatment.

As with other serious and mysterious diseases such as cancer, Alzheimer's, and AIDS, knowledge about alcoholism can come only through research and clinical experience. As outlined in chapter 4, today's treatment facilities and procedures reflect research carried out over the past three decades. Research findings in the 1990s may not be fully reflected in new treatment facilities and procedures before the year 2010. The quality of that research will determine the efficacy of those treatment programs.

Most scientists currently working in the field of addiction agree that alcoholism is the result—at least in part—of deficiencies or imbalances in brain chemistry—perhaps genetic in origin. Individuals experience the effects of these abnormalities through what have come to be known as the "reward centers" in the brain. As explained in chapters 8 and 9, if these centers are supplied with adequate amounts of certain brain chemicals, they initiate feelings of well-being and contentment. If the chemicals are undersupplied, or if the proportions of essential substances are out of balance, the individual may experience a wide range of unpleasant feelings ranging from restlessness and discontent to anxiety, anger, depression, or craving.

Through biogenetic and neuropharmacological research we are slowly moving toward solutions to this complex problem, learning what causes the deficiencies and imbalances and how they can be detected. We are developing formulae and methods that eventually may enable physicians to correct the problem and restore biochemical balance. We are not there yet, but with continued research we eventually will reach the goal.

2

Alcoholism: A Legacy of Pain for Alcoholics, Families, and Society

1
Alcohol and Society

For many thousands of years, human beings have had a love/hate relationship with alcohol. On the one hand, normal people want to protect their right to enjoy the pleasure that alcohol brings them. On the other hand, they want to deny alcohol to those who use it to damage or destroy their own lives or interfere with the lives of others. So in one decade or century people and governments may adopt a permissive attitude toward drinking, while in another they may mount a massive crusade to outlaw alcohol once and for all.[1]

No one knows when the first beer was brewed, but it was probably earlier than 5,000 B.C. Wine dates back to at least 3,000 B.C.; brandy appeared late in the twelfth or early thirteenth century, but grain-based "hard" liquors such as whiskey and gin had very little impact until the seventeenth century.

Whatever the form, alcohol aroused controversy. In about the fourth century B.C., Xenophon criticized the Greeks (except the Spartans) for their excessive drinking. Aristotle, Theophrastus, Chamaeleon, and Hieronomus wrote essays on drunkenness. In 36 B.C., Diodorus Siclus chastised the Gauls for their drinking. Pliny, writing in the first century A.D., described the alcoholic: "Pallor, pendulous cheeks, bloodshot eyes, tremulous hands which spill the full cup . . . sleep disturbed by the

9

furies." He added that "the habit of drinking increases the appetite for it . . ."

The sixth-century monk St. Gildas accused British chieftains of going into battle drunk and thereby leading Britain to ruin. In the mid-1300s, Emperor Charles IV of Germany said that the vice of drunkenness led to blasphemy, murder, and manslaughter, and that such vices and crimes have rendered the Germans "despised and condemned of all foreign nations." At the Diet of Worms in 1495, Emperor Maximilian I ordered all electors, princes, prelates, counts, knights, and gentlemen to "discountenance and severely punish drunkenness."

In 1524, an early temperance movement sprang up in Heidelberg, with goals prefiguring those of Alcoholics Anonymous. A brotherhood of princes, bishops, and nobles pledged themselves to abstain from "full swilling" and the drinking of healths—except in Lower Saxony, Pomerania, and Mecklenburg where, it was held, moderation was impossible!

The struggle in Great Britain was a classic one. Samuel Pepys struck some early blows for sobriety in his diary in the year 1662. On January 26, for example, he said:

> But thanks to God, since my leaving drinking of wine, I do find myself much better and do mind my business better and do spend less money, and less time lost in idle company . . .

Toward the end of the seventeenth century, the British government began a series of massive policy reversals on alcohol. The first action promoted the production of spirits as a means of utilizing surplus grain supplies, and was so successful that it touched off an epidemic of gin abuse among the lower classes of London. To put a halt to the epidemic, Parliament in 1729 passed a law requiring retailers to pay an excise tax, and forbidding the sale of spirits on the streets. The law reduced the gin trade, but the explosive reaction of gin lovers forced the government to repeal the law a few years later.

But the rising death rate, attributed largely to excessive gin drinking, could not be ignored. The sentiment for control was expressed in a quotation from Thomas Wilson's tract *Distilled Liquors the Bane of the Nation*, published in 1736:

> Everyone who now passes thro' the Streets of this great Metropolis, and looks into the Distillers Shops . . . must see . . . a Crowd of poor ragged People, cursing and quarreling with one another, over repeated glasses of these destructive Liquors. . . . [I]n one place . . .

a Trader has a large empty Room backward, where as his wretched
Guests get intoxicated, they are laid together in Heaps, promiscuously,
Men, Women, and Children, till they recover their Senses.

In 1736, Parliament passed a new and harsher Gin Act. The Preamble
to the Act stated that widespread drinking, especially among "people
of lower or inferior rank," was leading to "the destruction of their health,
rendering them unfit for labour and business, debauching their morals,
and inciting them to perpetuate all manner of vices." An outbreak of
bootlegging and smuggling soon forced the government to reconsider,
and in 1743 a less restrictive law was passed that proved to be more
enforceable, and the gin epidemic began to wane.

The controversy over alcohol extended into the medical profession,
too. Many physicians regarded alcohol as a panacea. It was prescribed
for a variety of ailments, was a component in many medications, was
widely used as an anesthetic, and was considered a protection against
exposure to cold and damp weather. But the medical community was
beginning to ask serious questions about alcohol. Many physicians were
becoming aware that moderate drinking for pleasure was quite different
from habitual drinking to excess. Blunt statements that alcoholism is a
disease were beginning to be heard.

The British physician Thomas Trotter in his "Essay, Medical, Philo-
sophical and Chemical on Drunkenness" made his views known, defining
drunkenness in medical terms as "strictly speaking . . . a disease; produced by a remote cause, and giving birth to actions and movements
in the living body that disorder the functions of health."

The American physician Benjamin Rush attracted wide attention in
1784 when he published *An Inquiry into the Effects of Ardent Spirits
upon the Human Body and Mind.* He provided powerful support for the
temperance movement when he questioned the beneficial effects of alcohol, and argued against its use in treatment. He stated that habitual
drinking is a disease caused by alcohol, and that its secondary effects
include liver disease, jaundice, consumption, epilepsy, gout, and mad-
ness. He said that the cure for habitual drinking is abstinence.[2]

Attitudes toward drinking in the United States underwent similar
painful reversals. In Colonial times, beer and cider were common beverages in the home as well as in the tavern. At weddings, barn raisings,
and harvest time, the jug and the cask were likely to be the center of
attention. During this period there was little opposition to alcohol itself,
but penalties for drunkenness included fines, jail terms, the stocks, or
public flogging.

By the late eighteenth century, however, there was a disturbing trend away from beer and ale toward distilled spirits. The result was that more people got drunker, faster, and thoughtful people in the post-Revolution era began to worry about the effect of "hard" liquor on individuals and society.

A sign of the times was the founding of the Washington Temperance Society in 1840 by six former heavy drinkers in Baltimore. Members vowed to "go dry" and to help others do likewise. The movement spread rapidly to New York and from there to other states. Of some 600,000 who had joined by the late 1840s, some 150,000 were listed as successfully recovered. The movement eventually declined, but its record remained to encourage others.

On June 2, 1851, the governor of Maine signed into law a bill prohibiting the sale of beverage alcohol in the state. By 1855, 12 additional states had enacted similar laws of their own. But politicians in the United States were soon to learn the lesson that politicians in other countries had learned before them: It is easier to pass prohibition laws than to enforce them. A reaction against the temperance movement set in, the Maine law was replaced by a weaker version, and eventually only three of the state prohibition laws remained on the books. By the beginning of the Civil War prohibition had collapsed as a major social and political issue.

To temperance advocates, however, such opposition was a mere setback. Women were now joining the crusade, holding "pray-ins" in front of saloons, hotels with bars, and drugstores that sold "medicinal" liquor. Wives of alcoholics brought suit against barkeepers in some areas, and scores of liquor-selling establishments were forced to close their doors.

In December 1874, at a women's convention in Cleveland, Ohio, the Women's Christian Temperance Union was organized. Their main target was the saloons, which they felt were a violation of the American moral code. Under the leadership of Frances Willard who took charge in 1879, the WCTU became the first genuine, broad-based women's political reform movement.

The stage was being set for Prohibition. In the 1890s, Carry Nation mounted a dramatic attack against saloons, rallying hundreds of supporters to her cause, but the movement was short-lived. Her tactics apparently were too violent for many believers who took the word "temperance" seriously in all of its connotations.

Also in the 1890s, the Anti-Saloon League was founded by the Reverend Dr. Howard Hyde Russell to rally religious support for the political movement against the liquor trade. Its tactics involved "local option," aimed at drying up individual towns and counties, and it quickly developed into a strong lobby for prohibition.

In 1916, their efforts paid off. So many League-endorsed candidates were elected that a national Prohibition Amendment was suddenly in reach, and in December 1917, the eighteenth Amendment was sent to the states for ratification. In January 1919, the Amendment was ratified by the thirty-sixth state. The enabling legislation was the Volstead Act.

Prohibition was destined to prove in dramatic fashion that a disease cannot be legislated away. Nonalcoholics joined alcoholics in a spreading national revolt that spun off crime like a hurricane spawns tornadoes. When the Act was repealed in 1933, the United States emerged from a bad dream just in time to enter the Depression.

But in retrospect we had been given a much-needed lesson from which we are only now beginning to benefit. The solution to the problem of alcoholism cannot be found in the ballot box, or in the policeman's club or gun. It can be found only in the laboratory where the disease process can be explored, in the hospital or treatment center where laboratory findings can be applied, and in the home, the classroom, and the media where people can be informed of the nature of the disease that makes individuals use alcohol destructively.

2
The Alcoholic

From *The First Special Report to the U.S. Congress on Alcohol & Health:*

The pain the alcoholic person feels is the pain of self-loathing and humiliation . . . from loss of the respect of his family and friends . . . from growing isolation and loneliness . . . from the awareness that he is throwing away much of his unique and creative self and gradually destroying his body and soul. He doesn't usually mean to get drunk, really drunk—he just wants to take the value from alcohol. Getting drunk, really drunk as only an alcoholic person becomes, is a nightmare of lost memories, retching, vertigo, the shakes, and a profound melancholy of regret. Sometimes it becomes a living nightmare of terrifying visions, screaming accusatory voices, and convulsions.

Who would seek such experiences knowingly? . . .[3]

To the normal individual, alcohol is a pleasant indulgence. It eases tension, releases inhibitions, promotes conviviality, and generates temporary feelings of well-being. Occasional overindulgence may lead to foolish or destructive behavior, but if used in moderation alcohol does not appear to injure health, or lead to habitual excessive drinking. (However, women should not drink during pregnancy to avoid possible danger to the developing fetus.) A summation of the normal person's attitude would be: "I enjoy drinking, but I can drink or leave it alone, and I don't understand why other people can't do the same."

The destructive potential of alcohol is apparent, however, even in this normal individual. When alcohol in sufficient quantity reaches the cerebral cortex, speech is slurred and thinking becomes confused. When the cerebellum is reached, balance and coordination are affected; the individual staggers and has trouble holding a match or cup. If the limbic system becomes involved, emotions are likely to be exaggerated, and boisterous or aggressive behavior, even violent behavior, may result. Judgment is clouded, and the individual tends to act in a primitive, unthinking manner.

If the normal person drinks until intoxicated, the ability to handle complex tasks is impaired, speech becomes even more slurred, and a loss of balance may make walking difficult or impossible. Speed and distance judgments are faulty, and accidental injury becomes a high probability.

To the alcoholic, who lives daily with a high level of anxiety and strong feelings of inadequacy and low self-esteem, and who may experience destructive pressures of anger or hostility, or the debilitating "low" of depression, alcohol seems not an indulgence but a necessity. The negative feelings are a constant source of emotional pain, a pain so powerful it cannot be ignored, and so unendurable it must be suppressed; an unending legacy of pain. Alcohol temporarily masks these feelings or reduces their intensity. That is why this chemical, in the early stages of alcoholism, seems such a welcome friend. For a little while it makes the pain go away.

Physicians have long theorized that alcoholism is a disease; now scientists are learning that the behavioral as well as the physical problems associated with alcoholism are all part of a disease syndrome. It is the *disease* that makes life unbearable for the alcoholic and the members of the alcoholic's family.

The early symptoms of the disease of alcoholism, even before drinking begins, are often intense forms of restlessness, anxiety, stubbornness, and anger that drive the alcoholic into self-destructive, asocial, or antisocial behavior. Alcohol sets the trap by demonstrating that it can ease the pressure temporarily, and provide brief feelings of pleasure and well-being.[4]

As the alcoholic takes the bait and begins drinking more and more, the nature of the trap becomes evident. When the initial "high" wears off, there is an increase in anxiety, hostility, or depression, and more alcohol must be consumed to regain the good feeling. As drinking continues over time, relationships with family, friends, and co-workers become progressively more difficult; body functions are damaged; mind functions such as memory and reasoning are disturbed or diminished; and a powerful craving for more alcohol is generated.

Once the trap has snapped shut, even though the alcoholic may realize the danger, the short-term rewards are so great and the urge is so powerful that the drinking habit has to be protected, and its adverse effects denied. At the same time, the alcoholic cannot escape the realization that he/she is different from normal people, is in trouble, and has lost control. Feelings of failure, irritability, or anger give rise to shame and guilt and they, too, must be denied. The overwhelming conviction is that alcohol cannot be given up.

Other psychological symptoms now begin to appear, and become more apparent as the disease progresses. Memory, reasoning, and judgment become increasingly faulty. Impulsiveness, irritability, and arrogance, even megalomania, may alternate with a growing need for sympathy and understanding. There may be a loss of inhibitions, leading to bizarre behavior and violations of personal ethics; reality may become hazy, giving way to a rich fantasy life sometimes accompanied by aggressive sexual behavior. Heavy drinking bouts may be followed by blackouts that leave no memory of events, or a distorted memory that ignores unpleasant happenings.

A complicating factor is that, as the alcoholic's own shortcomings multiply, the effort to shift the blame to others intensifies. This effort often leads to highly manipulative behavior and a disregard for truth.

Overall, the alcoholic is likely to experience a developing sense of panic, interspersed with irritability, quick outbursts of rage, or periods of deep depression. Such behavior, and the consequent adverse reaction of family, co-workers, and friends, inevitably leads to growing loneliness, and feelings of guilt or remorse that find expression in an all-pervading sadness.

Shame may now drive the alcoholic to enlist the aid of family members in hiding alcohol-related personal and family problems from friends and co-workers; but underneath there is an increasing concentration on self.

This apparent contradiction reflects a conflict between feelings of indifference toward others, and feelings of anxious dependence.

If depression or sadness persists, a preoccupation with suicide may develop. The seriousness of the intention in a particular individual is difficult to determine, but many alcoholics commit suicide, and many more attempt it—a higher proportion than in the normal population.[5]

As heavy drinking becomes habitual, serious physiological effects begin to appear. The lining of the esophagus may become irritated, leading to swelling. Irritation of the stomach and intestines may cause severe gastritis or ulceration. Unexcreted uric acid may crystallize in body tissues and joints, producing swelling and soreness. Hypoglycemia may interfere with the supply of glucose needed to raise blood sugar levels. An excess of catecholamines may cause excessive perspiration, tremor, fast pulse, and continuing waves of anxiety.

As nutritional deficiencies increase, the alcoholic may experience a loss of sensation in legs, ankles, and feet, and perhaps in hands and arms. Eventually the deep reflexes in these areas may weaken. If Wernicke's syndrome develops, it may bring vision problems, mental confusion, and a clouding of consciousness. If Korsakoff's psychosis develops, the alcoholic may experience severe memory defects and disorientation.

The liver becomes heavily involved. In the healthy body, the liver synthesizes proteins from amino acids, helps to metabolize fats and carbohydrates, detoxifies potentially dangerous compounds, and metabolizes alcohol. However, its capabilities are limited. The healthy adult liver can only metabolize the equivalent of one can of beer per hour, and heavy drinking can overload the system.

An early effect is an increase in liver fat, a condition called hepatosis. More drinking may lead to hepatitis, a condition which causes the death of liver cells. If heavy drinking continues, cirrhosis may develop with a consequent scarring of liver tissue. Scarring decreases blood flow in the liver, interferes with its detoxification processes, and reduces its ability to produce proteins needed for the maintenance of the body.

In pregnant women, heavy drinking can lead to the dangerous "fetal alcohol syndrome" as alcohol penetrates the placenta and reaches the unborn child. Continued exposure of the fetus to alcohol can lead to retardation as well as to structural and functional disorders such as incomplete hand development, defective eyelids, and brain abnormalities that cause impairment of both intellectual and motor abilities.

As heavy drinking continues in men or women, secondary physical deterioration may affect any cell, organ, function, or system in the body. Thus alcohol may become a factor in cancer, pneumonia, circulatory and heart ailments, and a wide variety of other physiological problems.

If the heavy drinker is suddenly deprived of alcohol, the withdrawal syndrome sets in: a response characterized by tremors, nausea, weakness, and a fast heart rate, followed by an increase in anxiety or hostility. If severe, withdrawal may be accompanied by delirium, clouding of consciousness, disorientation, seizures, and—in some instances—hallucinations. Breathing and pulse rate may become irregular, sleep is disturbed, tremors may recur, and the individual is likely to experience high levels of anxiety, frustration, irritability, or depression. Without careful treatment, this syndrome can lead to convulsions and death.

Probably the most frustrating effect of alcoholism for physicians, counselors, friends, and families is the phenomenon of *denial*. Convinced that alcohol is the only defense against his/her unbearable emotional pain and physiological need, the alcoholic regards any attempt to interfere with drinking as a personal attack that must be defeated at all costs. The lying, the evasions, the hiding of bottles, the broken promises, the attempts to shift blame, followed by pleas for patience and understanding—all are devices used to protect the drinking habit.

Characteristics of the Alcoholic

As a part of the disease syndrome, the typical alcoholic displays many or most of the following characteristics:

- restlessness, impulsiveness, anxiety
- selfishness, self-centeredness, lack of consideration
- stubbornness, ill humor, irritability, anger, rage
- depression, self-destructiveness, contactlessness
- physical cruelty, brawling, child or husband/wife abuse
- arrogance that may lead either to aggression or to coldness and withdrawal
- aggressive sexuality, often accompanied by infidelity, which may give way to sexual disinterest or impotence
- lying, deceit, broken promises
- low self-esteem, shame, guilt, remorse
- reduced mental and physical function; eventually, blackouts
- susceptibility to other diseases
- denial that there is a drinking problem
- and always, loneliness.

Types of Alcoholics

The particular set of characteristics exhibited will vary from case to case, determined in considerable part by the type to which the alcoholic belongs. The types have been variously classified, and I will discuss some of these classifications later. But for present purposes I will consider just two general types:

1. Alcoholics who inherit a predisposition to compulsive drinking. There is evidence that their brain wave patterns and brain chemistry are abnormal, and they may have trouble performing certain cognitive tasks. My observation, and that of others, has been that these genetic alcoholics, once they begin drinking heavily, are rarely able to achieve sobriety without professional assistance; have difficulty remaining in treatment programs; and have a comparatively low recovery rate. If they achieve sobriety through an act of will, without treatment, they are likely to become "dry drunks"; that is, they remain sober, but retain many of the behavioral characteristics of the alcoholic.

2. Alcoholics who may not have a genetic anomaly, but develop a habit of excessive drinking as the result of long-continued stress or long-term social drinking. Whatever the superficial motivation, pro-longed heavy drinking probably produces progressive changes in brain chemistry that lead to craving. If stress is removed, or if environmental conditions change so that drinking is not encouraged, these alcoholics respond well to treatment and their chances of recovery are favorable. They sometimes are able to stop drinking of their own volition, unaided.

In either case, the environment acts as the trigger, initiating the actual onset of the disease.

Prior to the beginning of scientific research into the causes and nature of alcoholism, these observational and anecdotal insights were the source of most of our knowledge about the disease. We knew how alcoholics looked and behaved when under the influence, but why they drank was a profound mystery. It was a question asked most frequently by their spouses and children.

3

Families of Alcoholics

Over the last century, people have begun to have some general under-standing of the plight of the alcoholic. We are slowly becoming aware that behind the drunken behavior, the lies and broken promises, the selfishness and stubbornness and anger is a frightened individual suffering from a deadly physical disease, in need of help.

But much of the public, and many physicians and psychiatrists, have no such insight into the peculiar hell family members experience as they attempt to adjust to life with an alcoholic. Only in recent years has there been a determined effort to study and understand their torment, and the abnormalities that develop in their behavior. Yet by conservative estimates there are at least 40 million family members directly involved with alcoholics in the United States today.

SPOUSES OF ALCOHOLICS

We have seen how the alcoholic experiences the disease. Now let us look briefly at the situation confronting spouses attempting to cope with an alcoholic. Two important determining factors are their own genetic predisposition, and the situation in their childhood home. The most common patterns are:

1. *Spouses who are not alcoholic, and whose parents were not alcoholic.* Without the blurring effect of alcohol, and without the behavioral problems common to adult children of alcoholics, they have the best chance of cooperating with their marital partner's recovery program, and helping to restore rationality to the alcoholic family.
2. *Spouses who are not practicing alcoholics, but who had one or more alcoholic parents.* Even though they are not suffering from the effects of excessive drinking, they may exhibit certain characteristics, common to adult children of alcoholics, that will interfere with the alcoholic's recovery process, and contribute to the irrationality of the family.
3. *Spouses who have a drinking problem, but whose parents were not alcoholic.* Their drinking problem will complicate the recovery process of the alcoholic, and add to the irrationality of the family, but they may not be burdened by some of the destructive characteristics of those who have the alcoholic inheritance.
4. *Spouses who are alcoholic, and who had one or more parents who were alcoholic.* With both a drinking problem and the behavioral distortions common to adult children of alcoholic parents, they will have a severe handicap as they try to achieve a joint recovery with their marital partner and rebuild the family.

Against this background, I will describe the experiences of two dysfunctional alcoholic families to illustrate some of the complex interactions that can develop. In the first case, the immediate families of both the husband and wife were nonalcoholic, but under stress the wife developed a drinking habit. In the second case, both the husband and wife were alcoholic, and came from alcoholic families.

The Case of John and Janette K.

John K. was a college professor whose family tree for at least three generations had been free of alcoholism. As a young man he had experimented with beer, but only briefly. He enjoyed the "high," but he did not like the "low" that followed.

When he was thirty he married Janette M. She, too, was a teacher, and the first two years of their life together were full of pleasure for them both. The first sign of trouble in their marriage came early in the third year when Janette learned that she could never have a child. She reacted first with disbelief, then with shame, then with anger. Although the doctor had said specifically that John was not at fault, she began to resent him, and her temper ignited at the least provocation.

When the superintendent of her school put her up for promotion to principal she was delighted, but as she moved into her new job she was dismayed to find how much work and responsibility were involved. Her stress level rose, and she began to have trouble sleeping.

At about this time her attitude toward alcohol began to change. Neither of her parents was alcoholic, and she had been a teetotaler since her marriage, but she now began to accept wine at parties, and with increasing frequency there was a strong smell of alcohol on her breath when John came home after an evening class. When he asked her about it she flared into anger. Later, she was penitent and admitted that she had drunk several glasses of wine, but said that she could handle it.

"I used to drink quite a bit in college," she said, "but it was never a problem, so don't worry."

Over the next year she drank only moderately when he was present, but he began to suspect that she was drinking more when she was alone in the house. Then at 3:00 A.M. one morning he wakened and found her in the kitchen with a half-empty bottle of gin. They had a terrible row, and she threatened to leave him if he did not stop harassing her about drinking. Finally she broke into tears, and he took her in his arms and comforted her.

But the next evening when he came home after his late class she had passed out on the sofa. He helped her into bed, and waited till morning to talk about it. She seemed confused and deeply ashamed. "I have been drinking too much," Janette admitted, "but I'm going to stop it. I've been thinking about children again, and it makes me crazy. I promise you, it won't happen again."

She seemed to become warmer and more affectionate during the remainder of the week, but on Monday when he came home late he found her passed out on the sofa again. Next morning she remembered little of the evening.

Now began for both of them a nightmare that was to last for nearly ten years. Every time she got drunk they would have terrible, endless arguments. The next day, she would apologize and promise to drink less, and he would believe her; but each time she broke her promise, and he felt betrayed.

Determined to help her break the habit, he began to empty bottles, and forbade her to buy more, but her response was to buy bottles and conceal them around the house. On one Saturday afternoon while she was out shopping he did a house search and found four bottles of blended liquor and three bottles of gin in various hiding places in the house, basement and garage. When he showed them to her she became enraged and screamed at him.

Janette's frustration about childlessness was continually on her mind. When she was sober she talked reasonably about the problem, but when she was drunk she questioned his virility and threatened to look for a man who could give her a child. When he reminded her of the doctor's report she said "Screw the doctor! You men hang together." When he suggested adopting a child she refused to discuss it. "I want my own child or nothing," she said hotly. "You can forget adoption."

Her blackouts were increasing in number, and he advised her to have a physical checkup. The doctor examined her, recommended that she cut down on her drinking, but said he saw no evidence of physical damage. With this professional sanction, she became defiant and began to drink openly. This continued until her inability to sleep and the physical effects of the heavy alcoholic intake brought on a near breakdown.

John now renewed his efforts to persuade or cajole her into a drastic reduction in her drinking. He bought her a new wardrobe, and over their holiday took her on a vacation to Mexico, but the vacation was a fiasco. The alcohol was rapidly destroying her sexual feelings, and she began to resent his efforts to make love.

Their entire life now revolved around her drinking, and he suddenly revolted. He gave her an ultimatum: go for treatment, or give him a divorce. Her reaction was shock, quickly followed by anger and recrimination. If he tried to divorce her she would ruin him; she would "get" his job, and shame him in front of his friends. But he was unmoved. He told her that he was already ruined, on the verge of being fired, and beyond shame. He repeated the ultimatum, and painted a merciless picture of what she had become, and what she was doing to her own career.

Faced with the reality of being alone for the first time she talked openly and honestly with John about her feelings: her disgust with herself, her fear of failing at her job, her growing conviction that her childlessness was a punishment, and the frequent wish that she could simply die and put an end to her misery. The next morning, without mentioning her intention to him, she enrolled in the outpatient program at a local alcohol treatment center.

The next two months were a revelation. In the other patients in her treatment group she began to see herself. She heard their excuses and self-deceptions. She saw the ravages of alcohol on their bodies and minds. She resolved to go all the way, join Alcoholics Anonymous, and put drinking behind her.

John, also, found this period a revelation. In going through "family week," his part of the treatment process, he learned how alcohol destroys families as well as individuals. He found that he had become a "co-dependent," and that his co-dependency had led him into three types of destructive behavior. First, he had become as dependent on Janette as she was on alcohol, and his love for her had been displaced by his need for her, leading to frantic efforts to win back her love and approval. Second, in his concern he had desperately tried to find ways to change her and solve "the problem," thereby arousing her resentment and locking her more tightly into her addiction. Third, he learned that by protecting her, making excuses for her, and overlooking her deterioration as a person, he was literally "enabling" her to continue drinking.

Only when he drew back, and she was forced to think and act for herself, did she find the determination and courage to do something about her life.

In the protected group environment at the treatment center, John was able to admit and accept his own pain. Aided by the group and a wise counselor, he came to grips with his confusion and hopelessness, and finally with the numb, cold anger that had made him deliver his ultimatum. Beyond that were tears, frank and unashamed—the pain of his frustration. And beyond the tears, suddenly, he rediscovered the love he had felt for Janette in the beginning.

By the end of family week he had learned the greatest lesson of all: *Nothing that a family member can do can cure an alcoholic's addiction or change an alcoholic's behavior.* At best, a loving family member can confront the alcoholic with the unbearable nature of the situation, and offer encouragement and support if the choice is made to seek professional help.

At the end of six months, Janette was sober and she and John were communicating freely. At the end of a year, Janette's sexual feelings were coming back and they were beginning to enjoy each other's company. At the end of two years she was still sober, and both of them felt that their lives were back on track.

The Case of Dr. Sam

The second case illustrates the destructive power of alcoholism when the genetic predisposition is strong.

Dr. Sam T. had a general family practice in a small Texas town. After medical school and residency he took over the practice of a retiring family doctor, and in a few years had endeared himself to the community. He was handsome, and had a bedside manner that reassured old and young. He was a good doctor. In a period when many physicians practiced "medical school medicine" all their lives, he read the journals and maintained a lively correspondence with other doctors who were interested in new insights and new treatments.

His father had been an alcoholic, prematurely aged and dead of liver disease at 54. His uncle had killed a man in a drunken brawl and spent 20 years in the penitentiary. An aunt on his mother's side had drunk herself through a tempestuous marriage and divorce, repeated the performance in a second marriage, and died childless at 45. He had lived with these stories as a child, but was always cautioned by his mother that they must never be repeated outside the family.

He resolved while still in his teens that he would never drink, and despite occasional impulses he held to that resolve through medical school, two years of bachelorhood while he was establishing his medical practice, and the first three years of his marriage to the daughter of the district judge.

Dr. Sam had been intensely proud of his new wife. Patricia was tall and stately, and carried herself with a serenity that he envied. But near the end of their third year of marriage he learned that she had been drinking heavily since she was fifteen. She had covered up her problem so cleverly he had not suspected until he accidentally discovered her cache of gin bottles. When he confronted her she calmly admitted that she was a secret drinker, "just like my father. Besides being an honored judge and a member of the Board of Stewards in the Methodist Church he is also the town's foremost closet alcoholic." With a numbing sense of shock, he realized that he was married to a woman he did not know.

Now he understood why she sipped wine daintily at intervals through the day; it was to cover the odor of the gin she was drinking in secret. Now he understood why they rarely visited and never talked about her family; she hated her father. Now he understood that her careful walk and seemingly calm personality were the walk and personality of a woman who, most of the time, was half anesthetized with alcohol.

"Don't worry about it," Patricia said. "I'm an alcoholic, but I can control it. My father has, and he's over sixty. I'm surprised you didn't find out before. But please do me a favor. Don't make a big deal of it. I promise not to embarrass you." And she did not. But he could not dismiss it from his mind. He was a physician; how had her alcoholism escaped his notice? He found the problem deeply upsetting.

During the following week he slept only fitfully, and eventually prescribed for himself a small whiskey to help him relax. The alcohol had the desired effect, so he decided to have a second small whiskey and enjoy the evening. After the third drink he suddenly had a feeling that he had never experienced before—a feeling that led him to take a fourth drink and a fifth. Within an hour the bottle was empty. As he fell into a drunken sleep his last thought was that he had liked the taste of alcohol.

When he waked the next morning he promised himself never to try that experiment again, and for several weeks he kept the promise. But again he made the mistake of taking a couple of drinks for his insomnia, and again the alcohol took over. At this point he exerted all his willpower and shut the door on drinking. Hard.

He was glad that he had found the strength, because shortly afterward Patricia told him quietly that she was pregnant. He was deeply moved, and while they were planning and overseeing the outfitting of the nursery they came closer than they had ever been. To avoid possible damage to the fetus he asked her to stop drinking during the pregnancy, and she agreed. He watched her carefully for several days, and decided that, for the most part, she was complying.

But she had lied to him. When her delivery time came, she gave birth to a stillborn son whose abnormal eye and hand structure made him suspect the fetal syndrome of babies born to some alcoholic mothers. When he asked her if she had continued drinking, tears came to her eyes.

"Yes," she said, "I couldn't stop."

Dr. Sam left the hospital and walked for hours. Eventually he found himself in a bar and began drinking. Toward evening he returned to the hospital and went to her room. She tried to smile, but the smile disappeared when she saw his face. The kind Dr. Sam had disappeared, and in his place was an accusing alcoholic husband she had never seen before.

"You killed our baby," he said with cold, deadly anger. "You murdered him with that goddamned bottle." When he saw the stricken look in her eyes he turned abruptly and left the room.

Patricia came home to a silent house. Dr. Sam spoke only when she asked a question, and he was drinking steadily. The next morning when he left for the office he did not say goodbye. The alcohol and the anger were dominating his behavior.

When he came home that evening he found his wife dressed in her most beautiful negligee and lying on their bed. By her side on the night table was a bottle that had once held sleeping pills. It was now empty. After a quick examination he knew that she must have killed herself shortly after he left that morning. His judgment of himself was that in his alcoholic stupor, despite his professional knowledge that alcoholism is a disease, he had condemned her to death.

The story then developed in classic fashion. He lost himself in alcohol, felt himself slipping professionally, made resolutions to stop drinking, and broke them. His pastor talked with him, and Dr. Sam tried to tell him about Patricia, but could not.

His loss of control was gradual but inexorable. He drank surreptitiously during office hours. He began to forget details of his patients' medical problems. He lost his temper and fired his highly competent nurse. In a single month he wrote three prescriptions that the pharmacist questioned, preventing a mistake.

His friends were slow to recognize the seriousness of his trouble. He was still handsome and charming, and everyone sympathized with him because of the death of his wife. But his patients began to notice that his hands were trembling more, and on more than one evening when friends stopped by his home they found him disheveled and incoherent. Soon people were shaking their heads about "poor Dr. Sam."

He tried to find help. He talked with other doctors, and with his pastor again, but he could never bring himself to talk about that scene with Patricia. One friend advised him to go to a treatment center, but the nearest was three hundred miles away, and with his reduced practice he could not afford the cost. He was still being consulted for simple ailments, but his patients were beginning to rely on doctors in nearby towns.

His story had no dramatic ending. Dr. Sam simply became the town drunk who had once been a fine doctor. Eventually he had to face the fact that his earnings would not support his Main Street office, and he set up an office in his home. He still had a few patients four years later when he died. The death certificate listed cirrhosis of the liver as the cause of death. It should have added "alcohol" and "shame" and "guilt."

There is no way to reproduce in case histories the loneliness and frustration, the pain and anger, the hopelessness that ravage alcoholics and their spouses. The essence of their experience is this: As there are no emotionally healthy, happy, well-adjusted genetic alcoholics, so there are few—if any—emotionally healthy, happy, well-adjusted spouses of alcoholics who are, themselves, children of alcoholics.

CHILDREN OF ALCOHOLICS (COAs)

There are an estimated 30 million children of alcoholics (COAs) in the United States. They represent a special problem because the probability is high that they have inherited the alcoholic gene or genes. Because of that legacy they are exposed to three basic hazards: (1) They, in their turn, are likely to become alcoholics; (2) they are likely to exhibit many characteristics of an alcoholic, even if they do not form a drinking habit; for example, intense anxiety, quick anger, and low self-esteem; and (3) the pressures of life in an alcoholic family are likely to force them into destructive patterns of adjustment.

The first two hazards are genetic; COAs must learn to live with them. The third is psychosocial, and can be modified.

The discussion of these psychological and family patterns presents a peculiar problem. There are few hard scientific data to draw on, yet many psychologists, clinicians, and counselors have provided us with observational and anecdotal information of great value. I will not cite their publications in the conventional manner, but I have drawn on them heavily and list them at the end of the chapter under Suggested Reading. To their wisdom and insight I have added my own observations, and I hope that, together, we present a picture of problems and adaptive patterns that COAs will recognize.

The Pressures on Children

The pressures on children of alcoholic families are remarkably consistent. The first pressure is *fear*. COAs live with high levels of fear and anxiety. They may fear a specific person or situation, or they may experience a generalized anxiety that surfaces as worry or dread, or a shrinking from feeling. They tend to be hypersensitive to threats in their environment. They lie to avoid trouble or punishment. They trust no one, and have difficulty relating to other children. They are ashamed of their situation, and feel they have no rights.

They fear physical abuse, sexual abuse, verbal abuse, inconsistency, and the physical manifestations of drunkenness; for example, staggering, slurred speech, passing out.

Fear distorts perceptions and destroys love and trust. It produces children who retreat into themselves, or hide behind a wall of family secrecy, alienated from the community and from each other.

The second pressure is *anger*. If a COA feels fear too long, or if the intensity is too great, the fear is transformed into anger. In the beginning the boy or girl will try to express the anger, but probably not often. Drunken parents do not approve of angry children. In some cases a strong-willed youngster will remain rebellious in spite of punishment; in other cases, anger and rebelliousness will be repressed only to surface later, in the teens or beyond.

When they try to express their anger physically, or "talk back" to their parents, COAs expose themselves to danger. The physical damage done to children by drunken parents is a blot on our society. A slap can dislocate a jaw or damage an eye. A blow can break a nose or a rib. A shove can lead to a fall that breaks an arm or causes a concussion. Drunken rage can lead to torture, savage beatings, severe internal damage, or even death. In a fight between a drunken parent and a child, the child loses.

The third pressure is *shame*. COAs are ashamed of the way their alcoholic parents look: disheveled, possibly dirty, vacant-faced, unsteady in their walk and hand movements. They are ashamed of the way they sound: loud and overly aggressive, or incoherent, slurring their words. They are ashamed of the way the alcoholic parents behave at home and outside the home: arrogant, overbearing, unreasonable, angry and abusive, or awash in self-pity and remorse. They are ashamed of what people say: the snickers and jokes, the half-amused or half-disgusted comments of adults, the cruel comments by other children. Because of these feelings, COAs tend to become hypersensitive and withdrawn; to overreact and carry a chip on their shoulder; or to develop sexual problems, or other distorted behavior.

The fourth pressure is a *sense of wrongness*—in their parents and in themselves. An alcoholic parent is painfully different from nondrinking parents, different in ways that the child cannot understand or defend. Something is wrong, but the wrongness is mysterious and not to be talked about. Often it is not clear to the child that alcohol is the cause of the parent's frequent change from loving to angry, responsible to irresponsible. And since COAs identify powerfully with the family, the sense of wrongness extends to themselves.

The feeling is intensified by their day-to-day experiences in the home. If a child is told repeatedly "You are no good," he or she eventually begins to believe it. If a husband and wife have repeated quarrels, and the father frequently yells at the son in exasperation: "Get out of here and let your mother and me have some peace!" the son may conclude that he is at fault and responsible for the trouble in the family.

The fifth pressure is *guilt*. If a COA begins to feel personally responsible for the problems of the family, a strong sense of guilt is likely to develop. A boy may feel that he has provoked his father into abusing his mother. A girl may feel that her secret relations with her father may have caused her parents to get a divorce. An older child may feel guilty for not protecting a younger; a brother may feel guilty for not coming to the defense of his sister.

Fear, anger, shame, the sense of wrongness, and guilt—these are powerful disruptive forces in the alcoholic family. They weaken or destroy the sense of self, and make it difficult for the child to develop.

Even if one parent is not alcoholic, the situation can still be traumatic for the child. Living with an alcoholic can generate stresses in the nondrinking spouse that lead to anxiety, frustration, anger, or depression. Add the distortions of codependency, and the family becomes so chaotic the child does not know where to turn for comfort or security.

Characteristics of COAs

In seeking to cope with their confusion and pain, COAs tend to develop certain characteristics in common. In general:

- They experience a high level of anxiety that generates feelings of worry and apprehension. As a result, they take themselves and their family very seriously, overreact to situations over which they have no control, have difficulty carrying projects through to completion, and generally are unable to relax and have fun. Under pressure, their anxiety is likely to convert into anger, and anger into hate or depression. Because of these negative emotions it is difficult for COAs to feel love or trust.

- They have no clear idea of personal boundaries and limits. Their picture of "self" is blurred and becomes confused with other "selves." If the mother is anxious, the COA tends to become anxious. If the father is angry, the COA tends to become defensive or angry. If COAs are accused, they are not sure whether the accusation is fair or unfair. They are not clear as to what they stand for, or what they believe.

- They are confused about right and wrong, and are never sure how they should respond in a given situation. Lacking a positive role model in their parents, COAs make decisions by guesswork and trial and error. As a result they tend to make impulsive decisions, and constantly seek affirmation and approval. If they make a mistake or feel threatened, they lie without thinking of consequences.

- They tend to avoid clear statements of opinion or judgment, or the expression of strong likes or dislikes. In this way they avoid confrontation and accusations of stupidity and error, or arrogance and insolence, either of which can lead to punishment.

- COAs identify with the alcoholic, accepting their parent's shame and wrongness as their own. With this attitude, they often blame themselves for the problems or unhappiness of their parents or other members of the family, feel a strong sense of guilt, and are harsh in their self-judgments.

- They see themselves and their family as different from others. This generates a sense of isolation; isolation generates defensiveness and often a kind of desperate loyalty. If circumstances worsen, COAs help to build a wall of secrecy around the family and its activities and a second wall around themselves. The first is to protect the family from the outside; the second is to protect themselves from the other family members. If the family comes under attack, or if it is threatened by internal dissension, COAs tend to reach out for too much responsibility, or throw up their hands in disgust or dismay and renounce responsibility entirely.
- They feel a strong resentment against outsiders who are critical or judgmental about the alcoholic or the family. This feeling may lead to defensiveness or angry denials that anything is wrong.
- They tend to avoid peer activities, and if such activities are unavoidable they try to arrange for them to take place somewhere else; anywhere, just so it is not at home.
- They tend to see things in black and white, and to insist on all-or-none responses to their wishes or demands: "If I can't have what I want, I don't want anything at all." This makes intimate relationships difficult, because COAs tend to be unwilling or unable to compromise.
- They come to believe that their private feelings of inadequacy and worthlessness are actually judgments of others, and that the judgments are accurate.
- They tend to live by the family rules, even if they complain and periodically rebel against them. Despite their feelings of fear, frustration, and anger toward their parents, most young COAs feel that home is preferable to "outside." At home, unhappy though it is, they have a place. Outside, they feel they will be rejected if people know the sordid truth about them and their parents. So, to help hold the family together, they try as long as they can to live by the rules, even contradictory rules that are subject to sudden and irrational change.

The most common rules are:

- Do what you are told; we have to control the family to keep it together.
- Do not talk to others about our problems; keep family affairs in the family; be silent.
- Do not admit to yourself, to your brothers and sisters, and particularly to outsiders that the family *has* a problem.

• Don't trust outsiders; keep them out of our family circle.

These characteristic feelings and attitudes are experienced by COAs in an intensely personal, inward-looking way. They may not understand that millions of other members of alcoholic families are undergoing the same or similar experiences.

The gravity of the problem comes more clearly into focus when we realize that these problems of childhood tend to carry over into adulthood.

Modes of Adaptation

As COAs seek to adjust to the turmoil and confusion of life in an alcoholic family, they develop one of at least four basic modes of adaptation. The modes were first identified in 1976 by Sharon Wegscheider-Cruse in a booklet entitled *The Family Trap . . . No One Escapes from a Chemically Dependent Family*, and have since been modified in various ways by other writers. The modes are not personality types, or rigid patterns of behavior; they should be regarded, rather, as tendencies commonly observable among children of alcoholic families. COAs may exhibit elements of two or more modes, but generally one mode will be dominant.

The Hero. The Hero develops a powerful anxiety that the family will fall apart, steadfastly denying "the problem" while trying desperately to do something about it. The boy becomes "the little man"; the girl, the "little woman." They each tend to assume responsibility for the other siblings and, to whatever extent possible, for their alcoholic parent(s). They often act as "fixers" or peacemakers, and may try to protect or control one or both of the parents, and the other siblings. The drive to assume responsibility is a powerful one, and the result is likely to be a child who becomes a juvenile overachiever.

Behind this facade, however, the Hero is likely to feel frightened and inadequate, full of hurt, shame, guilt, or resentment. The hurt is the result of feeling deprived or abused; the shame is the result of identity with the unhappy family; the guilt is the feeling of personal responsibility for the family's problems. The resentment, which may increase with time, grows out of a feeling that he/she can never do all that people have come to expect: "No matter how hard I try, it is never enough!"

The Scapegoat or Problem Child. The Problem Child is so deeply hurt by the chaotic family situation that he/she is forced beyond anxiety into hostility. Feelings of shame and guilt are pushed out of the way by defiance and anger. Efforts at early parental discipline are likely to be met with evasion ("I didn't do it!") or rebellion and provocation ("I won't! And you can't make me!"). Directed toward the parents at first, these reactions are likely to extend outward, eventually, to school and community ("To hell with everybody!")

The Problem Child tends to be a troublemaker in any situation, and eventually is likely to run afoul of the law. If the parents come to the rescue, this COA is likely to conclude that bad behavior is a surefire method of getting attention—and troublemaking becomes a way of life.

In the beginning, the other children in the family may regard the Problem Child as a lightning rod, drawing the wrath of the alcoholic parent(s). But the Problem Child's anger and bitterness are likely to generate reckless behavior that will reflect on the entire family: heavy drinking, brawling, promiscuity, unwanted pregnancy, or crime.

The Lost Child. The Lost Child also experiences feelings of rejection or abandonment, but the reaction is likely to be one of withdrawal, followed by the development of an exaggerated attitude of independence: "Nobody loves me, but I don't care!" Feeling unimportant to the family and, by extension, to friends and the community, the Lost Child tries to move through life as a loner, uninvolved and preferring daydreams to reality.

When arguments arise in the family, the Lost Child does not join in; when problems arise, he/she does not lend a helping hand; when the family is criticized, he/she tries not to be identified with them.

At times, out of loneliness, the Lost Child will be drawn into family activities but, if the atmosphere is threatening, soon retreats. Outside of the family, the story is the same. The Lost Child is "the child who isn't there."

The Mascot. The family Mascot is likely to be the cute one, childish and immature, but always lots of fun. Underneath, however, there is a bottomless pit of low self-esteem, loneliness, and nameless anxieties.

This child becomes an expert at "looking on the bright side," but tends to crumple at the first appearance of stress or opposition. Of all the COAs, the Mascot has the fewest defenses, but perhaps the greatest capacity to be a peacemaker. It is the Mascot who can deflect the alcoholic's anger, head off an argument with a bit of clowning, or help other family members laugh at themselves. A welcome safety valve for the family, the Mascot pays a heavy personal cost in loss of self-esteem.

For COAs, these modes of adaptation are patterns of survival. For a time they enable the individual to cope with the "craziness" of the dysfunctional family and maintain a degree of sanity. Eventually, however, the Hero, the Problem Child, the Lost Child, and the Mascot tend to become enmeshed in the irrationality and become, themselves, dysfunctional.

In treatment, COAs have to abandon these adaptive behaviors, and respond honestly to what is going on around them. If this is not accomplished, they are likely to carry their dysfunctional characteristics throughout life, creating a destructive environment for their children.

The greatest hope for COAs at the present time is that education and counseling will alert them to the fact that if their parents or grandparents, or even uncles or aunts, were alcoholic, they are at risk of carrying the gene(s). And if they have the gene(s) they are at risk of developing the craving if they expose themselves to alcohol. And even if they do not drink they may have a tendency to that special anxiety, restlessness, irritability, and anger that seem to be a part of the alcoholic legacy.

In the future we can hope for genetic markers that will clearly identify COAs who are at risk, but today their wisest course is abstinence. For them, the enemy is alcohol.

SUGGESTED READING

Ackerman, R. J. *Children of Alcoholics*, 2nd edition. Holmes Beach, Fla.: Learning Publications, 1983.

Bepko, C., and Krestan, J. *The Responsibility Trap: A Blueprint for Treating the Alcoholic Family*. New York: Free Press, 1985.

Black, C. *It Will Never Happen to Me*. New York: Ballantine Books, 1987.

Blane, H. T., and Chafetz, M. E., eds. *Youth, Alcohol, and Social Policy*. New York: Plenum Press, 1979.

Bradshaw, J. E. *Healing the Shame That Binds You*. Pompano Beach, Fla.: Health Communications, Inc., 1988.

Burgess, L. B. *Alcohol and Your Health*. Los Angeles: Charles Publishing, 1973.

Deutsch, C. *Broken Bottles—Broken Dreams: Understanding and Helping the Children of Alcoholics*. New York: Teachers College Press, 1982.

Johnson, V. *I'll Quit Tomorrow*. New York: Harper & Row, 1980.

Kritzberg, W. *The Adult Children of Alcoholics Syndrome*. Pompano Beach, Fla.: Health Communications, Inc., 1986.

McFarland, B., and Baker-Baumann, T. *Feeding the Empty Heart: Adult Children and Compulsive Eating*. New York: Harper & Row, 1988.

Pittman, Bill. A. A., *The Way It Began.* Seattle: Glen Abbey Books, 1988.

Russel, M., Henderson, C., and Blume, S. B. *Children of Alcoholics: A Review of the Literature.* New York: Children of Alcoholics Foundation, Inc., 1985.

Seixas, J. S., and Youcha, G. *Children of Alcoholics: A Survivor's Manual.* New York: Crown Publishers, 1985.

Wegscheider-Cruse, S. *The Family Trap . . . No One Escapes from a Chemically Dependent Family.* Rapid City, S. Dak.: Nurturing Networks, Inc., 1976.

———. *Another Chance: Hope and Health for the Alcoholic Family.* Palo Alto: Science and Behavior Books, Inc., 1981.

Woititz, J. G. *Adult Children of Alcoholics.* Pompano Beach, Fla.: Health Communications, Inc., 1983.

3

Self-Help Approaches to Treatment: Alcoholics Anonymous

It is an extraordinary coincidence that the first two successful methods for helping substantial numbers of alcoholics to break the drinking habit developed at about the same time in the mid-1930s. The first was a form of treatment called aversion therapy. The second was a self-help fellowship called Alcoholics Anonymous (AA). I will discuss aversion therapy in the next chapter. Here I will tell the story of AA, which serves alcoholics; Al-Anon, which serves families of alcoholics; and Alateen, which serves teenage children of alcoholics.

AA is not directly related to the story of research on alcoholism, but it has helped to focus world attention on the problem, and has supported the concept that alcoholism is a disease syndrome that responds to treatment.

AA had its origins in a meeting between two men in Akron, Ohio, in June 1935. One of the men was Bill W., a stockbroker. The other was Dr. Bob, a surgeon. Both were alcoholics who had lost control of their lives, and were desperately seeking a solution to their problem.

The meeting began when Bill W. sat down with Dr. Bob to talk about his drinking problem. Their conversation very quickly developed into an intense and far-ranging discussion of alcoholics and alcoholism. The details are not known, but the two seem to have emerged from the meeting with the basic concepts and the resolve that led to the formation of Alcoholics Anonymous.[1]

They agreed on at least six fundamental points:

- Alcoholics understand alcoholics
- Alcoholics can talk to other alcoholics
- Alcoholics tend to believe other alcoholics
- It is healing for alcoholics to help other alcoholics
- Alcoholics need the help of a Higher Power to achieve and maintain sobriety
- Abstinence is essential to recovery.

Out of their meeting came a commitment: to seek out alcoholics wherever they could be found and carry the message to them.

The first group formed was in Akron. The second was in New York. Progress was slow. In November 1937, Bill W. and Dr. Bob could number only 40 alcoholics they had benefited. By 1939, however, groups were forming in Cleveland and Chicago, and the movement began to gain momentum. The statistics from Alcoholics Anonymous World Services, Inc., tell the story of its phenomenal growth:

- 1968: approximately 170,000 members in the United States and Canada
- 1989: approximately 900,000 members in the United States and Canada.[2]

How did AA succeed where other groups had failed? For answers we have to turn to three publications that reveal the heart, method, and structure of the fellowship. The first is *Alcoholics Anonymous Comes of Age*. It presents a brief history of AA and the people who created it.[3] The second is *Alcoholics Anonymous*, the "big book" that tells the AA story and sets down its basic philosophy.[4] The third is the *Twelve Steps and Twelve Traditions*. The Twelve Steps constitute a kind of road map to recovery. The Twelve Traditions state the purpose and functions of AA and establish limits on the organization that protect the personal freedoms and anonymity of the members.[5] Together, these documents constitute AA's blueprint for success.

Superficially, AA appears to be unstructured to the point of anarchy. Individual groups are largely autonomous. There is a national board, but its members restrict themselves to general considerations of policy. There is a World Services Corporation, but it serves largely as an information arm for the publication and distribution of literature. There is only one requirement for membership: that you want to stop drinking. Once you are a member, your membership cannot be terminated. There are no dues, only voluntary contributions.

For many people coming upon AA for the first time, it is astonishing that an organization with such a loose structure could endure. Yet it has not only grown in size and strength, it has earned the respect of alcoholics and treatment professionals throughout the world. On my recent trip to Russia, for example, I found that interest in AA and Al-Anon was high, and groups are operating in both Moscow and Leningrad.

A common message from counselors and physicians to recovering alcoholics leaving clinical treatment or psychotherapy is: "Join AA, stay with AA, and you will have the best chance of staying sober."

THE TWELVE TRADITIONS

To begin to understand AA, let us look first at the Twelve Traditions. They were formulated later than the Twelve Steps, but were present in spirit from the beginning. A careful reading of the Traditions helps to explain how AA attracts and holds alcoholics as they struggle toward recovery.

The Twelve Traditions of AA

1. Our common welfare should come first; personal recovery depends upon AA unity.
2. For our group purpose there is but one ultimate authority—a loving God as He may express Himself in our group conscience. Our leaders are but trusted servants—they do not govern.
3. The only requirement for AA membership is a desire to stop drinking.
4. Each group should be autonomous, except in matters affecting other groups or AA as a whole.
5. Each group has but one primary purpose—to carry its message to the alcoholic who still suffers.
6. An AA group ought never to endorse, finance or lend the AA name to any related facility or outside enterprise lest problems of money, property, and prestige divert us from our primary purpose.
7. Every AA group ought to be fully self-supporting, declining outside contributions.
8. Alcoholics Anonymous should remain forever nonprofessional, but our service centers may employ special workers.
9. AA, as such, ought never to be organized; but we may create

service boards or committees directly responsible to those they serve.

10. Alcoholics Anonymous has no opinion on outside issues; hence the AA name ought never to be drawn into public controversy.

11. Our public relations policy is based on attraction rather than promotion; we need always maintain personal anonymity at the level of press, radio and films.

12. Anonymity is the spiritual foundation of all our traditions, ever reminding us to place principles before personalities.[*]

The Traditions have been a key factor in making AA a positive force for recovering alcoholics. Considering them one by one:

Tradition One. "Our common welfare should come first; personal recovery depends upon AA unity."

Alcoholics tend to be stubborn and uncooperative. Many have been rebels or outcasts. How does AA achieve unity?

The binding force is not commandments or persuasion. It is an imperative that all members share: the need for a safe environment and a fellowship in which they can be accepted as they work to achieve sobriety. AA provides that environment and fellowship.

Tradition Two. "For our group purpose there is but one ultimate authority—a loving God as He may express Himself in our group conscience. Our leaders are but trusted servants—they do not govern."

There are group leaders at AA meetings, but they are volunteers, and they change from time to time. Guidance comes from a spiritual source within each member. Some call this spiritual force "God"; others call it a "Higher Power"; others think of it as the power of the group—its collective love and understanding, and its willingness to share and support. But most members agree that the essence of the AA experience is some form of spirituality that transcends individual weaknesses and limitations.

Tradition Three: "The only requirement for AA membership is a desire to stop drinking."

[*] The Twelve Steps and Twelve Traditions are reprinted with permission of Alcoholics Anonymous World Services, Inc. Permission to reprint the Twelve Steps and Twelve Traditions does not mean that AA has reviewed or approved the contents of this publication, nor that AA agrees with the views expressed herein. AA is a program of recovery from alcoholism. Use of this material in connection with programs and activities which are patterned after AA but which address other problems does not imply otherwise.

The essence of this tradition is a solemn commitment to new members by AA and every current member of every group: "If you want to stop drinking you will be accepted here."

In AA, members find many others who have "been there" and share the same problem—and guilt and shame lessen. It is a fellowship where the alcoholic finds new friends, dedicated to sobriety, who slowly replace old friends who were associated with drinking.

Tradition Four. "Each group should be autonomous, except in matters affecting other groups or AA as a whole."

This tradition is a declaration of freedom. It means that each group can handle its affairs as it wants to unless a proposed action would endanger the group, or embarrass or jeopardize the national or world fellowship. For the alcoholic who is an outcast, a loner, a rebel, and for the one who distrusts institutions, this tradition provides a basic and essential reassurance.

Tradition Five. "Each group has but one primary purpose—to carry its message to the alcoholic who still suffers."

When an alcoholic finds sobriety in AA, that fact becomes a powerful tool. By sharing this experience, the alcoholic develops the power to help others. By using this power, the helper's own grip on sobriety is strengthened.

Tradition Six. "An AA group ought never to endorse, finance or lend the AA name to any related facility or outside enterprise, lest problems of money, property, and prestige divert us from our primary purpose."

The strength of AA is that it has one goal: to help the alcoholic by direct interaction of members; and one loyalty: to its membership. By keeping its goals and its loyalties simple, AA protects its singleness of purpose and its integrity.

Tradition Seven. "Every AA group ought to be fully self-supporting, declining outside contributions."

AA is supported entirely by member contributions and the sale of literature. It is indebted to no one. Large donations and bequests are refused. Absolute independence and freedom from outside influence are considered to be essential to the integrity of AA and the trust of its members.

Tradition Eight. "Alcoholics Anonymous should remain forever nonprofessional, but our service centers may employ special workers."

AA does not employ professional counselors or physicians. A group may, at times, engage a lecturer to address a particular topic, but the work of AA is to create an environment in which alcoholics can help themselves and each other.

> **Tradition Nine.** "AA, as such, ought never to be organized; but we may create service boards or committees directly responsible to those they serve."

This is another declaration of freedom. The General Services Office cannot issue orders to a local group, restrict membership, or levy assessments. The freedom, the autonomy of the local group is total and permanent.

> **Tradition Ten.** "Alcoholics Anonymous has no opinion on outside issues; hence the AA name ought never to be drawn into public controversy."

This tradition reaffirms the fellowship's singleness of purpose. To become involved in outside issues would dilute this effort, and divert attention of members from their personal goal of sobriety and recovery.

> **Tradition Eleven.** "Our public relations policy is based on attraction rather than promotion; we need always maintain personal anonymity at the level of press, radio and films."

AA does not need publicity. Members attract members, and treatment professionals, psychologists, and psychiatrists encourage their clients to attend AA meetings. Many books and articles are written about AA, and the General Services Office staff cooperates with writers and others seeking information. But AA members want primarily to be left alone to work out their problems and restore sanity to their lives.

> **Tradition Twelve.** "Anonymity is the spiritual foundation of all our traditions, ever reminding us to place principles before personalities."

Strangers may think that AA members carry secrecy too far in using only first names in meetings, but there are two major reasons for the "Anonymous" in "Alcoholics Anonymous." First, there is still a dark and dangerous prejudice among uninformed people who think that alcoholism is proof of weak moral fiber. Among such people, membership in AA can mean a question mark after the person's name. Anonymity is a practical precaution.

Second, in order for a member to be totally honest and forthcoming about something as painful as alcoholism, the environment must be *known* to be a safe place to tell the truth. By making anonymity a basic part of AA meetings, a sense of security is generated which all members strive to honor and protect.

Taken together, these traditions help to provide a secure environment where alcoholics can come together, share their experiences and their feelings, and know that they will be respected and protected. No matter how hostile and threatening the home, the workplace, or the community, a member knows that AA is a haven that can be trusted.

New members often find it difficult to participate in the first meeting with a group. Denial is a powerful force, and shyness is hard to overcome. But the moment a person finds the courage to share feelings and experiences, the recovery process begins.

THE TWELVE STEPS

It is doubtful, however, that simple group interaction and sharing of experiences would carry the process forward if it were not for the Twelve Steps that AA developed to help alcoholics change their attitudes and achieve sobriety. The steps are not rules of behavior; they are guidelines which, if adhered to, make it easier for the alcoholic to face reality, and begin the slow process of recovery.[6]

The Twelve Steps of AA

1. We admitted we were powerless over alcohol—that our lives had become unmanageable.
2. Came to believe that a Power greater than ourselves could restore us to sanity.
3. Made a decision to turn our will and our lives over to the care of God *as we understood Him.*
4. Made a searching and fearless moral inventory of ourselves.
5. Admitted to God, to ourselves, and to another human being the exact nature of our wrongs.
6. Were entirely ready to have God remove all these defects of character.
7. Humbly asked Him to remove our shortcomings.
8. Made a list of all persons we had harmed, and became willing to make amends to them all.
9. Made direct amends to such people wherever possible, except when to do so would injure them or others.

10. Continued to take personal inventory and when we were wrong promptly admitted it.
11. Sought through prayer and meditation to improve our conscious contact with God *as we understood Him,* praying only for knowledge of His will for us and the power to carry that out.
12. Having had a spiritual awakening as the result of these steps, we tried to carry this message to alcoholics and to practice these principles in all our affairs. *

Members hear the Twelve Steps read aloud at every meeting, and are encouraged to "work" or practice the steps in their personal life. Special "step" meetings are held in which members discuss their problems and progress in moving through a particular step. In addition to serving as guidelines, therefore, the Twelve Steps also provide a measure of progress. Considering them one by one:

Step One. "We admitted we were powerless over alcohol—that our lives had become unmanageable."

Denial is the first obstacle on the alcoholic's road to recovery. In the beginning, the alcoholic is reluctant to give up alcohol because it is a source of relief or pleasure, so the impulse is to deny that drinking is a problem. As the disease progresses, the alcoholic stubbornly refuses to admit to himself that alcohol is stronger than willpower, so again the impulse is to deny that drinking is a problem. In the final phase, the alcoholic is reluctant to give up the only thing that stops the pain of the disease, so the tendency becomes even more powerful to deny that the drinking is out of control. In extreme cases, the alcoholic may feel unable to live without alcohol.

The urge toward denial is so strong that most alcoholics cannot begin the recovery process until they recognize and admit the fact that they are powerless over alcohol. This admission is a difficult, often impossible step to take alone, or even in the privacy of the family.

But in AA meetings the alcoholic begins to see and hear himself or herself mirrored in the other alcoholics in the group, so that the self-deception and alibis; the stories of evasion and concealment; the fear, anger, pain, depression, and loneliness can no longer be denied.

Step Two. "Came to believe that a Power greater than ourselves could restore us to sanity."

---

* See footnote on page 37.

The typical alcoholic who comes to AA has tried to stop drinking, and failed; has failed over and over again, and now in taking Step One has finally admitted defeat. The family has tried to help, and failed. Friends have tried to help, and failed. Physicians and ministers have probably tried to help, and failed. Now AA is suggesting that a Higher Power can help where others have failed.

To the religious alcoholic, the course proposed in Step Two is simple: Trust in God. For many, the AA slogan "Let go and let God" seems to work. The alcoholic reaches out a trusting hand and lets God lead the way.

For those who are uncomfortable with the concept of God, help may come from a renewal of that inner sense of wonder, love, and faith that is the source of all spirituality. For them, the Higher Power flows from their connection with the world beyond themselves.

For others, turning to a Higher Power may mean trusting and identifying with the group and accepting their encouragement and support. In any case, an inner change begins when the individual begins to look beyond the self for insight, encouragement, and help.

Step Three. "Made a decision to turn our will and our lives over to the care of God *as we understood Him.*"

When the new AA member reaches this step there is likely to be a rise in anxiety, and a strong surge of resistance to the idea of powerlessness. Step Two called only for faith in a principle. Step Three calls for an actual surrender of control. Whether the concept "God" is translated as a literal Being, a spiritual principle, or the interaction of the group, it means that the individual must invest total trust in something outside of the self.

In practical terms, this step means the willingness to relinquish old attitudes and old patterns of living that have produced pain and disappointment, and to adopt new attitudes and patterns as an act of faith.

Step Four. "Made a searching and fearless moral inventory of ourselves."

Here the alcoholic is asked to do something that at first seems safe and not too difficult. As the process is undertaken, however, the power and difficulty of the step become evident.

To begin with, it reverses the familiar psychoanalytic process which places the emphasis on the question: "What has been done to you to make you behave as you do?" and asks instead: "What have you become?" and "What are you doing with what you are?"

Most alcoholics come back to Step Four again and again during their recovery. The effect of the personal inventory is to clarify what they have made of their life, and what their effect has been—for good or evil—on those around them. This inward look helps to remove alcohol as an excuse for failure; helps alcoholics face their own weaknesses and patterns of error; and helps them see and believe in those strengths and good qualities that have made it possible for them to survive in spite of the disease.

Step Five. "Admitted to God, to ourselves, and to another human being the exact nature of our wrongs."

This step invokes the power of confession. For those who believe in God, admission to Him of wrongdoing carries the implication of a plea for forgiveness. Admission to ourselves forces us to be honest, but may lead only to brooding and self-blame. But a confession to "another human being" carries some of the impact of the Catholic confessional, and some of the emotional discharge of the psychoanalytic couch. The result is often a marked improvement in self-image.

Another positive effect is that this interaction with a trusted person tends to remove some of the isolation and loneliness from the alcoholic. Barriers raised by years of increasing shame and guilt are breached, and as pain is shared, some feeling of belonging is restored.

For many alcoholics, sharing a painful secret with a trusted person may bring another major benefit: humility. To be accepted by another in spite of a confession of wrongdoing arouses a feeling of gratitude that permits humility to manifest itself.

Step Six. "Were entirely ready to have God remove all these defects of character."

Whether it is God, one's own spirituality, or the power of the group that is the operating influence, this step—even though it is purely introspective—can mark the beginning of the end of denial. If, in the process of giving up drinking and reaching for sobriety, the alcoholic can find the humility to be willing to change—to be consistently kinder, more loving, more cooperative—then healing has begun.

Step Seven. "Humbly asked Him to remove our shortcomings."

This step goes beyond humility. Taking the step is not a defeat, but a movement upward, and many AA members feel it as the beginning of a new kind of strength. By looking to God, or to an internal spirituality, or to the group and saying "I know I have been wrong, but I am still powerless to change. Help me!" the alcoholic is making a declaration of faith and a commitment to the goal of recovery.

Step Eight. "Made a list of all persons we had harmed, and became willing to make amends to them all."

This step recognizes a fundamental principle: the harm we do to others causes long-term damage to the self. Shame and guilt weaken and distort the self-image, reduce feelings of self-worth, and make it difficult for the alcoholic to mobilize strength to begin a new life. The willingness to make amends is another indication that recovery is under way.

Step Nine. "Made direct amends to such people wherever possible, except when to do so would injure them or others."

Here the wisdom of these related steps comes into focus. In the privacy of the introspective Step Four the alcoholic has faced the wrongdoing of the past, and in Step Five admitted it to God, to him- or herself, and to *another human being.* That made it easier in Step Eight to become willing to make amends; and now Step Nine can be taken with less emotional turmoil.

Many alcoholics find that Step Nine dissolves the last of the denial, removes much of the remaining feelings of shame and guilt, enhances feelings of self-worth, and strengthens the grip on sobriety.

Step Ten. "Continued to take personal inventory and when we were wrong promptly admitted it."

The cumulative payoff of the steps now begins to be apparent. The new inventory probably looks less to the past, and more to the present and future. "What am I thinking, doing, feeling today? What am I hoping, planning, working toward for the future?"

The self-image that emerges is probably not the final image, but it is closer to health than the earlier versions.

Step Eleven. "Sought through prayer and meditation to improve our conscious contact with God *as we understood Him,* praying only for knowledge of His will for us and the power to carry that out."

The operating word in Step Eleven is "contact." Whether it be with the Judeo-Christian God, with that inner sense of spirituality, or with the power of the group, the alcoholic works toward feeling more closely attuned. The sense of isolation is dropping away, and with it may go much of the anxiety or depression that was so painful in the past.

The recovering alcoholic is now beginning to experience a more powerful sense of self, and to rediscover the simple joys of living and functioning. In a moment of revelation, realization may come that the pleasure of sobriety is greater than the escape and the "high" once derived from drinking.

Step Twelve. "Having had a spiritual awakening as the result of these steps, we tried to carry the message to alcoholics and to practice these principles in all our affairs."

The alcoholic has now come full circle: after a voyage of self-discovery and recovery, the time has come to help others find their way. For the alcoholic this is an affirmation ("I have something to share that can help others!"); a new reason for staying sober ("I want to set a good example."); and an intense feeling of pleasure and satisfaction ("I'm making it! Thank God I'm making it!")

AN EVALUATION OF AA

Alcoholics Anonymous is not for everyone. Some people are put off by the emphasis on God. Some do not like the club-like informality of the meetings. Others reject the idea of dedicating two to ten hours per week to attending meetings—often dull meetings—as the long-term price of sobriety.

AA has been criticized for being anti-professional, and in some groups there seems to be some justification for the charge. Psychiatrists and psychoanalysts are held in low esteem by many members, and some reject the idea that science will one day find a cure for alcoholism.

But AA champions the disease concept of alcoholism, and works in close cooperation with psychiatrists, psychoanalysts, and treatment centers. Indeed, it has become an informal but integral part of both inpatient and outpatient treatment programs throughout the United States, and now is spreading throughout the world.

The lack of meaningful statistics on the efficacy of AA is frustrating. For example, there are no dependable figures on the number of alcoholics who attend AA for a time and then drop out. But a 1986 survey of active members conducted by the World Services Office of Alcoholics Anonymous revealed that of those who attend meetings:

- A randomly selected member of the AA population with less than a year's sobriety has an approximate 40 percent chance of remaining sober another year.

- A randomly selected member with one to five years' sobriety has an approximate 80 percent chance of remaining sober another year.
- A randomly selected member with more than five years' sobriety has an approximate 90 percent chance of remaining sober another year.[7]

These figures are gratifying, but since AA membership in the United States and Canada is under 1 million, and there are many million who have alcohol problems, the reality is that most of those who need the fellowship never see the inside of an AA meeting room. This is not intended as a criticism. Alcoholics Anonymous has made a noble beginning. Despite the growth of the professional treatment field, AA is reaching approximately two-thirds as many alcoholics as all of the hospitals, clinics, and treatment centers combined, and now is regarded by many as the single most effective institution for dealing with alcoholism. But Alcoholics Anonymous is not a final solution. Practical methods of prevention of alcoholism, and more effective methods of medical treatment, are among the most urgent needs confronting our society today.

AL-ANON: THE SELF-HELP INSTITUTION FOR FAMILIES

Al-Anon was founded in 1951 by Lois W., wife of Bill W., co-founder of Alcoholics Anonymous, and her friend Anne B. Its objective was to help spouses and children of alcoholics as AA was helping alcoholics. Long before the problem was widely recognized by treatment professionals, Lois and Anne had seen the confusion, pain, and irrational behavior among family members who were trying to live with alcoholics.

Informal groups were already springing up; Al-Anon brought them together and provided coordination and a coherent philosophy. The program was designed around the Twelve Steps and Twelve Traditions that had already proved of value to alcoholics.

Because of a lack of funds, Al-Anon was a purely volunteer service to begin with, but as new groups formed around the country and donations began to trickle in, the founders were able slowly to build an organization similar to that of Alcoholics Anonymous.[8]

The Al-Anon World Services Office serves as a clearinghouse for information, provides guidance for those wanting to start new groups, compiles and distributes literature, and handles public inquiries. It acts as liaison between AA hospital and prison groups and the families of inmates, corresponds with groups all over the world, as well as with lone members in isolated areas, and maintains files and records of all active Al-Anon groups.

Since Al-Anon offers understanding, hope, and practical guidance to some 40 million men, women, and children whose lives have been disrupted or distorted by an alcoholic family member, it is not surprising that the organization has grown rapidly. According to Al-Anon Family Group Headquarters, as of September 1988, there were over 29,000 Al-Anon groups in some 100 countries around the world, including 3,000 Alateen groups for teenagers.[9]

Membership is open to any family member who is living with, has lived with, or is in some way connected to an alcoholic. As in AA, there are no dues, but voluntary contributions are welcome. The groups usually meet in places of worship, or in a community facility such as a public library. Meetings are informal, with a volunteer leader for the day's discussion. When groups grow too large, they generally break up into smaller groups where communication is easier.

In all the groups we have visited over the years, the atmosphere is always one of warmth and friendliness, and there is a sense that any problem or any emotion, no matter how painful, can be shared.

It quickly becomes apparent to new members that many of these husbands, wives, mothers, fathers, sons, daughters, girlfriends, and boy-friends are experiencing problems similar to, and as painful as, their own. The stories they share are of disappointment, frustration, neglect, and physical and mental abuse. The feelings and emotions they share are loneliness, anxiety, shame, guilt, anger, rage, or a pent-up sadness that brings them quickly to tears.

They learn that the efforts they have been making to help or change the alcoholic—the alibi-making, the cover-ups, the assumption of added responsibility, the pleading, the hiding of bottles, the threats—have in fact been enabling the alcoholic to continue drinking without paying the penalty.

The older children, and the adults who themselves are children of alcoholics, begin to see in others—as in a mirror—the roles they have played in the family: for example, the Hero, the Problem Child, the Lost Child, and the Mascot. They slowly come to understand that these roles, adopted in a desperate attempt to hold the family together, are actually frustrating their own needs, and blocking their growth and development.

Many begin to see in themselves some of the behavioral symptoms that accompany the genetic predisposition: the persistent anxiety, the impatience and anger, the rigidity, the unwillingness to compromise, the exaggeration of problems, the tendency toward depression. As they hear the others talk, they begin to see how their family has generated in them the self-doubt, and the feelings of inadequacy and low self-worth. They begin to understand the destructiveness of the isolation, the distrust, the secrecy which the family has developed to hide the truth of the alcoholic's behavior.

Al-Anon helps to relieve these problems in two ways. The first is to encourage members to focus on themselves. The emotional stress of attempting to help the alcoholic and the other family members has made the co-dependent psychologically and perhaps physically ill. To recover, the co-dependent must abandon the effort to change the alcoholic and protect the family, and focus on the needs and rights of the self. This is not selfishness in the usual sense of the word; it is a necessary act of survival.

The other main thrust of Al-Anon is to encourage members to "work" or practice the program of the Twelve Steps. As it does for the alcoholic, the reaching for a Higher Power (in the sense of God, spirituality, or the support of the group) brings to the Al-Anon member a degree of peace and strength. The self-inventory, and the admission of errors and wrongs carries the process forward. Making amends helps to remove shame and guilt, and reaching out to help other members who are hurting strengthens the feeling of self-worth.

In that atmosphere, family problems can be approached more realistically. Family members find reassurance in the knowledge that alcoholism is not a moral problem, but a physiological disease with emotional components. Their shame and guilt slowly dissipate as they accept the fact that they are not responsible for the alcoholic's disease, and that recovery is the responsibility of the alcoholic, not of the family.

Family members can plan their lives around a simple set of principles: recovering alcoholics are responsible for their own recovery; co-dependent spouses and children are responsible for their own recovery; and all are responsible for decisions and interactions that affect the family as a whole.

ALATEEN

Some young people from alcoholic families attend Al-Anon meetings seeking assistance, but many are ill at ease, and few participate freely. They may be angry with adults, or intimidated, but in either case, they are not comfortable with the adult group.

To fill their need, the first Alateen group was formed in California in 1957 by the teenage son of parents who were in AA and Al-Anon. The program was patterned after Al-Anon, using the Twelve Steps and the Twelve Traditions as a model. The growth of Alateen has been almost as phenomenal as that of AA and Al-Anon. According to Al-Anon Family Group Headquarters, by the end of 1988, some three thousand groups were meeting worldwide.

The approach and program are similar to those of Al-Anon, but are geared directly to the problems and needs of teenagers. The goal is to help young people from alcoholic homes cope with other family members, with the community, and with their own internal needs and stresses.

Members are encouraged to be frank and open in their discussions, and the meetings can be highly emotional. When they feel the need, individuals are encouraged to seek sponsors among Al-Anon members who can help them understand their problems and find solutions.

The programs of Alcoholics Anonymous, Al-Anon, and Alateen are not therapies; they do not "cure" alcoholism or co-dependency. But they provide a healing atmosphere and support for alcoholics and the members of their family, and serve as powerful psychological adjuncts to treatment programs.

But the physiological problem and the mystery remain. And the pain.

SUGGESTED READING

Al-Anon Faces Alcoholism. 2nd ed. New York: Al-Anon Family Group Headquarters, Inc., 1984.

Earle, M. *Physician, Heal Thyself.* Minneapolis: CompCare Publishers, 1989.

Fishman, R. *Alcohol and Alcoholism.* New York: Chelsea House Publishers, 1986.

Kurtz, E. A. A. *The Story.* San Francisco: Harper & Row, 1988.

Mendelson, J. H., and Mello, N. K., eds. *The Diagnosis and Treatment of Alcoholism.* New York: McGraw-Hill, 1979.

Milam, J. R., and Ketcham, Katherine. *Under the Influence.* New York: Bantam Books, 1985.

Pittman, Bill. *A. A., The Way It Began.* Seattle: Glen Abbey Books, 1988.

Powell, D. J., ed. *Alcoholism and Sexual Dysfunction: Issues in Clinical Management.* New York: Haworth Press, 1984.

Shore, R. S., and Luce, J. M. *To Your Health: The Pleasures, Problems, and Politics of Alcohol.* New York: Seabury Press, 1976.

4

Biopsychic Approaches to Treatment: Frustration and Progress

Although the conviction that alcoholism was a disease rather than a symptom of moral weakness was growing in the late nineteenth and early twentieth centuries, there was no knowledge of how the disease might be acquired or treated. As a consequence, early efforts at treatment were largely guesswork or trial and error.

EARLY TREATMENT THEORIES

One theory held that alcoholism was the result of an infection, so a few patients were treated with germicidal agents. The results were negative.

Another advanced the idea that alcoholism could be prevented by vaccination. In France, horses were injected with alcohol till they exhibited signs of physical dependence, then blood was drawn and the antibody was separated from the serum. This substance was then injected into human alcoholics. In the United States, a similar antibody called Equisine was developed from horse blood and applied to scarified tissue on the alcoholic's arm or leg over a nine-week period. The results in both cases were negative.

Under the theory that alcoholism was the result of a nutritional deficiency—a brilliant insight, but one based on insufficient information leading to an ineffective treatment—diets were tried that relied heavily on apples, oranges, grapes, dates, figs, lemons, bananas, and onions. Eliminated from the diet were coffee, tea, fat or overcooked meats, pork, oils, syrups, butter, and cheese. Light work, rest, and massage were also prescribed. Undoubtedly the patient felt better under this regimen, but the effect on the drinking habit was minimal.

More bizarre treatments featured direct and alternating electrical current, hot air boxes, ultraviolet light, and hypnotism. Claims were made for each method, but success was elusive.[1]

The most dramatic development came in 1880 when Dr. Leslie Keeley announced that he had discovered a specific remedy for alcoholism. The scientific basis for his discovery remained obscure, but he was a promotional genius, and the first Keeley Institute soon opened at Dwight, Illinois. Soon other Institutes were opened, and by the end of the century there was at least one Keeley Institute in every state.

Keeley was besieged with requests for information about his formula, but the most that could be determined was that it was based on a secret ingredient called either "bichloride" or "double chloride" of gold. Inevitably, the treatment process became popularly known as "the Gold Cure." Altogether, it was estimated that 400,000 people were treated with the Gold Cure before the movement died out.[2]

EARLY THERAPIES: AVERSION THERAPY

The first successful professional treatment for alcoholism, based on scientific principles, had its beginnings in the mid-1930s when Charles Shadel, a businessman in Seattle, Washington, conceived the idea of a hospital where conditioned reflex therapy would be used to treat alcoholics. He enlisted the aid of gastroenterologist Walter Voegtlin and psychiatrist Fred Lemere, and the enterprise was launched.[3]

The idea was not new. The ancient Romans had tried to discourage heavy drinkers by hiding spiders and other unpleasant substances in their wine cups. But it remained for the Russian scientist Pavlov to provide the insights that would later make aversive conditioning possible. He found that if he presented the sound of a metronome to a dog just before it was given meat powder, causing saliva to flow, a conditioned linkage would be established. Afterward, the sound of the metronome, alone, would cause a saliva flow. This is *positive* conditioning.

Similarly, by linking a sound to the unpleasant taste of acid, a negative conditioning linkage could be established that would reduce or halt the flow of saliva when the sound was repeated, without the reinforcement of acid. This is *negative* or *aversive* conditioning.

Voegtlin and Lemere found that aversive conditioning could be used with many alcoholic patients to block the desire to drink. Around this technique they built a program that, during the last half century, has helped over thirty thousand alcoholics achieve and maintain sobriety.

In a Schick Shadel Hospital, patients are interviewed to obtain their history, and then given a medical examination. About 50 percent require detoxification over a two- or three-day period, and sometimes longer. If no detox is needed, they begin aversion therapy without further delay.

The patient is taken first to a small treatment room whose walls are covered with liquor advertisements, and whose shelves are filled with a wide variety of alcoholic beverages in their original bottles. The patient sits in a comfortable chair equipped with a basin, in anticipation of the forthcoming nausea.

A drug mixture is then administered. Emetine creates nausea within five to eight minutes; pilocarpine contracts the pyloric sphincter and inhibits the emptying of the stomach into the duodenum; and ephedrine controls blood pressure fluctuations. The patient then drinks warm, dilute salt water to provide a volume of easily vomited material, and to prevent excessive loss of electrolyte. This salt water also contains oral emetine.

Shortly before the nausea is expected to begin, the patient is given a drink of his or her favorite beverage mixed with warm water. The instructions are to sniff the drink to get the full odor sensation, take a mouthful and swish it around to get the full taste, and then spit it out into the basin.

After the nausea hits, the instructions are changed to sniff, swish, and swallow. Usually the reaction is instantaneous—it all comes back up, along with part of the salt water. Very little alcohol remains in the stomach to be absorbed. During the remainder of the first session the patient receives four or five more drinks, each of a different kind of alcoholic beverage. By the fifth session, as many as 20 drinks will be given, including beer to provide a larger volume of liquid for the extended vomiting.

During the ten-day treatment, drinking sessions alternate with interview sessions in which patients are under the influence of equal parts of diluted sodium pentothal and sodium amytal in normal saline. The overall effect is like that of a sleeping pill, but there is an intermediate phase called the pentothal or "truth serum" phase in which the patient will answer questions freely and without censoring.

The pentothal interview has two goals. The first is to gain answers to psychologically oriented questions of value in diagnosis and counseling.

The second is to monitor the effectiveness of the aversion conditioning. If the patient is asked "How would you like to have a drink of bourbon (or scotch or vodka) and the answer is "I would love it—make it a double!" the aversion is not yet established. If the response is negative, or if the patient gags and exhibits signs of nausea, the conditioning is beginning to work.[4]

Dr. James Smith, then president of Schick Shadel Hospitals, commented in a 1988 interview:

The conditioning is very specific. We could condition against bourbon, and they could drink scotch without batting an eye. So let's say at the third pentothal interview (after three aversion treatments) we find we have a good aversion to scotch and bourbon, but beer and white wine still seem to be attractive, the next day we will hit the beer and wine harder. We guide the treatment process with the information we get from the pentothal interviews.

The process is powerful, but it does have certain basic limitations. Dr. Smith continued:

We could build aversion so powerful that patients would vomit at the sight of a whiskey advertisement in a magazine, but we could not make it impossible for them to drink. What we aim for is to make it possible for them *not* to drink. If we were to overshoot the mark and arouse their antagonism, they might say "Listen, you miserable so and so's, you can't make me stop drinking. I'm going to the first bar I see and have a drink! I'll show you who's in charge of my life!" And they could do it. They would probably throw up everything they drank for the first few days, but eventually they'd get enough to stay down to build up the blood level, and over time that could wipe out the conditioning. So we concentrate on giving them back their free will so that they can stay sober. And we find that when they can, they do.

In addition to the aversion therapy, patients at Schick Shadel also receive counseling, both individual and group, and instruction as to the nature of alcoholism and its effects on the individual and on the family.

Toward the end of the ten-day program, a counselor works with each patient to develop an aftercare plan. Among other things, patients learn to identify and avoid the "danger spots" in their normal environment that might trigger the desire to drink: a street with a favorite bar, the hour of five o'clock, a special drinking buddy, or anything in the past strongly associated with drinking.

At the end of the ten-day program (plus any detoxification time that may have been needed before aversion therapy began), the patients go home for one month, then come back for two days of reinforcement treatment. This consists of one aversion treatment, one pentothal interview, and contact with the counselor to update the aftercare plan and discuss problems that have arisen.

On weekends there are formalized family programs. In one of the groups, both the patient and the family are involved. In the other, only the spouse and children are involved. Couples counseling is provided if needed, and there is an ongoing couples group that in the beginning meets every week, then at less frequent intervals.

After treatment, patients are followed up weekly at first, then at longer intervals for a year.

The treatment program does not incorporate the Twelve Steps of Alcoholics Anonymous, but patients are encouraged to join AA and attend meetings as a means of supporting the recovery process.

Dr. Smith estimates that approximately 100,000 patients have undergone aversion therapy for alcoholism.

A 1985 study of 654 former Schick Shadel patients who had been discharged an average of 16 months after treatment showed that 82.8 percent received emetine aversion therapy. Of this number, 94.6 percent completed the standard course of treatment, and 55.3 percent completed two follow-up treatments. Contact was made with 412 of the patients, and 315 agreed to be interviewed by telephone. Of those who were interviewed, 71.4 percent claimed to have been abstinent since discharge, 5.7 percent admitted to having had one drink, usually to "try out" the aversion response, 5.1 percent reported having "slipped" one drink since treatment, and 17.8 percent reported drinking more than once since treatment.[5]

NONAVERSIVE THERAPY: INPATIENT

Most alcohol treatment programs in hospitals and treatment centers do not use aversive therapy, but combine medical treatment for physical problems with psychosocial therapy that has evolved from the Twelve-Step philosophy of Alcoholics Anonymous, psychoanalytic theory, learning theory, and group dynamics.

Gradually, drawing upon the findings of science and the practical insights growing out of clinical practice, physicians and counselors have developed treatment methods that ease the patient's transition from alcoholism to sobriety, and provide follow-up support that makes it easier to maintain sobriety once it has been achieved.[6]

Typical of such programs is that of the Faulkner Center in Austin, Texas, a treatment facility of Parkside Medical Services of Chicago. Faulkner provides both inpatient and outpatient therapy, with special programs for members of the alcoholic's family.

The Alcoholic

On admission to the inpatient program at Faulkner, the patient's history is taken, followed by a complete examination to determine physical condition, measure vital signs, and determine the severity of withdrawal symptoms. Some patients may experience no more than mild anxiety and tremulousness accompanied by insomnia, and can enter immediately into the treatment program. Others experience symptoms of much greater severity including sweating, heart palpitations, nausea, fever, hallucinations, disorientation and—in some cases—delirium or seizures, and must undergo a detoxification process to bring their feelings and behavior under control. At Faulkner, about 40 percent of the patients require detoxification.

In the detoxification process, patients receive two cc's of a 50 percent solution of magnesium sulfate shortly after admission to replace magnesium lost because of drinking. It also helps to reduce brain irritability and offsets any tendency toward hallucination or seizure.

If the possibility of *grand mal* seizure is high, the patient will also be sedated with chlordiazepoxide (Librium), a tranquilizer, until the withdrawal symptoms subside. The goal is to bring the symptoms under control and have the patient drug free in three to five days.

Along with the Librium, the patient is given 200 milligrams (mg) of phenytoin (Dilantin) twice a day. As the Librium dosage is reduced, Dilantin levels remain high enough to prevent seizures. Dilantin also helps to prevent the heart arhythmias common to patients coming off alcohol, and enhances the potassium/sodium balance in brain nerve cells. In most instances, Dilantin is continued for the first ten days of treatment.

If the patient is having the gastric problems that are common to alcoholics, 1,000 mg of vitamin B and 100 mg of thiamine are given intramuscularly once a day for three days. After that time, a multiple vitamin can be given orally. All patients receive a well-balanced diet, and are required to participate in planned exercise.

The program at Faulkner places great emphasis on a structured environment during the treatment process.

Dr. Larry Wharton, former medical director at Faulkner, said in a 1988 interview:

> There does not appear to be a typical "alcoholic personality," but as I continued to work with alcoholics I found that heavy drinking produces personality effects that alcoholics share. These include dependency, decreased ability to handle anxiety and responsibility, decreased ability to set long-range goals and work stepwise toward achieving them, emotional immaturity and isolation, and an extreme degree of manipulativeness. We found it essential to create an environment for patients that would help to restore a sense of structure in their lives. To offset pathological dependency, for example, we have a policy that staff does nothing for the patient that the patient can do unaided. This extends from bed making to planning recreation programs.

Patients are slowly made aware that alcoholism is a disease for which there is, as yet, no cure, and that the main problem is for them to learn to live with it on a day-to-day basis for the rest of their lives. Dr. Wharton continued, "We have two 30-minute lectures per day. In content, the lectures are short on theory and long on practice. The goals are to help them understand the disease, prepare them for sobriety, and help them learn to handle problems without hiding behind alcohol."

In community meetings that everyone attends, the schedule for the day is read and the staff makes it clear that patients are expected to adhere to the schedule rigidly. This discipline helps them restore structure to their lives so that they will have stable routines once the treatment is over. This stability helps to create a sense of security.

Each person participates in group therapy every morning. This is not psychotherapy; there is no effort to dig deeply into the past. Most of the patients could not handle analytical insights at this early point. They are not in touch with their past or with their deep feelings, which they have spent years learning to conceal or disguise. The goal is to help them recognize and accept these feelings. Then, with some guidance from their counselor, they learn to deal with their feelings in the group.

The "cross talk" is part of the healing process. They learn from each other.

They learn that they are not alone, and that their problems are not unique. Between lectures and sessions, they are encouraged to share meals, coffee breaks, exercise sessions, and whatever clean-up chores may be assigned. This helps them develop a sense of community.

Counselors quickly identify denial and other less extreme defenses, and patients are helped to recognize the role these defenses play in maintaining their dependency. As each patient sees his or her own defenses and denial in others of the group, the defenses weaken, the rationalizations and self-deceptions lose their power, and the patient becomes more responsive.

When repressed material breaks through in group or individual therapy, the counselor helps the patient understand and express the emerging feelings. It is a permissive atmosphere, and patients learn that they can express anxiety, anger, grief, sadness, or depression without embarrassment. According to Dr. Wharton, "We avoid psychoanalytic probing or other forms of depth therapy, but in our sensitivity to childhood influences, and our handling of emotion and denial, we owe a great deal to psychoanalytic theory and practice."

As treatment progresses, patients experience extremely painful emotions. Resentment, anger, and depression; uncertainty and confusion; fear, anxiety, and sadness come pouring out. It is difficult for them, at first; but as they express their feelings and share them with others the intensity gradually lessens, and they begin to experience pleasure as well as pain. In the group sessions there is often laughter as well as tears.

Each person works with a specific counselor to identify and tackle problems. A special goal for the counselor is to help patients, through individual counseling, explore and solve problems that are not common to the group. For example, if a patient has a problem with an angry father, he may be encouraged to write a letter to the father explaining his reaction to his father's outbursts. Even if the patient does not mail the letter, in writing it he or she will gain insight into the damage the anger has caused.

The first stage of recovery comes when patients admit that they cannot control their drinking, and accept the fact that they have the disease of alcoholism.

The second stage comes when patients begin to explore the disease through talking about it and its problems with the counselor and others in the group.

The third stage comes when they begin to see how alcoholism has affected, and is continuing to affect their lives.

The fourth stage comes when they can put aside their defenses and accept the fact that their only hope is to give up drinking and begin to learn a new way of life.

Dr. Wharton said:

We place a heavy emphasis on the Twelve-Step recovery program of Alcoholics Anonymous. We have the patients do written exercises on the first three to five steps while they are in the program. We also escort them to four or five AA meetings away from the Center each week during their 28-day program. There is no question but that AA helps them stick it out through the treatment program, and helps them stay sober once they are out on the town again.

The aftercare program begins when the 28-day treatment program is completed. The 90-minute group sessions held once each week encourage group interaction under the guidance of a counselor. Patients find that the group is a safe place for discussing problems and asking advice, and a source of friendly encouragement and support from other patients they have come to know and trust in the program. Patients are free to attend these meetings as long as they feel the need.

The attitudes of the staff are of crucial importance during the treatment, as Dr. Wharton explained:

If I had to single out one factor that is most responsible for our success in treating patients, I would say it is the gentle, loving care the staff provides for every patient. That includes everyone: waiters, receptionists, secretaries, counselors, nurses, and physicians alike. The patient has to know that Faulkner is a safe place for being honest and letting feelings emerge without fear of censure.

The program works because we are able to restore hope. Successful patients learn that they are suffering from a disease, rather than a moral weakness. They learn that others who were in the same boat have made it and have rebuilt their lives, free of drugs and alcohol. They rebuild a sense of pride and competence. Through Faulkner and AA they become part of a community of people who are comfortable with each other. They find that the continuing pleasure of being sober is greater than the intermittent "highs" that once were so important to them. They rejoin society, and find that society welcomes them back. They still have problems, but they have begun to learn how to cope with them.

The Family

While the alcoholic patient is moving through the early phases of the inpatient program, family members are strongly encouraged to participate in "family week." This is a series of five all-day sessions in which groups of 10 to 20 spouses, children, brothers, sisters, and parents of alcoholics work with a counselor to come to grips with the meaning of "co-dependence."

In the language of therapists, this word refers to the fact that the family member is as dependent on the alcoholic as the alcoholic is on alcohol. The spouse may feel an absolute compulsion to stop the alcoholic from drinking, or to lie and dissemble in a desperate effort to hide the illness from friends, employers, and even from relatives outside the immediate family group. Or he or she may feel compelled to hide personal feelings and endure neglect, abuse, deceit, broken promises and, often, economic disaster brought on by the drinking.

Children may feel neglected, abused, and betrayed, and equally embarrassed in the community. More importantly, they often take onto themselves the blame for the alcoholic parent's behavior. They may feel inferior, ashamed, and guilt-ridden. Many of them also feel a bitter, often explosive anger toward the alcoholic which adds to their feeling of guilt.

As a consequence, the members of alcoholic families who come together in family week share a legacy of deep emotional trauma. It is not surprising, therefore, that the first session for a given group generally begins in an abnormally quiet, distrustful, extremely awkward atmosphere. The individual members are not reassured when they see boxes of tissues in strategic locations around the room.

The counselor who was responsible for a recent group undergoing family week at the Faulkner Center opened the session by asking the participants to identify themselves, and state their relationship to the person in treatment for alcoholism. The answers were quiet, defensive, or grudging, depending on the individual.

The counselor talked briefly about alcoholism and the painful consequences it has for family members, then asked if anyone wanted to talk about an experience or a problem. The resulting silence was a long one. Eventually, a woman made an embarrassed comment, with a self-conscious laugh; then more silence.

An older woman expressed her anxiety about her child who was in treatment, and was the first to reach for the tissue box while the other members of the group looked at her more in curiosity than in sympathy.

She did not talk long, but cried quietly for several minutes before she regained her composure.

The group broke for lunch without anyone's having lost control or let feelings come through freely. Probably most of the people were wondering why they were there. Probably all were convinced that, whatever was supposed to happen, it wouldn't work.

After lunch there was a lecture by one of the counselors in which alcoholism was described as a disease.

In mid-afternoon a man started talking quietly and then suddenly broke into agonized sobs as he tried to tell what it had been like living with an alcoholic wife. He worried briefly that he was betraying his wife's confidence by talking about her problem, but after a minute or two he stopped trying to censor and cried unashamedly. A woman sitting across from him, a total stranger, went over and patted him on the shoulder. She stood by him until he was quiet, then went back to her chair. She looked around in mild embarrassment. Two women and one of the men smiled at her encouragingly.

A man who had been struggling with his impatience and anger suddenly burst out: "This is nonsense!" he exclaimed. "My wife is the lush! There's nothing wrong with me. I don't know why I'm here!"

A young girl whose sister was in treatment ignored him and began to cry. "I think my sister is going to die," she said. "We tried to tell her . . ."

After a long silence, a middle-aged woman said suddenly, "My son doesn't want to live with me when he gets out. He wants to live with two of his drugging friends, and I don't trust them. He should stay with me."

"How old is he?" the counselor asked.

"He's 35. He's a bachelor and he's always lived at home."

"Don't you think he is old enough to be on his own and make his own decisions?" the counselor asked.

"I've always looked after him . . ."

"So you want to continue to make his decisions for him?"

"I get so afraid for him . . ."

"You can't run your son's life. You need to begin concentrating on your own life, deciding what is best for you. What has it been like, living with your son?"

"He's a good boy . . ."

"What has it been like living with him?"

"He drinks, and he doesn't listen to me . . ."

"Is he good to you when he isn't drinking?"

The woman shook her head and began to sob. The man sitting next to her handed her the tissue box.

By the time the second day was over the people in the room, one by one, had come to the conclusion that in this room it was safe to speak the truth, to reveal the family secrets, to feel the forbidden emotions, to be angry, to cry, to express shame and guilt, to be selfish. They had also come face to face with a shocking fact: The efforts they had made to control their alcoholic's drinking had been a major factor in maintaining that drinking habit; and the sacrifices they had made to protect their alcoholic had literally enabled him or her to continue drinking.

By the end of family week, the walls of guilt and shame were coming down, and most of the people in the group were talking freely about their experience, their fears and hopes, and the realities they would have to face when their alcoholic came home. They had arrived at a new understanding of their own worth, and of their right to express their needs and take steps to fulfill them. Most of them felt more relaxed, more hopeful, and more honest than they could remember feeling before.

In general, when recovering alcoholics return to families who have been through family week, they find a healthier atmosphere and an incentive to remain sober.

NONAVERSIVE THERAPY: OUTPATIENT

For patients still in the early to middle stages of alcoholism, outpatient treatment can be quite successful, and offers two advantages: (1) Most patients are able to remain on the job and with their families during treatment, and (2) the cost is lower than that of a comparable inpatient program.

Pace Health Services in New York City, for example, offers a yearlong, medically oriented program tailored to the individual's specific needs. Primary Care is a three-month program that includes a preliminary internal medical and physical examination, evaluation, detoxification if needed, weekly medical visits, individual and group counseling sessions, biofeedback therapy, and lectures on alcoholism and the recovery process.

If withdrawal symptoms are severe, the patient may be required to go through a detoxification process, either on site or at a local hospital, before beginning his or her outpatient program; but if the patient has a cooperative husband or wife, detox can often be handled at home, under careful medical supervision at the outpatient center, over a period of from five to twelve days.

Dr. Nicholas Pace, medical director of Pace Health Services/Parkside Recovery Center, said in a 1988 interview:

> For a patient with less serious problems we might simply combine Librium with your nutritional supplement. We find that most of our new patients do not require detoxification. They are able to begin treatment immediately. However, whether they require detox or not, I follow these people as if they had diabetes. I follow their physical recovery; that is, their blood pressure, their liver size, and try to correct any specific medical problem they may have. But above all, I monitor their progress in the program. I ask "How are you doing with your counselor? With your group? How are the lectures going? Are you going to AA?" If I don't like the answers I modify their program.

During the three-month Primary Care period the patient works with the physician and an assigned counselor. In addition, all patients are required to attend two different series of 12 lectures for a total of 24. Some lectures give patients general information about alcoholism. Others help patients understand how alcohol has affected them in relation to their family, their job, and the community.

Throughout the program there is strong emphasis on group work. In addition to the permanent group for lectures, patients undergo three types of group therapy: early recovery training, relapse prevention, and supportive group training.

In the Early Recovery Training group, patients learn to carry out detailed self-analyses of their progress. These sessions require a lot of homework, and help the patients learn to look at their behavior honestly and with increasing objectivity.

In the Relapse Prevention Training group patients learn strategies that help them maintain their sobriety after they achieve it. Literally, the program teaches patients how *not* to drink.

In their Support group, they learn to rely on each other for mutual support throughout the year. Pace explained:

> Although we are a medically oriented program and spend a great deal of time orienting the patient to the medical aspects of alcoholism, we place a strong emphasis on Alcoholics Anonymous. There is no doubt in my mind that attendance at AA meetings makes it easier for patients to get through the program, and remain sober after they are on their own. We hold two mandatory AA meetings on the

premises each week, and take patients as a group to a meeting in the community once a week. This community activity helps them establish ties to nondrinking, recovering alcoholics in areas where they will be living and working.

We also attach great importance to our work with families. We have programs for spouses and their children, and we pay special attention to spouses of alcoholics who are also children of alcoholics. These spouses are highly vulnerable, highly stressed, and sometimes as sick as the alcoholic husband or wife. We move very cautiously with them, and help them to adjust slowly to the realities of their family situation, with the primary emphasis on their own personal feelings and needs. Eighty percent of the patients who have completed our program have been sober for more than a year.

1988 CATOR REPORT

A significant measure of the effectiveness of a cross section of treatment programs in general can be found in the 1988 Chemical Abuse/Addiction Treatment Outcome Registry (CATOR) report. In a survey of 2,303 adults discharged from 22 chemical dependency treatment programs, with interviews at four consecutive six-month intervals, the following results were noted:

- Approximately two-thirds of the patients were reportedly abstinent during either the first or second year after treatment.
- 57 percent reported total abstinence for the full two-year period.
- Of those who attended AA weekly, 76 percent reported abstinence in the first year.
- In the second year, 83 percent of the regular AA attenders reported abstinence for the twelve months.[7]

Such reports must be viewed with caution. Self-reporting by recovering alcoholics is not always reliable; only those who completed the treatment programs were questioned, and no effort was made to evaluate the residual emotional or behavioral disturbances patients were experiencing while maintaining their sobriety. But even with these reservations, it is clear that the programs are benefiting a high percentage of alcoholics who seek treatment, even though many aspects of the disease are still unclear.

Treatment professionals are virtually unanimous in the recognition that their programs do not cure the disease of alcoholism, and AA makes it clear that their members are always recovering, never recovered.

The disease remains. But the surveys show that treatment unquestionably helps many patients achieve sobriety if they complete the program, and if they attend AA their chances of maintaining sobriety increase sharply.

A major problem is to get the alcoholic to treatment. In some cases, intervention—a concerted effort by family, friends, an employer, a family physician, or a clergyman to show "tough love" and persuade an alcoholic to seek help—is effective. But generally the alcoholic must "hit bottom" and be willing to accept treatment before it can be effective.

A crucially important part of the treatment process is the counselor. These dedicated individuals, many of whom are recovering alcoholics, provide the understanding, the caring, the dedication, and hard work needed to build an environment for recovery.

In the early 1950s, few trained professionals were available for work with alcoholics. The treatment teams consisted of physicians, social workers, psychologists, nurses, and clergy. Dr. Daniel J. Anderson, a psychologist at Willmar State Hospital in Minneapolis, was the first to use a recovering person who was a practicing member of AA, and understood the philosophy of the fellowship of AA, to serve on a treatment team. As a result of his efforts, in 1954 the Minnesota Civil Service Commission developed a formal employment category designated as Counselor on Alcoholism.

Since then, the profession of counselors of alcoholism has grown rapidly, and now the training, the standards of certification, and the continuing education of the counselor ensure the quality of care essential for the success of treatment programs, both inpatient and outpatient, aversive and nonaversive.[8]

OTHER NONAVERSIVE TREATMENT APPROACHES

Other treatment procedures have developed in recent years, but although each has had its champions, none has proved to be of significant value. The approaches that have attracted the most attention have been those based in psychoanalytic theory and social learning theory.

Approaches Based in Psychoanalytic Theory

Many psychoanalysts have found alcoholism to be a tantalizing challenge. When clinicians were asked to name the principal emotional and personality characteristics of problem drinkers, they selected dependency, imma-

turity, anxiety, hostility, depression, compulsiveness, and self-deprecia-
tion. Such problems are viewed by the psychoanalyst as arising from
conflicts among the unconscious, the superego, and the ego, with special
emphasis on ego-superego conflicts.[9]

In discussions with psychologists and psychoanalysts over the years,
I have heard a variety of possible psychological causes of alcoholism:

- Fixation at or regression to the oral stage, with resulting narcissism
  and the need for self-indulgence
- Fixation at or regression to the anal stage, with resulting aggressive-
  ness or rebelliousness
- Fixation at the phallic stage, resulting in the development of a
  superficial attitude of competence and friendliness covering feelings
  of low self-esteem, anger, or rebelliousness
- A flight from homosexual impulses
- Incestuous urges
- Sadistic drives and oedipal conflicts
- An effort to reach a compromise between hysterical and obsessive-
  compulsive neuroses
- A self-destructive drive: a kind of "chronic suicide"
- Feelings of inadequacy, fear of failure, and poor social relationships
- An unconscious need to dominate, together with feelings of loneli-
  ness and frustration
- Excessive dependence that prevents the individual from achieving
  independence
- Overly punitive parents who serve as role models for the development
  of attitudes of self-punishment expressed in excessive drinking.

The principal assumption has been that if conflicts could be resolved
the associated addiction would disappear spontaneously. But clinical
experience has proved otherwise.

Dr. John O. Stocks, founder and former medical director of Woodland
Hills Psychiatric Center in New Orleans, stated in an extended interview
in 1988:

In working with alcoholics I found that . . . treating the pathology
did not remove the addiction. The cause lay elsewhere.

My first insight was the realization that many individuals seem to
have a built-in capacity for addicting themselves to alcohol; a predisposition. I found it exciting, therefore, when scientists began to find
evidence that this predisposition is the result of physiological—probably genetic—anomalies, and that these anomalies lead to deficiencies

or imbalances of the neurotransmitters in the brain. But that left
the question: How does the addictive capacity become established
in our personality, and in our family systems? How does it affect the
developmental process?

Psychologically, we know that for individuals having this capacity
for addiction, alcohol in the beginning is an agent for reducing emotional pain. It masks or suppresses the anxiety, depression, loneliness,
despair, and disorganization that grow out of the physical anomaly.
In the mind of alcoholics, drinking gradually becomes essential to
life; they build their lifestyle around alcohol, and establish two goals.

The first goal is simple: they drink to escape pain and feelings of
inferiority and low self-esteem; to dull anxiety and anger; to find a
way to live with loneliness and isolation. The second goal is more
complex: they drink to regain a lost feeling that they can do anything
they want to do if they only try hard enough.

Stocks calls that feeling "omnipotentiality" and he explained it:

Most of us have that feeling when we are young. The future seems
boundless, but as life progresses we are forced more and more to the
crashing conclusion that our options are limited; that the life we
have today is probably a preview of the life we will have tomorrow.
Alcohol, in the beginning, changes that; it tends to restore the feeling
of omnipotentiality. When we first begin to drink we feel again that
we are undiminished; that we do not have to hurt; that we *can* be
desirable; that we *can* achieve our goals. Trouble comes when alcohol
begins to poison the body and cloud the mind, further limiting the
options. This is the trap, and most alcoholics mobilize all their forces
to deny that the trap exists.

In this context the concept of the "addictive personality" makes
sense. I think we can say that alcoholics are individuals who will
maintain and protect their addiction at whatever cost to themselves
or others. . . . Many patients report that in the early stages of recovery
they are afraid they will die if they give up alcohol.

In treatment, today, we can help the patient understand the nature
of the disease, build determination and resolve through group support
and counseling, and provide follow-up programs that help to maintain
that determination and resolve to stay sober. But as a treatment profession we are waiting for two developments.

On the one hand we are waiting for the pharmacologists and neurobiologists to come up with the "magic potion" that will change the

biological imbalance or deficiency that causes addiction—not to enable the patient to drink safely, but to enable him or her to refrain from drinking without undue discomfort. I think this development will come in our lifetime.

On the other hand, we are waiting for the psychoanalytic and psychiatric professions to learn how to correct the psychological anomalies of the addictive mind. We do not know enough about how deficiencies or imbalances in the brain bring about the behavioral alterations—the anxiety, the anger, the depression, the stubbornness, the self-destructiveness—that characterize the alcoholic.

Dr. Stocks finds regrettable the current effort by a few psychoanalysts to question the importance of the search for a medical solution to the problem of alcoholism:

There have been unfortunate efforts by some psychoanalysts in recent years to make unsupported claims for the psychoanalytic method as a curative tool for alcoholism, and to make equally unsupported attacks on the efforts of pharmacologists and neurobiologists to find the biological causes of alcoholism. It is my hope that, in the future, these disciplines will come together: the biological scientists to find the physical and chemical anomalies in the addictive brain and nervous system; the psychological scientists to find the mechanisms and patterns that characterize addictive behavior and lifestyles.

The Behavioral and Social Learning Approach

Behavioral and social learning theorists generally hold that alcoholism is the consequence of learned behavior. The three primary viewpoints that I have found to be of interest in the treatment field are:

1. That drinking styles and attitudes toward drinking are transmitted to the individual by way of "models"; for example, family, peers, television, and newspapers.

The drinking behavior of parents is considered of particular importance. In a family where the use of alcohol is limited to occasions such as special meals or religious rituals, children are unlikely to become heavy drinkers. In a family where one or both parents drink to excess, children are likely to follow their example. Once an individual develops a pattern of heavy drinking, physical or psychological dependence may develop and lead to problem drinking.

Television and movies not only provide information about drinking, but also reinforce the idea that alcohol is a useful and socially acceptable means of easing social contacts, solving problems, and having fun. The situation is beginning to change, but the media often fail to show the adverse affects of heavy drinking.

Peer pressures on young people are held to be a major factor. Individuals who can "hold their liquor" are considered to be admirable; heavy drinking is associated with "having a good time"; and the presence of one heavy drinker in a group can influence others to drink more.

2. That alcohol reduces tension, and this relief of tension reinforces further alcohol use. In this view, each new experience of tension release through the use of alcohol reinforces the pattern.

Despite early acceptance of this theory, both animal experiments and human experiences have proved inconclusive. Alcohol may decrease tension and stress in the short term, and increase it in the long term. Thus alcohol may reduce anxiety in the moderate drinker, but increase it to the level of a serious problem in the heavy drinker.

3. That our expectations concerning alcohol influence our reaction to it. Our expectations are influenced by the social situation in which we drink, the way we respond to alcohol, and social reactions to that response. Young drinkers expect that alcohol will help them "have a good time," ease social situations, and excuse boisterous or even outrageous behavior.

The cognitive-behavioral viewpoint is also guiding investigation of the problem of relapse. In one model, the tendency toward relapse is determined by the degree to which the drinker feels helpless and easily influenced by others; by the degree to which environmental events are beyond his or her control; by the availability of alcohol in the environment; by feelings of constraint on drinking behavior; by the availability of adequate alternatives to drinking; and by the individual's expectations as to the effects of alcohol as a means of coping with a given situation.[10]

The study of such factors undoubtedly yields information about the manner and to some extent the degree to which alcoholism develops, but it has provided little useful insight into the causes of alcoholism, and few practical guidelines for building a treatment program.

However, as Elliot L. Richardson, secretary of health, education and welfare, suggested over two decades ago:

The search for a single cause of alcoholism may be an unrealistic goal . . . Many theorists . . . suggest a multifaceted approach which incorporates elements from two or more hypotheses. Generally, such an approach selects from each of the broad areas discussed: physiology, psychology, and sociology.[11]

THE NEED FOR RESEARCH

Despite the advances that have been made in the treatment of alcoholism during the past four decades, the inescapable fact is that *alcoholism remains a largely unsolved medical problem*. Through pharmacological and nutritional means we can support the treatment process and offset, to some extent, the brain chemical deficiency or imbalance that causes alcoholism, but we are only beginning to identify and understand the underlying genetic anomalies that may be the basic cause. Similarly, we are only beginning to identify and understand the mechanisms by which neurochemical deficiencies or imbalances alter psychological patterns.

Until we can solve these problems we cannot bring the alcoholic into the "comfort zone": the feeling of normalcy and well-being that can come only from being free of the physical abnormality and the emotional distress that accompanies it.

The best that we can do to help alcoholics with today's limited knowledge is to help them understand the nature of their disease; provide support through AA; use aversive methods to condition them against drinking; use nonaversive methods to build up their courage and desire to gain and maintain sobriety; and employ pharmacological and nutritional adjuncts to ease the treatment process and improve their chances of avoiding relapse.

There is only one key that will unlock the necessary knowledge and make it available to the clinician: scientific research. Working in some 18 allied disciplines, scientists in the past 50 years have explored many of the peripheral areas that surround the mystery of alcoholism. We have learned that it is a disease involving brain chemistry dysfunction, and that for much and perhaps most of the alcoholic population the disease is genetic in origin.

But we need to know much more. In the biological sciences, we need to identify all of the neurotransmitters involved in alcoholism; identify the receptor sites they activate; follow neuronal activity through the entire sequence of alcoholic behavior; find the specific pharmacological and/or nutritional agents the physician needs to treat the disease; pinpoint the gene(s) responsible for the anomalies; learn how to determine which children in an alcoholic family are at risk; and modify the gene(s) to break the line of transmission.

In the psychological sciences, we need to learn how biological deficiencies or imbalances trigger anxiety, anger, aggression, depression, craving, and denial, the behavioral components of craving; and the attitudinal factors involved in relapse.

SUGGESTED READING

Blum, K. *Handbook of Abusable Drugs.* New York: Gardner Press, 1984.

Chafetz, M. E., and Demone, H. W., Jr. *Alcoholism and Society.* New York: Oxford University Press, 1962.

Ewing, J. A., and Rouse, B. A., eds. *Drinking: Alcohol in American Society—Issues and Current Research.* Chicago: Nelson-Hall, 1978.

Johnson, V. E. *I'll Quit Tomorrow.* San Francisco: Harper & Row, 1980.

Kaufman, E., and Kaufman, P., eds. *Family Therapy of Drug and Alcohol Abuse.* New York: Gardner Press, 1979.

Mendelson, J. H., and Mello, N. K., eds. *The Diagnosis and Treatment of Alcoholism.* New York: McGraw-Hill, 1979.

O'Donnell, M. P., and Ainsworth, T. H., eds. *Health Promotion in the Workplace.* New York: John Wiley, 1984.

Pace, N. A. Early identification of the alcoholic as viewed by the internist in industry and private practice. *NAAPH Journal* 12, no. 3 (March 1980): 102–8.

Pace, N. A., and Cross, W. *Guidelines to Safe Drinking.* New York: McGraw-Hill, 1984.

Powell, D. J., ed. *Alcoholism and Sexual Dysfunction: Issues in Clinical Management.* New York: Haworth Press, 1984.

Vaillant, G. E. *The Natural History of Alcoholism.* Cambridge, Mass.: Harvard University Press, 1983.

SECTION TWO

THE SEARCH FOR THE SOLUTION

5

The Neuron: A Primer of Brain Function

In order to follow the story of research on the causes of addiction, readers will need to know some basic facts of brain neurochemistry. In this chapter, I will describe the key structures in brain neurons, and chemical reactions between them that generate feelings of well-being and satisfaction, or frustration, anxiety, anger, or depression.

The chapter may be difficult reading for many, but it will be well worth the time and effort. It provides a foundation for understanding the work of the scientists described in subsequent chapters.

IN THE NEURON

The brain is composed largely of linked nerve cells or neurons. They perform two broad functions: they send messages to other neurons, and receive messages from other neurons. This interaction determines our mental and emotional functioning.

- The *cell body* (a, Fig. 5–1) is a chemical factory where messenger and control substances are manufactured.
- The *nucleus* (b) contains the chromosomes which, in turn, contain the genes that are made up of long chains of nucleotides. The nucleotides make up deoxyribonucleic acid (DNA). The DNA lays down the code for ribonucleic acid (RNA), and RNA, in turn, controls the synthesis of proteins which form neurotransmitters and enzymes.

- The tiny, treelike elements on one end of the neuron are called *dendrites* (c). They are the receivers that accept messages from other neurons. A given neuron may have hundreds or even thousands of dendrites linking it to other neurons. Since there are some 50 billion neurons, the total number of possible interactions is too great for comprehension.

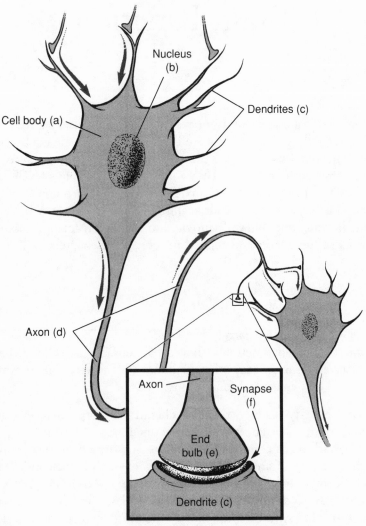

Figure 5–1 The Structure of the Neuron. Structural representation of the neuron. Close-up in box illustrates the anatomy of the synapse.

- A single large element extending outward from the other end of the cell body is called the *axon* (d). It carries messages to dendrites of adjacent neurons. Together, the axon and the dendrites act as "wired connectors" linking the neurons.
- Located at the end of the axon is a spherical protuberance called the *end bulb* (e). Or the axon may proliferate into multiple end bulbs. The outer surface of an end bulb constitutes one wall of the *synapse* (f) which acts as a chemical switch to control communication between the neurons.
- In the nucleus of the neuron (a, Fig. 5–2), the *DNA* molecules provide the blueprint which controls ribonucleic acid (RNA) manufacture.
- *RNA*, in turn, transmits instructions to the "factory" to control the design and production of neuronal proteins which act as building blocks for the neurotransmitters that carry messages between neurons, and for enzymes that regulate the synthesis and breakdown of neurotransmitters.

DNA and RNA are produced inside the nucleus. Proteins are produced in the cell body outside the nucleus in the *endoplasmic reticulum* (b). The work of the endoplasmic reticulum is to produce certain neurotransmitters and enzymes.

Some neurons produce *excitatory neurotransmitters* such as norepinephrine; some produce *inhibitory neurotransmitters* such as gamma-aminobutyric acid (GABA); and some produce both excitatory and inhibitory neurotransmitters, enabling a neuron to transmit more than one type of message. *But a particular neurotransmitter in a particular neuron can transmit only one specific message: stimulate or inhibit.* All neurotransmitter molecules of a given type—for example, norepinephrine—are structurally identical.

Neurotransmitters and certain enzymes are carried from the cell body through *microtubules* (c); along the axon (d); into the end bulb (e); and into small, spherical sacs called *synaptic vesicles* (f) whose position along the membrane is controlled by the genes. These vesicles are only 400 to 1200 angstroms in diameter. (An angstrom is one ten billionth of a meter.)

All of the molecules in a given vesicle are identical; that is, a vesicle will contain *only* norepinephrine molecules or *only* GABA molecules. If a particular neuron manufactures both norepinephrine and GABA, some of the vesicles will be filled with norepinephrine molecules, and some with GABA molecules.

Within the end bulb, *enzymes* which have migrated from the cell body act to regulate the supply of neurotransmitters by controlling their metabolism, or breakdown. This action prevents an oversupply of neurotransmitters that would result in overstimulation or overinhibition of the dendrite of the next neuron in the sequence. For example, monoamine

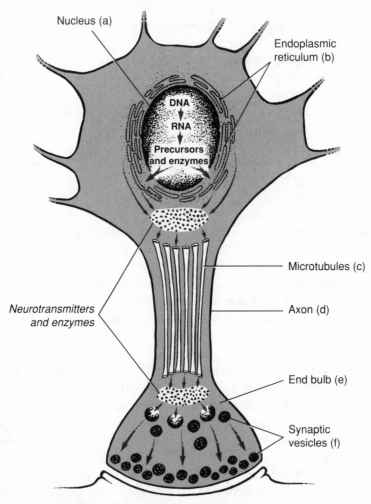

Figure 5–2 Nucleus and End Bulb. Expanded representation of the nucleus and end bulb. Arrows show the flow of neurotransmitters out of the endoplasmic reticulum (b) through the microtubules (c) to the end bulb (e).

oxidase prevents an oversupply of the neurotransmitter norepinephrine by converting it into a nonactive compound.

AT THE SYNAPSE

Also within the end bulb, substructures called mitochondrions (a, Fig. 5–3) convert sugar and oxygen into energy-releasing molecules for use by the neuron as needed. Across from the surface of the end bulb (b) is the *receptor area* of the dendrite of an adjacent neuron (c). The two surfaces are separated by the *synaptic gap* (d), 50 to 200 angstroms in width. This space is filled with a *synaptic fluid* (e), similar to salty water. It acts as an electrolyte to promote electrical activity at the interface.

The two surfaces and the intervening fluid constitute a *synapse* (f). The synaptic fluid contains positively charged ions such as sodium, potassium, calcium, and magnesium; and negatively charged ions such as chloride and phosphate.

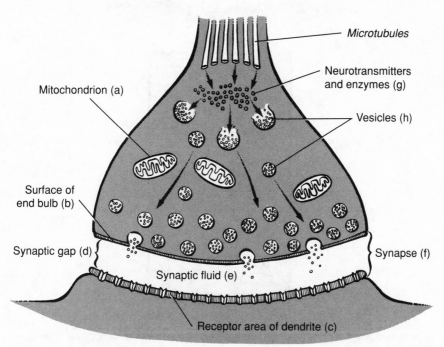

Figure 5–3 End Bulb and Synapse. Close-up of the axonal end bulb and the synapse. Arrows show flow of neurotransmitter release.

NEURONAL TRANSMISSION

Transmission of neurotransmitters across the synapse involves the following actions:

- Neurotransmitters (g)—and sometimes enzymes—*migrate* into the vesicles (h).
- In the *resting phase*, the ions (a) in the synaptic fluid (b, Fig. 5–4) are in electrical balance but the area is positive relative to the end bulb. Inside the bulb (c) there is a deficiency of positively

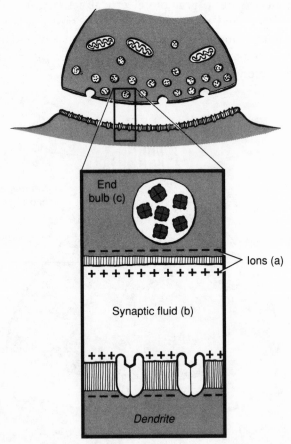

Figure 5–4 Resting Phase of the Neuron. Close-up of the resting phase, illustrating the axon-dendrite resting change.

charged ions, creating a net negative charge. The reason is that in the resting phase the neuronal membrane does not permit the entry of positively charged ions.

- In the *action phase*, the neuronal membrane changes its permeability (A, Fig. 5–5) to permit positively charged sodium (Na) and calcium (Ca) ions from the synaptic fluid to enter the end bulb. Simultaneously, potassium (K) is pumped out to maintain a balance and prevent an excessive positive charge.

- During this brief action phase, external calcium ions penetrate the membrane that encloses the end bulb. This action involves several other enzymes and proteins, and causes a *fusion of the walls of the vesicles with the membrane.* When this occurs, packets of neurotransmitter molecules are released (B) through the end bulb membrane into the synaptic fluid.

- Some of these molecules are immediately returned to the neuron

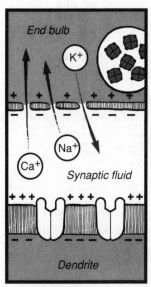

A. Permeability Change

B. Neurotransmitter Release and Receptor Binding

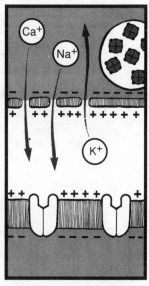

C. Return to Resting

Figure 5–5 Action Phase of the Neuron. In the action phase, ions and neurotransmitters flow from synaptic fluid to end bulb and from axon to dendrite, and return to rest. Arrows indicate direction of flow.

by a pumping action involving sodium and potassium ions (d): the *"re-uptake mechanism."*

- Some molecules are *metabolized or destroyed* by enzymes in the synaptic fluid.
- The remainder move across the synaptic gap and come into contact with specialized molecules called *receptors* (e) in the membrane of a dendrite of the second neuron.

At the height of this action phase, the interior of the cell has a strong positive charge relative to the synaptic fluid. This positive state lasts only 1/10,000 of a second, followed by a pumping out of positive sodium and calcium ions to bring the cell to a negative state again: the *resting state* (C).

- When one of the *neurotransmitter molecules* (a, Fig. 5–6) comes into contact with a *receptor cell* (b) that has the right shape and electrical charge, it fits it "like a key in a lock" and binds to the receptor to form a *neurotransmitter-receptor complex* (c).

If we take a closer look, when an excitatory neurotransmitter molecule (a, Fig. 5–7) approaches the receptor (b) and forms a neurotransmitter-receptor complex (c), it opens a channel for the exit of potassium ions, and the entry of sodium and calcium ions into the second neuron (d), activating it and initiating a new neuronal sequence.

- After activating the receptor, the neurotransmitter molecule is dissociated from the receptor, and is either metabolized by an enzyme in the synapse, or is returned to the end bulb of the first neuron to reenter a vesicle or be metabolized by internal enzymes.

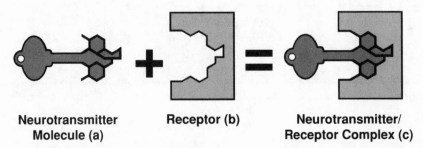

**Neurotransmitter   Receptor (b)   Neurotransmitter/
Molecule (a)   Receptor Complex (c)**

Figure 5–6 Neurotransmitter-Receptor Complex. Schematic of the structure of the neurotransmitter-receptor complex. The "lock and key" concept is shown.

- The *effect of an excitatory neurotransmitter on a receptor* (A, Fig. 5–8) is to permit positively charged sodium and calcium to enter, and potassium to exit the dendrite. These actions excite the second neuron in a controlled manner. The action requires approximately 2/10,000 of a second. An example would be the excitatory action of norepinephrine; for example, increasing neuronal firing.
- The *effect of an inhibitory neurotransmitter on a receptor* (B) is to permit negatively charged chloride ions to enter the dendrite, and potassium to exit. These actions inhibit cell activity. An example would be the inhibitory action of GABA, reducing neuronal firing.

If an excitatory neurotransmitter is involved, three "second-messenger" systems affect the function of the adjacent neuron:

- A compound called *adenosine monophosphate* (*cyclic* AMP) is activated. This initiation of the second messenger response sequence prepares the way for the eventual release of neurotransmitters from the vesicles in the axon.
- The *Protein Phosphorylation System* (PPS) provides energy for the eventual release of neurotransmitters from vesicles in the end bulb.

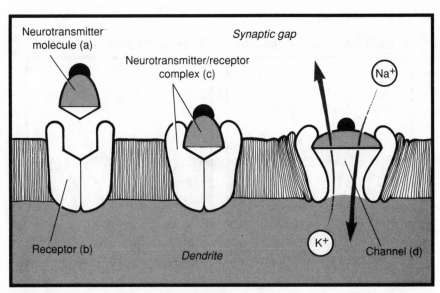

Figure 5–7 Excitatory Action at the Synapse. Action of an excitatory neurotransmitter molecule in the synaptic gap.

• *Intraneuronal calcium* enables the fusion of the vesicles with the membrane of the end bulb, opening the way for movement of a neurotransmitter across the synapse to an adjacent neuron.

This completes one full cycle of neuronal activity, the fundamental sequence of stimulus and response that determines behavior.

NEUROTRANSMITTERS

Essential to understanding the function of the neuron is an understanding of the nature and function of *neurotransmitters*. These substances are manufactured in the neuron, and can be divided into two types, both of which are made from amino acids, the basic building blocks of protein. The first type is the *monoamines*. They are composed entirely of single amino acids derived from food and carried by the blood into the brain. The second type is the *neuropeptides*. They are made from giant, linked amino acids called peptides produced in the endoplasmic reticulum. In the giant form they are inactive; that is, they have no biological activity, but are broken down into smaller, active neuropeptides.

A. Excitatory Neurotransmitter   B. Inhibitory Neurotransmitter

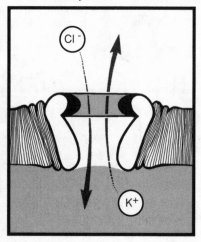

Figure 5–8 Comparison of Excitatory Neurotransmitter Action and Inhibitory Neurotransmitter Action at the Synapse

Monoamines

The key monoamines are:

1. Serotonin. Serotonin is made from the amino acid trypto-phan through the action of two enzymes: tryptophan hydroxylase and amino acid decarboxylase. It is metabolized or broken down in the brain by two other enzymes: monoamine oxidase, and aldehyde dehy-drogenase.

Serotonin messages promote feelings of well-being and sleep, tend to reduce aggression and compulsive behaviors such as drug abuse and excessive drinking or eating, elevate the pain threshold, and aid in the regulation of the cardiovascular system.

2. Dopamine. Dopamine is made from the amino acids phenylalanine and tyrosine through the action of three enzymes: phenylalanine hydroxy-lase, tyrosine hydroxylase, and amino acid decarboxylase. It is metabolized by the enzymes monoamine oxidase, catechol-O-methyl transferase, al-dehyde reductase, and alcohol dehydrogenase.

Dopamine messages increase feelings of well-being, tend to increase aggression, increase alertness and sexual excitement, and reduce compul-sive behavior. In some individuals, however, an excess of dopamine may cause psychotic behavior.

3. Norepinephrine. Norepinephrine is made from dopamine, through the action of a single enzyme: dopamine beta-hydroxylase. It is metabo-lized by the enzymes monoamine oxidase, catechol-O-methyl transferase, aldehyde reductase, and alcohol dehydrogenase.

Norepinephrine messages increase feelings of well-being, and reduce compulsive behavior. An excess may induce anxiety, increase heart rate and blood pressure, and cause tremors in patients undergoing with-drawal from alcohol and drug addiction.

4. GABA. GABA is made from the amino acid glutamic acid, which in turn is derived either from another amino acid called glutamine, or from the sugar glucose. The activating enzyme in the synthesis is glutamic acid decarboxylase. It is metabolized by the enzymes GABA transaminase and succinic semi-aldehyde dehydrogenase.

GABA messages reduce anxiety and compulsive behavior; elevate the pain threshold; and reduce heart rate, blood pressure, tremors, and the tendency toward convulsions in patients undergoing withdrawal.

Neuropeptides

The key neuropeptides are:

1. *Endorphins.* Endorphins are made from propiomelanocortin, a large amino acid peptide that is manufactured in the endoplasmic reticulum. Some six endorphins have been found, containing from 15 to 32 linked amino acids. The activating enzymes in endorphin synthesis are members of a class called endorphin convertase. Endorphins are metabolized by the enzymes acetyltransferase, carboxypeptidase B, or other endopeptidases.

2. *Enkephalins.* Enkephalins are made from pro-enkephalin proteins that originate in the endoplasmic reticulum. Three members of the class are found in large quantities in the brain: methionine-enkephalin and leucine-enkephalin, which contain five linked amino acids; and methionine-enkephalin-arginine-phenylalanine, which contains seven amino acids. The activating enzymes are members of a class called enkephalin convertase. They are metabolized by three independent inactivating enzymes: amino-peptidase, dipeptidylaminopeptidase, or endopeptidase. This latter, which is the most important of the three, has been given the name enkephalinase.

3. *Dynorphins.* Dynorphins are made from pro-dynorphin peptides that originate in the endoplasmic reticulum. There are four major types: dynorphin A and B, and neoendorphin Alpha and Beta, which contain from 8 to 18 amino acids. The activating enzyme is a member of a class called dynorphin convertase. They are metabolized by a trypsinlike endopeptidase, carboxypeptidase B, and endo-oligopeptidase A.

These three peptides—endorphins, enkephalins, and dynorphins—are called "opioid peptides" because they behave in the brain like a natural opiate such as morphine. Their functions include regulating the immune response, raising the pain threshold, stimulating feelings of well-being, regulating sexual activity, reducing compulsive behavior, promoting emotional balance, and enhancing mental activity such as learning.

NEURONAL RECEPTORS

Receptor molecules are of two types:

- *Presynaptic* receptors are located in the membrane of the end bulb of the axon near the synapse. They act to regulate the synthesis, metabolism, and release of neurotransmitters.
- *Postsynaptic* receptors are located in the membrane of the dendrite across the synapse of the adjacent neuron. They accept neurotransmitter molecules that cross the synaptic gap and initiate a new cycle of response.

Receptors respond only to their own neurotransmitters, or to drugs that resemble a given neurotransmitter substance. There are three types of serotonin receptors, two types of dopamine receptors, four types of norepinephrine receptors, two types of GABA receptors, and five types of opioid receptors.

The sensitivity of presynaptic receptors is affected by a change in the firing rate of the neuron, in re-uptake activity, or in the ion conductance of sodium, potassium, calcium, or chloride across the synaptic membrane.

The sensitivity of the postsynaptic receptor system is affected by a change in the number of receptors, in the supply of neurotransmitter molecules, or in ion conductance across the synaptic membrane.

BLOOD BRAIN BARRIER

Certain essential amino acids that are precursors to, or give rise to, neurotransmitters are derived from the blood. Therefore the availability of neurotransmitters is dependent on the permeability of the brain capillaries that supply the neurons. These capillaries are tiny tubules made up of endothelial cells which control the passage of substances from the blood to the brain and vice versa. Their permeability, in turn, is affected by the molecular size of the amino acid, its charge, its solubility, and the availability of substances that act as carrier systems across the barrier.

For amino acids, one carrier system is a protein attached to the endothelial cells. When an amino acid passes through the capillary, the carrier sucks it out of the blood and, to the best of our knowledge, rotates and discharges it through the barrier into the brain.

Stress, or drug or alcohol abuse increases permeability; lowering of the pH factor (acidity) decreases permeability. For example, if the amino acids isoleucine and tryptophan are in competition for the same carrier proteins to penetrate the blood brain barrier:

- An increase in the intake of carbohydrates into the diet will have the effect of diverting isoleucine into the muscles. The result will be that more tryptophan molecules will be picked up by the carrier molecules and transported into the neuron.
- An increase in protein in the diet will have a reverse effect, and the number of tryptophan molecules entering the neuron will decrease.

AGONISTS AND ANTAGONISTS

Two final concepts are crucial in understanding the function of the neurons. Substances that affect axons and dendrites fall into two classes: agonists and antagonists. As scientists define them:

- An *agonist* is a substance that binds to a receptor. For example, when morphine binds to a receptor, it activates a dendrite, leading to a reduction in pain.
- An *antagonist* is a substance that binds to a receptor, has no effect on the receptor itself, but prevents the bonding of an agonist to that receptor. For example, naltrexone may strip away an agonist like morphine that has already bonded to a receptor, ending its painkilling activity.

These activities produce specific action sequences in the neuron, leading to transmission of impulses—excitatory or inhibitory—that generate behavior.

In summary, when a stimulus impinges upon a dendrite it triggers the neuron factory to make neurotransmitters for carrying messages, and enzymes for regulating neurotransmitter supply. Neurotransmitters that move down through the axon and cross the synapse carry a message that either stimulates or inhibits receptors in a dendrite of the next neuron in the chain, initiating or continuing a behavioral response.

SUGGESTED READING

Angier, N. Storming the wall. *Discover* 11 (May 1990): 66–72.

Bousfield, D., ed. *Neurotransmitters in Action: A Collection of Articles from Trends in Neurosciences.* New York: Elsevier Biomedical Press, 1985.

Bloom, F. E., Lazerson, A., and Hofstadter, L. *Brain, Mind and Behavior,* New York: W. H. Freeman, 1985.

Bradford, H. F. *Chemical Neurobiology.* New York: W. H. Freeman, 1986.

Cohen, S. *The Chemical Brain: The Neurochemistry of Addictive Disorders.* Irvine, Calif.: Care Institute, 1988.

Cooper, J. R., Bloom, F. E., and Roth, R. H. *The Biochemical Basis of Neuropharmacology.* 5th ed.: Oxford University Press, 1986.

Daigle, R. D., Clark, H. W., and Landry, M. J. A primer on neurotransmitters and cocaine. *Journal of Psychoactive Drugs* 20(1988):283–95.

Drlica, K. *Understanding DNA and Gene Cloning: A Guide for the Curious.* New York: John Wiley, 1984.

Gilman, A. G. and Goodman, L. S., eds. *The Pharmacological Basis of Therapeutics, 8th edition.* New York: Pergamon, 1990.

Goldstein, G. W. and Betz, A. L. The blood-brain barrier. *Scientific American* 255(September 1986):74–83.

Restak, R. M. *The Mind.* New York: Bantam Books, 1988.

Snyder, S. H. *Drugs and the Brain.* New York: Scientific American Books, 1986.

———. Drugs and neurotransmitter receptors in the brain. *Science* 224(1984):22–34.

Tokay, E. *The Fundamentals of Physiology.* New York: Barnes & Noble, 1967.

Zucker, R. S., and Lando, L. Mechanisms of transmitter release: Voltage hypothesis and calcium hypothesis. *Science* 231(1986):574–79.

6

Science and the Disease Concept

This book is not a critical review of research on the neurological, pharmacological, and genetic bases of alcoholism. It would be impossible in a book of this length to summarize four or five decades of work in all of the relevant disciplines. My intentions are to inform readers about the main findings, and to give them some sense of how and when they were arrived at.

Given the second intention, I will thus describe in a reasonable amount of detail—perhaps too much for some readers!—those experiments that, in my view, made basic contributions to our understanding; make briefer mention of experiments that clarified or extended those contributions; note significant questions or controversies that arose; and reference books and papers that may be of interest to the serious reader. To rank the order of importance of individual experiments would be beyond the abilities of even a prestigious panel of experts. My selection is necessarily personal and arbitrary, but it represents my best judgment as to the discoveries, integrations, and major concepts that have contributed most to clarifying the nature and progression of alcoholism and the addictive disease process.

To help the reader maintain a sense of direction as the ideas develop, I will present the findings in approximate chronological sequence—just as we in the field learned of them—with occasional flashbacks to earlier work that took on new significance because of new insights. Readers who want more information on certain of the more complex experiments, should consult the end notes that provide additional detail.

At the beginning of the 1940s, most research into alcoholism could be classified under three main headings: observation and analysis of psychological or behavioral variables; observation and analysis of social and cultural variable; and laboratory investigations of the effects of alcohol upon bodily organs and the nervous system.

There were few efforts to study neurological, endocrinological, metabolic, and genetic causes of alcoholism. Scientists in the biological disciplines could not use human subjects as guinea pigs, and they had not yet bred animals that could be used as models to simulate human alcoholics. But the major brake on research into alcoholism was the prevailing belief that it was nothing more than a psychological or sociological aberration.

THE DISEASE CONCEPT

Dr. E. M. Jellinek probably deserves the credit for focusing the attention of scientists on the idea that alcoholism was a disease. Born in the United States in 1890, Jellinek first became interested in alcoholism while working as assistant director of research for the United Fruit Company in Honduras. There he saw the destructive effects of heavy drinking on the company's professional staff.

This interest eventually led him to Massachusetts State Hospital, and then to Yale University where, with Dr. Howard W. Haggard, he founded the Yale Center of Alcohol Studies in 1942. He was also one of the founders of the National Council on Alcoholism. His work culminated in *The Disease Concept of Alcoholism* (1960), a controversial book that aroused wide interest among scientists and treatment professionals. His thesis was that alcoholism is a chronic illness to which several factors contribute.

1. A *constitutional liability factor.* He postulated that certain individuals have an inborn vulnerability to alcohol. They have a tendency to lose control of their drinking because they have a biochemical sensitivity to alcohol. This sensitivity may be genetic or congenital, and may reflect a nutritional deficiency, a pathological condition of the brain, or a dysfunction of the endocrine system.
2. A *personality or psychological factor.* He suggested that psychological strain, a feeling of personal inadequacy, and an alienation from society might make an individual vulnerable to alcohol.
3. A *social factor.* He considered that the alcoholic gains relief from his pain and his problems by turning to the culturally acceptable pleasures of the bar and the cocktail party.

Jellinek identified five basic types of alcoholism:

1. *Alpha alcoholism* is a psychological dependence that leads the individual to rely on alcohol to relieve physical or emotional pain. The drinking is heavy enough to violate accepted rules of behavior, but does not lead to loss of control.
2. *Beta alcoholism* leads to complications such as nerve disorders, gastritis, and liver ailments, without the development of physical or psychological dependence. Withdrawal symptoms do not occur.
3. *Gamma alcoholism* involves increased tissue tolerance to alcohol, adaptive cell metabolism, and withdrawal symptoms. There is a definite progression from psychological to physical dependence, and pronounced behavioral changes. Under certain conditions, alpha and beta alcoholism may develop into gamma alcoholism. The gamma alcoholic experiences the most serious physical and psychological damage.
4. *Delta alcoholism* entails not so much a loss of control as an inability to abstain. The delta alcoholic may never drink enough to lose control, but maintains a constant level of alcohol in the body, and cannot do without it even for a short period of time without experiencing withdrawal symptoms.
5. *Epsilon alcoholism* leads to episodic or binge drinking.

Jellinek's conclusion was that gamma and delta types are diseases because they involve disturbances of cell metabolism and increased tissue tolerance, along with loss of control or inability to abstain. He saw that the physiopathological conditions arising from alcoholism were analogous to those caused by the continued abuse of drugs such as morphine, cocaine, and barbiturates. He pointed out that these drugs, as well as alcohol, can lead to craving.[1] This was the first clear, coherent statement of the disease concept of alcoholism.

But Jellinek's theory left three basic questions unanswered: What are the underlying biogenetic mechanisms that cause alcoholism? Do stress and social influences alter cell function and lead to alcoholism? Does long-term excessive drinking alter cell function and lead to alcoholism?

GENETIC INDIVIDUALITY AND NUTRITION AS FACTORS IN ALCOHOLISM

As with so many other human medical problems, real progress in answering these questions began to be made when scientists turned to experiments on animals. Laboratory animals have been used in thousands of experiments conducted by hundreds of scientists investigating alcohol and drug abuse. The results of these experiments have stimulated a generation of other research projects involving human subjects. Together, animal and human experiments have opened the way to a new understanding of the disease process, and provided medical insights that have strengthened methods of treatment. They may eventually lead to prevention and cure.

Jorge Mardones was one of the pioneers in scientific research into alcoholism. His principal interests were alcohol metabolism and its effects on the liver, and the human genetics of alcoholism. He became director of the Institute for Alcoholism Research at the University of Chile in 1949.

In an experiment with two groups of rats, he fed one group a well-balanced diet, and the other a diet deficient in vitamin B-complex. When offered a choice of water or an alcohol solution, the deprived rats chose the alcohol over the water. When he added liver or yeast, these rich sources of vitamin B complex caused a marked reduction in alcohol intake.

When he experimented with rats housed separately in individual cages, he found that some of them, when deprived of vitamin B complex, were more prone to increase their alcohol intake than others. He attributed this phenomenon to a nutritional factor naturally occurring in the liver. He called this the "N 1" factor.[2]

Later, in an extension of this research in which he tested voluntary consumption of alcohol under conditions of dietary deficiency, he used rats that had been inbred for seven generations. He found that young rats preferred alcohol if their parents had preferred alcohol before them.[3] These results were among the first to support the theory that both nutrition and genetics might affect alcohol preference.

When he visited me two decades later, he said that he began this series of experiments because of his dissatisfaction with the prevailing idea that alcoholism was a moral problem reflecting weak willpower and a sinful nature.

THE GLUTAMINE FACTOR

Biochemist Roger Williams, born in Ootacumund, India, of missionary parents, was for many years director of the Clayton Foundation at The University of Texas at Austin. In his research into the causes of alcoholism, he found evidence of an important role for both genetics and nutrition. In experiments with rats, he found that there are pronounced differences in the amount of alcohol that individual rats will drink if they have a choice between alcohol and water. He attributed these differences to "metabolic individuality," and—drawing to some extent on the work of Mardones—advanced what he called the "genotropic theory" of alcoholism. This theory held that some individuals need alcohol to replace a nutritional fault, probably genetic, and probably due to an enzyme anomaly.

In 1955, Williams contributed to our understanding of the pharmacology of alcoholism when he found that an amino acid called L-glutamine markedly reduced alcohol consumption in rats given a choice of water and an alcohol solution. When we visited him in 1987, in retirement, he told us the story of this research:

> My associate Bill Shive had been investigating the toxicity of alcohol. In an experiment, he found that when he added alcohol to a medium supporting the growth of a bacterium called *Streptococcus faecalis*, further growth was inhibited. Recalling the work of Mardones, he added liver extract to see if it would offset the toxic effect of the alcohol. When the bacteria began to grow again, Shive analyzed the liver extract and isolated the active component responsible for this effect. It proved to be an amino acid called *L-glutamine*.[4]
>
> This really sparked my interest. If glutamine would work in a test tube, perhaps it would work in a living animal. I gave 30 rats a choice of water or a 10 percent solution of alcohol, and measured their alcohol consumption over a period of 55 days. I then took 19 of these animals and gave them 100 mg of glutamine orally over a period of 26 days. I then measured their alcohol intake, and found it to be 35 percent lower than their intake prior to the glutamine administration.[5]
>
> However, glutamine was almost wholly ineffective in reducing alcohol consumption in three rats of this group. Furthermore, the effect of glutamine in reducing alcohol consumption in the other animals slowly diminished, and eventually disappeared. These results suggested to me that in experimental animals an individuality in metabolism exists, confirming the genetropic concept.[6]

INBRED LABORATORY ANIMALS:
A GENETIC MODEL OF ALCOHOLISM

Utilizing a strain of black mice called C57, Leonora Mirone made an early contribution to the development of an animal model when she found that C57 mice, when confronted with a choice of water or 5 percent ethanol in water solution, chose more ethanol than water.[7]

Mirone also found that certain diets either increased or decreased this preference. Based on this work she suggested that dietary changes accentuate the genotropic condition hypothesized by Williams.[8]

At this point, scientists were considering the role of both genetics and environment in predisposition to alcoholism, but there was no insight into the mechanisms involved, and no means available for determining their relative importance. An animal model of alcoholism was needed that could be more precisely controlled, so that experimental data could be more accurately quantified. That was the situation when Gerald McClearn stepped into the picture.

While still an undergraduate psychology major at Allegheny College, McClearn became curious about genetic differences such as coat color in laboratory animals, and decided to take a course in genetics. It seemed clear to him that all parts of the animal/human organism (and their functions) could be influenced, at least in theory, by genetic differences. Psychology was clearly wrong, he felt, to assume that the roots of individuality were to be found primarily in the environment.

As McClearn explained in a 1988 interview:

My first thought was that I ought to get out of psychology and take up this genetics stuff, but then I had a second thought. Why not study the genetics of behavior?

I completed my doctoral work at the University of Wisconsin, started a project on the genetics of learning ability in mice, and then moved to the University of California at Berkeley, where I met Dave Rogers, a clinical psychologist. After several good-natured discussions about his kind of psychology and my kind of psychology we decided to collaborate. We had to come up with something in a hurry, because we had ordered a bunch of laboratory mice, and they were at the right age, and time was passing.

Out of the depths of a cloudy memory I recalled that someone had looked at alcohol preference in mice, and when I looked up the reference it turned out to be a paper by Roger Williams in which he reported that certain strains of both rats and mice showed individual differences in their preference for alcohol over water. There was considerable variability among strains, probably due to a lack of rigorous inbreeding, but the possibility of inheritable difference seemed to be there.

I had also read papers by Mirone in which she had used, among others, the C57 strain which seemed to exhibit this preference for alcohol over water. Dave and I decided to set up an experiment, using five different strains: C57BLs, A/Cals, DBAs, BALBs, and C3Hs. These specific strains had been inbred for many generations, so we could be reasonably sure they would breed true.

In that first experiment with the animals, water and a 10 percent ethyl alcohol solution were both available so that they could drink when they felt like it. Within three or four days, the C57s were showing a strong preference for alcohol over water, the C3Hs were divided in their preference, and the other strains preferred water. Since there were no environmental variables, it was clear that the C57s were genetically predisposed to drink alcohol. In other words, we had a strain of alcoholic mice!

McClearn then began to refine his mouse model through selective breeding. For example, animals that go to sleep quickly after drinking alcohol are assumed to be highly sensitive to alcohol, while animals that resist sleep after drinking are assumed to have a low sensitivity to alcohol. To develop this sleep behavior into a research tool, he mated "short-sleeping" males and females, and "long-sleeping" males and females, and after 17 generations the lines bred true.[9]

With these strains of mice available, scientists could use sleep as a tool for investigating differential sensitivity to alcohol. Later, other strains were developed that showed differences in preference, tolerance, or withdrawal, or combinations of these characteristics. McClearn explained:

> With selective breeding, a scientist can specify in advance the characteristics wanted in the mouse model. For example, you can develop an animal tolerant to alcohol, or a tolerant animal who likes to drink but has strong withdrawal reactions. These subtypes are the key to the whole thing.
>
> If we are right in assuming that alcoholism is genetic in origin, we are not likely to find that it originates in a single gene, but in many genes, and each of these genes may generate a particular behavior pattern. If we have the appropriate animal model, we can explore these patterns independently and with precision.

The development of these genetically bred alcohol-preferring and non-preferring animals produced a research tool of great power. It has enabled neurobiologists and pharmacologists to study alcoholism in living organisms without the constraints imposed by the use of human subjects.

Using alcoholic mice, a scientist can go into the brain and explore the changes brought about by alcohol at the molecular and cellular level; explore the differences in brain chemistry of animals that prefer alcohol over water; and look for the genetic anomalies at the DNA and RNA levels that are responsible for that preference.

CAN NURTURE CHANGE NATURE?

John R. Nichols, in a little-known but fascinating experiment, injected morphine into rats that normally did not drink morphine solutions, and continued until morphine drinking was an addiction. When the morphine was withheld, and the animals went into withdrawal symptoms (indicating addiction), he selected those animals that had shown a high tendency to drink morphine, and those that had shown a low tendency to drink morphine. He then used selective breeding techniques to develop a strain of rats that showed a high preference for morphine, and a strain that showed a low preference for morphine. When the strains began to breed true after the third generation, he found that the animals highly susceptible to morphine were similarly susceptible to drinking alcohol.[10]

Nichols' findings suggested (1) that environmental influences (such as forced injection of drugs) can unmask a genetic propensity for addiction to morphine and (2) addiction proneness to morphine and alcohol may be due to a common genetic influence.

As we shall see, in the intervening years there has been ample support for the idea of common genetic factors in addiction to opiates and alcohol, but Nichols' suggestion that the heavy consumption of opiates or alcohol by a previously normal person can lead to addiction has not been properly explored.

STRESS AND ALCOHOL CRAVING

Several pioneering investigators established stress as a motivator for alcohol-seeking behavior. J. H. Masserman and K. S. Yum created experimental neuroses in cats by subjecting them to severe stress, and then offered them a choice of plain milk or an alcoholic "milk cocktail." Whereas normal cats preferred plain milk, the stressed cats preferred the alcoholic beverage.[11]

J. Conger formulated what he called the "tension reduction hypothesis"

(TRH) which later became widely accepted by behavioral scientists. The hypothesis, based on the principle of instrumental learning, held that alcohol drinking reduces tension, and that some individuals learn to use alcohol to feel calmer in tense situations.[12]

Albert Casey found that when water-preferring rats were exposed to electrical shock at intervals over a period of 16 days they developed a preference for alcohol over water, and that this preference continued long after the shocks were eliminated. Rats that received no shocks continued to prefer water. His conclusion was that stress causes changes in the organism that can lead to above-normal alcohol intake, and that this pattern continues for a period of time after the stress is removed.[13]

These results were among the first indications that stress can alter the chemistry of the brain, and that this alteration can change alcohol-craving behavior.

Ernest Noble and his associates used inbred strains of mice—some alcohol-loving, and some alcohol-hating—to investigate genetic differences in their biochemical response to alcohol.

They injected the animals with alcohol as a stressor, and then took blood samples to measure the levels of corticosterone, a substance that is secreted by the adrenal gland under conditions of stress. They found that the alcohol-loving animals had a reduced level of corticosterone, compared to alcohol-hating animals.[14]

These results provided some of the first evidence that sensitivity to alcohol may be under genetic control, and that the alcohol-loving animals have an inborn resistance to stressful stimuli.

ALCOHOL CAUSES ALCOHOLISM

Robert D. Myers at Purdue University in Indiana had been intrigued by the work of Casey which suggested that alcohol craving increases following stress. He formed the hypothesis that, whereas occasional or short-term use of alcohol relieves stress, long-term use—instead of relieving stress—may permanently change brain chemistry in such a way as to generate craving. To test this hypothesis he implanted plastic tubes into the cerebral spinal fluid of rats that had never drunk alcohol. Through these tubes he pumped regulated quantities of different alcohol solutions directly into the brain. In all, each rat received 1,000 brain injections during the period of the experiment.

Afterward, the rats were deprived of food and water on alternate days, and tested for their preference for alcohol or water. He found that the greater the infusion of alcohol directly into the brain, the greater the tendency to drink larger amounts of alcohol.

In the second part of the experiment he stopped the infusions, and over a two-week period tested the animals' preference for alcohol. He found that the induced increase in alcohol preference persisted until the end of the test period.[15] Myers commented:

> These results clearly indicate that repeated and direct alterations of the brain's biochemical environment, caused by alcohol, can produce significant changes in later alcohol-seeking behavior.
>
> A new biochemical theory of alcoholism may have to be evolved with its primary focus on metabolic aberrations of the central nervous system.

We were now seeing the first evidence linking an increase in alcohol-craving behavior to permanent biochemical changes induced by long-term ingestion of alcohol—in itself a scientific confirmation of the folk belief that alcohol can cause alcoholism.

EMERGING INSIGHTS

Earlier we stated that the work of Jellinek raised three questions. By the end of the 1960s, the questions were still unanswered, but new insights were emerging.

1. *What are the underlying biogenetic mechanisms that cause alcoholism?* Mardones, Williams, and others suggested the existence of differences in individual preference for and sensitivity to alcohol. McClearn and others showed that these differences can indeed be produced through selective breeding.
2. *Do stress and social influences alter cell metabolism and lead to alcoholism?* Masserman and Yum found that stress increases alcohol consumption in experimental animals. Conger concluded that alcohol consumption reduces tension, and thereby generates a learned response that relates the drinking of alcohol to feeling calmer in difficult situations.

   Casey verified the Masserman and Yum findings, and further showed that the effects of stress extend long after the stress is removed.
3. *Does long-term excessive drinking alter cell metabolism and lead to*

alcoholism? Myers demonstrated that the intake of alcohol created a preference for alcohol in animals that previously had preferred water, and went beyond Casey to suggest that this takes place because alcohol alters the biochemical environment of the brain. Or to paraphrase: "The more you drink the more you want."

Nichols went still further and suggested, admittedly on scanty evidence, that alcohol and other drugs may produce a permanent genetic change in the brain that transfers to later generations. This is still a "chicken or egg?" question, but evidence is slowly accumulating. With the theory of alcoholism as a disease process gaining wider acceptance, and with animal models available for experiments on the role of genetics and environment in alcohol preference, scientists were now ready to move ahead in their investigations of the biochemical nature of alcoholism.

SUGGESTED READING

Blum, K. *Handbook of Abusable Drugs.* New York: Gardner Press, 1984.

Cahn, S. *The Treatment of Alcoholics.* New York: Oxford University Press, 1970.

Chafetz, M. E., and Demone, H. W., Jr. *Alcoholism and Society.* New York: Oxford University Press, 1962.

Fishman, R. *Alcohol and Alcoholism.* New York: Chelsea House, 1986.

Fitzgerald, K. *Alcoholism: The Genetic Inheritance.* New York: Doubleday, 1988.

Fox, R. *Aspects of Alcoholism,* vol. 2. Philadelphia: J. B. Lippincott, 1966.

Gallant, D. M. *Alcoholism: A Guide to Diagnosis, Intervention and Treatment.* New York: W. W. Norton, 1987.

Mendelson, J. H., and Mello, N. K., eds. *The Diagnosis and Treatment of Alcoholism.* New York: McGraw-Hill, 1979.

Williams, R. J. *The Prevention of Alcoholism through Nutrition.* New York: Bantam, 1981.

————. *Physicians Handbook of Nutritional Science.* Springfield, Ill.: Charles C Thomas, 1975.

7

The Biochemistry of Alcoholism: Early Clues

S everal research initiatives now began to clarify some of the basic physiological phenomena associated with behavior, pointing toward biochemical factors that had previously been unknown or ignored.

CHEMICAL COMMUNICATION

The first suggestion that communication between and among neurons takes place not only through electrical action currents, but also through the transfer of chemical substances at nerve terminals had been made by DuBose-Reymond in 1877. He suggested ammonia or lactic acid as the active agent.

Fourteen years later, J. N. Langley noticed a similarity of effect between the injection of extracts made from adrenal glands, and direct excitation of the sympathetic nerves which control these glands.[1] He added to the picture in 1905 when he suggested that neurons respond to both excitatory and inhibitory chemical substances. It was later pointed out by T. R. Elliot that the material released through stimulation of the sympathetic nerves resembled epinephrine, a product of the adrenal glands. He considered this material to be an important chemical step in neurotransmission.[2]

CHEMICAL RECEPTOR SITES

W. E. Dixon took a long step into the unknown in 1907 when he advanced the hypothesis that when a nerve is stimulated it liberates a hormone which combines with an unknown constituent on an end organ, muscle, or gland.

This was probably the first reference—though an obscure one—to the concept of chemical receptor sites.[3]

NEUROCHEMICAL CONTROL THROUGH EXCITATION AND INHIBITION

In 1921 Otto Loerwi, a German scientist, established the first proof of chemical control of nerve impulses. In a classic experiment he stimulated the vagus nerve of a frog heart, causing it to slow its rate of beating. When he channeled fluid from this heart into a second heart, it also slowed in apparent reaction to chemicals transferred from the first heart. He found that the chemical in the fluid that caused the heart to slow was a substance he named *vagus-substance*, or *parasympathin*, now known as *acetylcholine*. Later, he found a chemical that increased the heart rate. This substance he named *acceleran*, now known as *epinephrine*.[4]

In that same year, W. B. Cannon found an accelerator substance released by the sympathetic nerves, and called it *sympathin*.[5] It was later shown by U.S. von Euler to be a combination of epinephrine and a similar substance called norepinephrine.[6] Cannon went on to characterize the function of the sympathetic (norepinephrine) and para-sympathetic (acetylcholine) divisions of the autonomic nervous system.

EARLY RESEARCH INTO THE EFFECTS OF ALCOHOL

Growing out of these insights into the role of chemical messengers in the nervous system, a number of studies in the early 1960s began to explore the effects of *alcohol* on the nervous system. Many of the results were contradictory. D. Gursey and P. E. Olson found, for example, that when they injected ethanol into the brain of a rabbit the levels of brain serotonin and norepinephrine were reduced.[7] But when D. H. Efron and G. L. Gessa tried a similar experiment with rats, they found no reduction in serotonin.[8]

We now understand that many such small controversies grew out of the fact that a variety of factors influence the effect of alcohol on the brain. For example, a measurement taken shortly after injection of a test substance may vary sharply from one taken after a longer delay. Or the size of the dosage may radically alter the result. Or an animal from an alcohol-preferring genetic strain may show diametrically opposite results from an animal belonging to a non-alcohol-preferring strain.

The behavioral aspects of brain chemical changes resulting from alcohol intake were also receiving more attention. G. Rosenfeld, for example, became interested in the fact that when he injected a mouse with an alcohol solution it went to sleep. When he injected the mouse with the neurotransmitter serotonin or dopamine before it received the alcohol, it slept longer. No one knew why these chemicals lengthened sleep time, but the finding helped to stimulate research into the neurotransmitters and their role in alcoholism.[9]

PRELUDE TO NEUROPHARMACOLOGICAL INTERVENTION

Robert D. Myers, whom we met earlier, came back into the picture in 1968. He and his associate, W. L. Veale, devised an experiment to explore the effect of neurotransmitter imbalances on alcohol preference. They chose serotonin and norepinephrine for their tests on laboratory rats.

Three sets of rats were installed in individual cages and offered a choice of an alcohol solution or water. Over the first 11 days of the experiment, the percentage of alcohol in the solution was gradually raised from 3 percent to 30 percent to establish a preference curve. They found that as the alcohol concentration increased the animals drank less alcohol and more water.

During a second 11-day period, to one set of rats they administered a substance called pCPA that was known to reduce the amount of serotonin in the brain. To a second set of rats they administered a substance called alpha-MpT that reduces the amount of norepinephrine in the brain. To a third set of rats, for a control, they administered a neutral saline solution that affects neither serotonin nor norepinephrine.

During this 11-day period, they measured the drinking behavior of the rats in each set. They found that:

- The pCPA group with reduced serotonin developed a strong aversion to alcohol.
- The alpha-MpT group with reduced norepinephrine developed a mild aversion to alcohol.
- The saline control group showed no change in preference.

A month later, they again tested the drinking behavior of the pCPA group, and found that the strong aversion was still present.[10]

From this experiment Myers and Veale concluded that both serotonin and norepinephrine are involved in alcohol preference; that serotonin is more potent; and that the effects of both persist over time. They then made a creative leap in a paper that appeared in *Science* in 1968. Although admitting that treatment with pCPA might not be applicable to the problem of human alcoholism, they concluded that "the findings do suggest that restoration of normal neurochemical function in an organism that drinks excessively may now be within the realm of possibility."

This was probably the first explicit statement of the potential use of neuropharmacological intervention in the treatment of abnormal drinking behavior in the human alcoholic. The precise role of serotonin in craving behavior came under question in later years, but Myers' conclusion provided a powerful rationale for future experiments.

TETRAHYDROISOQUINOLINES (TIQS): THE ALCOHOL-OPIATE LINK

Virginia Davis at the Veterans Administration Hospital at Baylor College of Medicine was considering two startling questions:

- When people drink alcohol, do their brains use the alcohol molecule to manufacture an opiate-like substance that resembles morphine?
- Is it possible that the biochemical bases of alcohol addiction and opiate addiction are similar?

These questions had been provoked by experimental evidence that led to a tantalizing hypothesis. Her reasoning was complex, but I will summarize as simply as I can:

1. In the brain, the neurotransmitter dopamine is converted first to *dopamine aldehyde* and finally to dopamine acid.
2. The final conversion is carried out by a natural enzyme called acetaldehyde dehydrogenase.
3. When alcohol is consumed, it is converted first to *acetaldehyde* and finally to carbon dioxide and water. This final conversion is also carried out by acetaldehyde dehydrogenase.
4. This means that dopamine aldehyde, naturally present in the neuron, competes with acetaldehyde, derived from alcohol, for the available acetaldehyde dehydrogenase enzyme.
5. Acetaldehyde, however, is much more strongly attracted to the

enzyme than is dopamine aldehyde. As a result, a greater amount of acetaldehyde reacts with the enzyme and is destroyed. This action leaves an excess of dopamine aldehyde in the brain.

6. The excess dopamine aldehyde molecules may combine with unconverted dopamine molecules, yielding an alkaloid with the formidable name of tetrahydropapaveroline (THP).

And THP strongly resembles the raw material from which the poppy plant manufactures morphine!

To test this intriguing hypothesis, Davis teamed up with Michael Walsh, an assistant professor of biochemistry, and set up an elegant experiment. They homogenized material from the brain stem area of rats and combined it in a test tube with radioactive dopamine, vitamin C, and a chemical derived from nucleic acid called NAD. They knew that this combination would yield dopamine aldehyde, but would it also yield THP?

Painstaking analysis yielded unmistakable proof of the presence of THP. The striking resemblance between the two molecules can be seen in Figure 7–1. In other words, both the brain and the poppy plant manufacture the raw materials from which morphine is made.

In a second experiment they incubated the same materials with alcohol, in one case, and acetaldehyde in the other. In both cases they found that the production of THP was increased. Clearly, increasing the supply of alcohol or its breakdown product, acetaldehyde, led to increased THP production.

For a quantitative test, they injected radioactive THP into rats and analyzed the results. About half of the material was converted into opiate compounds such as normorphine, morphine, norcodeine, and

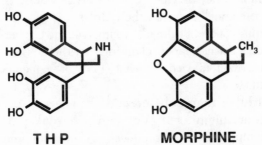

T H P   **MORPHINE**

Figure 7–1 THP and Morphine. Chemical structure of tetrahydropapaveroline (THP), a known precursor of morphine in the poppy plant.

codeine. The report on their experiment appeared in the February 1970 issue of *Science*. [11]

On the basis of this work, Davis and Walsh suggested that the consumption of alcohol may lead to the production of addictive compounds of the opiate type; and that alcohol abuse is a true addiction that may involve biochemical processes similar to those associated with opiate dependence.

There was clinical support for this hypothesis. Many opiate addicts, during a period of abstinence, will substitute alcohol for their drug of choice. Conversely, it is not uncommon for opiate addicts to have previous histories of alcohol abuse, suggesting a cross-dependence between alcohol and opiates.

Despite supporting scientific and clinical evidence, the findings of Davis and Walsh caused heated debate in the scientific community, and even in the popular press. Maurice H. Seevers at the University of Chicago Medical School led the attack, also in *Science* in 1970, arguing:

> A major portion of the signs of alcohol abstinence resembles the effects produced by convulsant drugs. . . . Morphine not only has psychomotor effects which are quite different from those of alcohol, but, in addition, it relieves pain, depresses respiration, and alters greatly the central [brain] and peripheral regulation of autonomic function. . . .
>
> . . . if the concept of Davis and Walsh was tenable, the morphine antagonists (nalorphine, naloxone, and so forth) would antagonize short-term alcohol intoxication as they do specifically for morphine-like drugs. [12]

Seevers also pointed out that there is no evidence that alcohol lessens the effect of morphine, or vice versa; in other words, there appears to be no "cross-tolerance" between these drugs.

Perry V. Halushka and Philip C. Hoffman at the University of Chicago also objected in a *Science* paper, claiming that there is no direct evidence that THP is formed *in vivo*, or that THP or a metabolite has high addictive liability.

Davis replied that their only intention had been to define "a possible biochemical concomitant of alcoholism which would provide a common link between the addiction produced by ethanol and the narcotic alkaloids."[13]

The controversy became so heated that Michael Walsh was denied membership in the American Society for Pharmacology and Experimental Therapeutics. Following his death ten years later, however, in view of later findings he was posthumously elected to membership in the Society.

The Davis and Walsh experiments did not provide answers to the questions of where and how these opiate-like substances act in the brain to influence behavior, but they opened an important new area of investigation.

TIQS: A NEUROTOXIN

In the March issue of *Science* in that same year, Gerald Cohen and his postdoctoral student, Michael Collins, at the Columbia University College of Physicians and Surgeons published a paper that provided support for the biochemical basis for alcoholism.

In a 1988 interview, Cohen said:

The question in my mind at the time was, can aldehydes convert to TIQs in the body? For our experiment we took adrenal glands from cows, and into one inserted a dilute solution of acetaldehyde, and into another, a solution of saline. The tissues were then homogenized, stored overnight, run through a centrifuge, and analyzed by chromatography. The tissues receiving acetaldehyde showed the presence of TIQs; the tissues receiving saline showed no TIQs. The higher the amount of aldehyde, and the longer the aldehyde remained in the tissues, the greater the amount of TIQs converted.[14]

This experiment demonstrated the fact that acetaldehyde, the major by-product of alcohol, does convert to TIQs in animal tissues.

In another experiment, Cohen and Collins gave methanol (a form of alcohol) to rats until they were intoxicated, removed their adrenal glands, and tested them for TIQs. The fluorescence of the tissues revealed the presence of TIQs, demonstrating the conversion of TIQs in living bodies.

From these experiments it was reasonable for Cohen to hypothesize that TIQs can form in the brain in the presence of an aldehyde. The implication was that they may be associated with biochemical changes that take place in the brain in connection with intoxication and, possibly, dependence on alcohol. Furthermore, since TIQs are chemically similar to neurotransmitters such as dopamine and norepinephrine, they may act as a toxin to interfere with the normal action of those neurotransmitters.[15]

Cohen saw the following possible modes of interference. By mimicking some of the actions of dopamine, the TIQs may function as false neurotransmitters. They may occupy dopamine receptor sites, blocking them; or, by interfering with normal metabolism, they may prolong the actions of dopamine. By modulating some of the physiologic changes normally brought about by dopamine, TIQs may provoke undesirable changes in physical, mental, or emotional states.

These actions had not been tested at the time, but they seemed reasonable. It was known, for example, that TIQs can induce changes in blood pressure and temperature, hyperexcitability leading to withdrawal seizure, and hallucinosis.

Cohen and Collins were challenged, because other researchers at first were unable to find TIQs in animals exposed to alcohol. Several years would pass before other experiments yielded unmistakable proof of the presence of TIQs in animal and human brains.

It is a remarkable coincidence that Davis and Cohen, working independently, published such closely related findings in Science one month apart; Davis in February, and Cohen in March. Davis suggested a common biochemical basis for alcohol and opiate dependence; Cohen suggested that many of the actions of alcohol are due to the formation of morphine-like TIQs.

ALCOHOL AND OPIATES: LACK OF RELATIONSHIP

A year later at Stanford University, Avram Goldstein, an internationally known authority in the field of opiate pharmacology, and an associate attacked the Davis and Walsh view that physical dependence on alcohol is due to the formation of a natural opiate in the brain. Their paper, entitled "Alcohol Dependence and Opiate Dependence: Lack of Relationship in Mice," was published in Science.

In their paper they stated that the presence of morphine or codeine in mammalian tissue had never been demonstrated, and that the amount of alcohol needed to make even the small amounts of THP found by Davis and Walsh would be a lethal dose in humans.

On these grounds they questioned the validity of the Davis and Walsh hypothesis, and designed a counter-experiment to examine further the alcohol-opiate relationship. It was based on two well-known observations:

1. If mice are made dependent on morphine, and then injected with the narcotic antagonist naloxone, they exhibit a frantic leaping

behavior within minutes. This is an exaggerated morphine with-drawal response that can be precipitated only with a narcotic antago-nist such as naloxone.

2. If mice are made dependent on alcohol, and then alcohol is with-held, they exhibit convulsions after approximately an hour as the alcohol concentration drops. This is a typical alcohol withdrawal response.

In their experiment they used a vapor chamber to addict mice to alcohol, then divided them randomly into two groups. After one hour, when withdrawal signs were just beginning to appear, they injected one group with naloxone, the opiate antagonist, and left the other group untreated. The naloxone group did not exhibit the typical leaping behavior that mice exhibit during withdrawal from opiates. Goldstein interpreted this result to mean that there was no opiate present for naloxone to block, suggesting that alcohol had not been converted to an opiate-like material such as TIQs.

They followed the withdrawal behavior of the mice for 50 hours, and found only the typical pattern of alcohol withdrawal in both groups, with no indication of an opiate-like effect. Goldstein observed, "Since even a mild degree of opiate dependence can be detected by the naloxone test, we conclude that alcohol dependence is not a manifestation of dependence upon any endogenous opiate, as proposed by Davis and Walsh."[16]

This controversy stimulated numerous investigations by other scientists into the alcohol-opiate relationship, focusing much-needed attention on the pharmacology of the nervous system.

A CLUE TO ALCOHOL-RECEPTOR INTERACTION

While I was working as an assistant research scientist at the Southwest Foundation for Research and Education in San Antonio, I became inter-ested in alcoholism through my association with Irving Geller, a psycho-pharmacologist whose work on rodents had led to a method used by the drug industry for identifying and measuring the effects of tranquilizers on humans.

Among our first research projects was an investigation into the nature of the alcohol-receptor interaction. My interest in this subject had been stimulated by a study in Germany which we confirmed in our laboratory. Simply, a substance called diethanolamine partially blocks the effect of alcohol on animals. What intrigued me was that alcohol contains a hydroxyl (OH) radical, as you can see in Figure 7–2, and diethanolamine contains two of them.[17]

Could it be that these hydroxyl radicals, among the simplest of all compounds, were in some way responsible for the blocking action of diethanolamine? I decided to find out.

We set up an experiment around the known sleep-inducing effect of alcohol on laboratory mice:

- Group One mice, for a control, were injected with alcohol two hours after the injection of a saline solution. Shortly after the injection 100 percent of the mice slept.
- Group Two mice were injected with alcohol two hours after the injection of diethanolamine, a drug that we believed might block the hydroxyl radical in alcohol. Only 40 percent of the mice slept, suggesting a mild blocking action.
- Group Three mice were injected with alcohol two hours after the injection of dimethoxyethylamine, a substance that resembles diethanolamine, but has no hydroxyl radical. All of the mice slept, indicating that in the absence of the radical there was no blocking action.

There was a possibility that this change in sleep response could have been due to a speedup of alcohol metabolism in the brain, but our measurements showed that this was not the case; there was no decrease in the amount of alcohol present. We concluded, therefore, that the hydroxyl radical in diethanolamine was in some manner and to some degree interfering with the action of the hydroxyl radical in alcohol on specific receptor sites in the brain.

This was a novel idea, and it took one whole year for us to get our paper accepted by the *European Journal of Pharmacology*. The consensus at the time was that alcohol acted as a general anesthetic; our findings

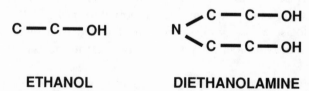

ETHANOL   DIETHANOLAMINE

Figure 7–2 Structural Resemblance of Ethanol and Diethanolamine. Chemical structural comparison of ethanol and the ethanol antagonist diethanolamine. The hydroxyl groups are common to both substances.

suggested, instead, that alcohol has selective effects on receptors on specific neurons.[18]

In a parallel experiment we investigated another prevailing assumption. G. Duritz and E. B. Truitt, Jr., had suggested that acetaldehyde is the intoxicating agent in alcohol, formed when alcohol is metabolized in the body.[19] The idea was intriguing, and it was soon being widely assumed that acetaldehyde was the *only* agent involved in intoxication.

But our findings raised a question about this assumption. We had shown that intoxification can take place through the action of the hydroxyl radical, and acetaldehyde has no hydroxyl radical. Could alcohol, which has a hydroxyl radical, cause intoxication if it is not metabolized into acetaldehyde?

When I discussed this question with Geller he was interested, and we designed an experiment to find a possible answer. After injecting rodents with methyl-pyrazole, a substance known to prevent the breakdown of alcohol into acetaldehyde, we injected them with alcohol and observed its effect on sleep time and motor coordination. After the alcohol injection (1) the mice quickly went to sleep, indicating intoxication and (2) when roused and placed on a slowly rotating bar they quickly fell off, also indicating intoxication.[20]

These results suggested that alcohol, alone, will produce intoxification; the intermediate step of acetaldehyde is not necessary. The findings also provided further evidence of the direct action of the hydroxyl radical on the nervous system.

DARKNESS AND ALCOHOL INTAKE

Geller and I had been puzzled by a mystery we uncovered when we were carrying out an experiment on shock-induced stress in rats. The mystery was that alcohol intake increased over the weekends when no shocks were administered. We could think of no explanation for this peculiar behavior. Were the rats going on weekend binges?

Our first clue came in 1971 at a meeting in Atlantic City when we heard a paper delivered by Julius Axelrod, who had recently won a Nobel Prize for his work on the metabolism of neurotransmitters. In discussing the role of the biological clock on neurotransmitter activity in the brain, he showed that a change from night to day can alter neurotransmitter function.

After the meeting, Geller and I found ourselves asking the same question: Was it possible that the increase in drinking we had observed earlier was the result of our habit of leaving the laboratory comparatively dark over the weekends?

When he returned to the laboratory, Geller placed a group of rats in a dark closet and gave them a choice of alcohol or water. In normal light conditions these rats would drink very little alcohol, but after approximately a week in the dark they were all drinking alcohol in copious amounts. He then showed me the data.

The implication was clear: darkness was affecting drinking behavior. The more we talked about it, the more plausible it became. It was well known that rats kept in constant darkness develop larger pineal glands than those kept in constant light, and that under those circumstances they convert comparatively large quantities of serotonin into a substance called melatonin. We designed an experiment to test the assumption that melatonin was the active agent that had stimulated drinking in the rats kept in a low-light environment.

As reported by Geller the results were:

- Under natural, daily cycles of light and dark, laboratory rats when given a preference drank more water than alcohol.
- After living in total darkness for two and a half weeks, the rats developed a strong preference for alcohol.
- When the lights were switched back on and constant illumination was maintained for two weeks, the alcohol intake of the rats dropped sharply.[21]

In a later experiment with two laboratory rats we gave them daily injections of melatonin, one for two weeks, and one for four weeks. In both animals, the alcohol intake rose sharply, just as it would have if they had been kept in total darkness.

Clearly, drinking behavior in these experimental animals was influenced by light and darkness, and melatonin in the pineal gland, derived from serotonin, appeared to be the active agent that brought about this response.

This finding tied back into the previously noted conclusion of Myers that serotonin was involved in alcohol preference.

THE PINEAL GLAND AND ALCOHOL CRAVING

When I joined Arthur H. Briggs at the University of Texas Health Science Center at San Antonio, I decided to test the hypothesis that darkness, the pineal gland, and melatonin interact to influence alcohol preference. I teamed up with Russel Reiter who was internationally known for his work on the pineal gland. Using rats that preferred water over alcohol, we divided them into two groups. In the test group we removed the pineal gland; in the control group we left the gland intact.

After a period of rest, we placed both groups in total darkness and kept them in that environment for three weeks. In the first week, the animals in Group One—whose pineal glands had been removed—drank 67 percent less alcohol than those in Group Two—whose pineal glands were intact. A significant reduction in alcohol consumption in these rats remained even after they were returned to a normal day-night cycle.

Clearly, the pineal gland was a factor in alcohol preference, as had been suggested by Geller, but more work was needed to characterize its role.[22]

Knowing that rats who are born blind drink more alcohol than animals with normal sight, we set up an additional experiment in which we used two groups of congenitally blind rats to test the physiological effects of constant darkness on alcohol-craving behavior. Our finding was that blind animals with intact pineal glands drank much more alcohol than similar animals whose glands had been removed.[23]

Our conclusions from these experiments were that Geller was right in suggesting that darkness induces alcohol consumption in rats, and that the pineal gland plays a major role in this darkness-induced alcohol preference.

ALCOHOL AND OPIATES: EVIDENCE
FOR A RELATIONSHIP

A paper by Geller's group reporting that a TIQ called beta-carboline, derived from acetaldehyde and serotonin, increases alcohol intake in rats stimulated anew my interest in the TIQ hypothesis.[24]

I decided to use a variation of Goldstein's earlier experiment to determine whether or not the narcotic antagonist *naloxone* would alter the sleep behavior of animals injected with alcohol. If the answer proved to be yes it would tend to support the Davis and Walsh hypothesis that alcohol converts into a morphinelike substance in the body. If the answer was no it would support Goldstein's findings, and raise a question about the work of Davis and Walsh.

In the experiment my associates and I used two groups of mice. One group was injected with saline, the other with naloxone. After 30 minutes we injected a dose of alcohol large enough to cause sleep in untreated mice. The effects were as follows: the saline group slept 50 minutes on the average, while the naloxone group slept only 10 minutes on the average. When they waked, we measured the concentration of alcohol in the blood and brain and found it to be the same in both groups.[25]

From these results we drew two conclusions: Naloxone does not affect alcohol metabolism, but it does reduce sleep time, which can be interpreted to mean that it reduces intoxication.

These findings suggested one of two possibilities:

- Naloxone was blocking an opiatelike substance derived from alcohol, perhaps a TIQ, as suggested by Davis and Walsh.
- Naloxone was blocking the direct action of alcohol at a receptor site shared by alcohol and opiates.

In either case, our results raised a serious question about Goldstein's view that there was no biochemical relationship between alcohol and opiates.

Biochemical support for the view that alcohol and opiates share a common mechanism was provided by two other experiments. E. Long Way and H. H. Loh at the University of California, San Francisco, had shown that the long-term administration of morphine to animals increases the synthesis of the neurotransmitter serotonin which had previously been implicated by Myers in alcohol-drinking behavior.[26]

K. Kuriyama and P. Y. Sze at the State University of New York, Brooklyn, had found that long-term administration of alcohol increases the synthesis of serotonin. Sze summarized this work, saying, "The fact that both alcohol and morphine change the synthesis of serotonin under similar experimental conditions, suggests that the alteration of serotonin synthesis in the brain may be an important factor in inducing the well-known addictive processes produced by these agents."[27] The linkage between alcohol and opiates was becoming stronger.

NEUROTRANSMITTERS AND ALCOHOL WITHDRAWAL

Early in 1973, two experiments had shown the effects of alcohol on neurotransmitters. Avrid Carlsson and his associates in Sweden demonstrated that alcohol reduces the concentration of norepinephrine and dopamine in the brain. Both of these substances have an excitatory effect on neuronal activity.[28]

At about the same time, I. Sutton and Michael A. Simmonds in London demonstrated that, although short-term administration of alcohol had no significant effect on the supply of GABA in the brain of rats, long-term administration increased the concentration of GABA by almost 50 percent. GABA is an inhibitory substance that reduces neuronal activity.[29]

In one instance, alcohol interfered with an excitatory effect; in another, long-term alcohol intake increased an inhibitory effect.

Meanwhile, Dora Goldstein at Stanford University was investigating the role of neurotransmitters in animals undergoing withdrawal from alcohol dependence. She had developed a vapor chamber which she used as a tool to induce rapid dependence on alcohol in laboratory mice. It consisted of a transparent box into which alcohol vapor was pumped. As the animals breathed the vapor, they quickly became intoxicated. In three days they were demonstrably dependent on alcohol. If they were removed from the box, and left untreated, after about an hour they began to exhibit the typical convulsive behavior associated with withdrawal. This behavior peaked at eight to ten hours.

In a series of experiments, test animals were injected with chemical agents known to (1) block or stimulate the action of neurotransmitters on their natural brain receptors, or (2) block or stimulate the action of enzymes that alter neurotransmitter synthesis or breakdown.

The neurotransmitters under investigation were acetylcholine, serotonin, GABA, dopamine, and norepinephrine.

Goldstein's *negative* findings from the experiments were:

- Blocking acetylcholine receptors had no effect on withdrawal.
- Preventing the breakdown of acetylcholine, thereby raising its concentration, had no effect on withdrawal.
- Stimulating serotonin receptors had no effect on withdrawal.
- Inhibiting serotonin synthesis, thereby reducing its concentration, had no effect on withdrawal.

Apparently, neither acetylcholine nor serotonin was significantly involved in alcohol withdrawal.

Her *positive* findings were:

- Inhibiting the breakdown of GABA, thereby increasing its concentration, sharply reduced the withdrawal response.
- Blocking GABA receptors increased the withdrawal response.
- Depleting the catecholamines (dopamine and norepinephrine) increased the withdrawal response.
- Inhibiting the synthesis of catecholamines, thereby lowering their concentration, increased the withdrawal response.

- Blocking the catecholamine receptors increased the withdrawal response.

Goldstein's conclusions were:

Drugs that interfere with catecholamine pathways aggravate the withdrawal seizures. . . . GABA and catecholamine pathways tend to suppress the hyperexcitability of the alcohol withdrawal state. . . .
. . . effective drugs to treat alcohol withdrawal in Man may eventually be found among compounds that activate brain GABA or catecholamine pathways.[30]

ALCOHOL AND BRAIN PROTEIN PRODUCTION

The effect of alcohol on the brain's ability to manufacture proteins, such as enzymes, necessary for conversion of amino acids into neurotransmitters was explored by S. Tewari and E. P. Noble at the University of California, Irvine. In their experiments, they took C57 black mice that preferred alcohol, and divided them into two groups. The test group received alcohol, the control group received only water. After varying periods of time—up to 47 days—the investigators found that (1) the alcohol-receiving mice had a 50 percent reduction in ribosomal protein in the brain which is controlled by RNA, compared to the water-receiving mice, and (2) the alcohol-receiving mice could incorporate into the ribosomal protein only 20 percent as much of the amino acid leucine as the water-receiving mice.

These findings indicated that alcohol affects the RNA processing system, interfering with the formation of proteins, and thereby interfering with or distorting neurotransmission.[31]

SOME FOCAL QUESTIONS

At this point in the investigation of the disease theory of alcoholism, there was growing evidence that:

- There is a complex interaction between alcohol and the complex chemistry of the brain.
- Alcohol preference involves the neurotransmitters.
- The metabolism of alcohol in the body produces opiate-like substances.
- The behavioral effects of alcohol can be blocked or altered by substances that act as opiate antagonists.

- Alcohol and opiates may operate through some common receptor.
- Alcohol can act on certain receptors before conversion to acetaldehyde.
- Darkness operating on the pineal gland can increase drinking behavior.
- Neurotransmitters are involved in the withdrawal response to alcohol.
- Alcohol affects RNA processing of proteins.

The research community was now poised to attack some of the most basic questions about the nature of the disease process of alcoholism:

1. *The alcohol-opiate relation:* How do opiates act on the neuron? Are there specific receptor sites? What are the behavioral similarities and differences in the action of alcohol and opiates? What are the biochemical similarities and differences in the action of alcohol and opiates in the brain? Do they share common receptor sites?

2. *The TIQ conundrum:* Are TIQs the link between the action of alcohol and opiates in the brain? Are they formed in the brain of human alcoholics in sufficient concentration to alter neurochemical balance and functions? Do TIQs induce alcohol craving and dependence?

3. *The role of the neurotransmitters:* What are the specific neurotransmitters involved in alcoholism? At what sites do they operate? Which neurotransmitters mediate craving, tolerance, and withdrawal response? Do they mediate these brain functions through alterations in the reward process?

4. *The role of brain opioids:* Are there opiatelike endogenous substances in the brain, separate from the opiates and TIQs, that mediate behavior in the alcoholic? Do they act on specific receptor sites? Are their actions similar to those of the opiates?

5. *The role of genetics:* Are some individuals born with a greater risk of alcoholism than others? Is this risk due to inheritance of one or more defective genes that distort neurotransmission? Do individuals genetically at risk have larger amounts of natural TIQs in their brain than normal individuals?

All these exciting questions were stimulated by the assumption that alcoholism is a disease process caused by a biochemical imbalance in the brain.

SUGGESTED READING

Galanter, M., ed. *Currents in Alcoholism*, vol. 7. New York: Grune & Stratton, 1980.

Kissin, B., and Begleiter, H., eds. *The Biology of Alcoholism*, vol. 1. New York: Plenum Press, 1971.

Leake, C. D., and Silverman, M. *Alcoholic Beverages in Clinical Medicine*. Chicago: Yearbook Medical Publishers, 1966.

Lucia, S. P., ed. *Alcohol and Civilization*. New York: McGraw-Hill, 1963.

Majchrowicz, E., and Noble, E. P., eds. *Biochemistry and Pharmacology of Ethanol*. New York: Plenum Press, 1979.

Ray, O. S. *Drugs, Society, and Human Behavior*. St. Louis: C. V. Mosby, 1972.

8

The Opiate Connection

One of the most interesting ideas circulating in the early 1970s was that there is a basic relationship between the actions of alcohol and those of opiates in the brain. Davis and Walsh had shown that alcohol metabolism produces a substance that is a source from which morphine is made in the opium poppy plant. I had shown that we can block alcohol-induced sleep by administering the opiate antagonist naloxone. Davis and I, independently, had suggested that alcohol and opiates may share a common receptor site in the brain. There was no direct evidence to support this suggestion, as yet, but we were building on a hypothesis that had been under consideration for several years.

This hypothesis was that opiates must bind to specific sites, or "receptors," in the brain. This binding, or tissue interaction, induces a pharmacological response to the drug; for example, blocking pain or inducing euphoria. These sites can be occupied only by molecules of very specific structure so that there is a "fit" between the drug molecule and the receptor site. This may explain the specific action of opiates: they bind to these sites and no other.

THE DISCOVERY OF OPIATE RECEPTORS

In the early 1960s, Eric J. Simon, at the New York University Medical Center, had been impressed by the fact that pharmaceutical companies can manufacture a substance that acts like morphine but, through a slight chemical change in the compound, can be converted into an "opiate antagonist," a substance that blocks the action of morphine. He was working at the time with D. Van Praag. In a 1987 interview, Simon explained that "this gave us the idea way back in the mid '60s that there must be highly specific differences in the sites where incoming substances bind to the receptors. We tried to locate such sites, but were unable to find conclusive proof that we had identified specific receptors."[1]

Avram Goldstein also attempted to isolate an opiate receptor in brain tissue in 1971. He took homogenized brain tissue and mixed it with an artificial form of morphine that had been made radioactive. When he fractionated the mixture, he found that only about 2 percent of the radioactive material had bound to the brain tissue. This was not sufficient to indicate that he had isolated opiate receptors, but he suggested that "the material responsible for specific binding might be the opiate receptor."[2]

In a curious case of virtually simultaneous discovery, three independent laboratories found direct evidence of specific binding sites for opiates. The first report of experimental evidence was from Lars Terenius at the University of Uppsala in Sweden. His paper was accepted for publication in *Acta Pharmacologica et Toxicologica,* Copenhagen, on November 8, 1972. It did not actually appear, however, until March 1973.

In his experiment he used an artificial radioactive form of morphine similar to the one Goldstein had used, and measured the degree of binding to a fraction of rat brain cortex. He then repeated the experiment, but added the opiate antagonists nalorphine and naloxone. He found that the antagonists reduced the amount of binding of the radioactive material by 14 to 24 percent, indicating that this large percentage of radioactive artificial morphine was binding to specific sites in the brain material. This was a much larger percentage than Goldstein had found, and the use of the antagonists pinned the binding action down specifically to the opiates.[3]

Intrigued again by the problem of the opiate receptor site in Goldstein's paper, Eric Simon designed an experiment focused on an opiate agonist 1,000–10,000 times more powerful than morphine itself (etorphine). At the time he had not yet seen Terenius' paper, which had not yet appeared. Simon succeeded in demonstrating the existence of the opiate receptor in the fall of 1972.

On April 18, 1973, he made a report on his findings at a symposium on the current status of pharmacological receptors at the annual spring meeting of the American Society for Pharmacology and Experimental Therapeutics in Atlantic City, but for some reason the Proceedings were not published that year.

On March 9, 1973, a paper by Candace Pert and Solomon Snyder at Johns Hopkins School of Medicine was published in *Science,* describing the isolation of the opiate receptor. The paper had been accepted on January 15, 1973.

In the first of these experiments, Pert and Snyder used rats, guinea pigs, and mice. Brain material from each of the animals was extracted; small amounts were placed in beakers and mixed with one of 20 drugs being tested—some opiates, and some not—and incubated. Then, to each beaker they added radioactive naloxone. If the radioactive naloxone displaced the drug and bound to the receptor site, the amount of radioactivity remaining in the sample was reduced. The amount of the reduction, therefore, could be taken as a measure of the amount of the drug that had been displaced.

Two measurements stood out. Approximately 70 percent of the potent painkiller levorphanol had bound to the opiate receptor in the rat, guinea pig, and mouse brain. Dextrorphan, an opiate but not a painkiller, showed no binding effect. This strongly suggested that opiates bind only to specific receptor sites. Furthermore, the potency of a given opiate—morphine, codeine, propoxyphene (Darvon), methadone, Levorphanol, etc.—proved to be proportional to its binding activity.[4]

Snyder and Pert later sought to determine precisely where opiate receptors can be found in the brain. They also wanted to know if receptors are located in nonneural as well as neural tissues. To obtain neural material, they homogenized rat brain tissues and separated the various components with a high speed centrifuge. Nonneural materials were taken from guinea pig intestine, rat liver, human red blood cells, and baker's yeast. The materials were incubated with radioactive naloxone to reveal binding to the opiate receptors.

They found that binding occurred only in the neural tissues. The nonneural tissues showed no binding effect. As Snyder and Pert summed it up in their paper:

> Only drugs that present a high degree of molecular complementarity toward the site at which they act are believed to be able to form this drug-receptor complex. . . . Since this binding is highly stereospecific and corresponds with the previously reported pharmacological potencies of opiates, we believe that our results represent a direct demonstration of "opiate receptor" binding.[5]

In a 1987 interview, Simon reflected on the timing of these events:

> Being somewhat lazy in writing papers, and thinking that no one else was working in this area (Terenius was carrying out research on

cancer, and Snyder was working on mescaline and LSD), I took my time. I knew that I was presenting my paper in April, so I didn't worry about the competition. But they published first, and that's history.

THE FORMATION OF TIQS IN HUMANS

The TIQ story unfolded further when Merton Sandler and his associates at Queen Charlotte's Maternity Hospital, London, carried out an experiment which demonstrated for the first time that TIQs are formed in the living *human* body.

In the experiment they began with two normal human subjects who were not receiving either alcohol or drugs. Urine samples were analyzed, and two types of TIQ were found in small amounts: salsolinol and tetrahydropapaveroline (THP).

Since it was known that TIQs are formed directly from dopamine and aldehyde, the next step was to see if the TIQ concentration could be increased by raising the level of dopamine in the brain. Four patients were selected who were suffering from Parkinson's disease—characterized by low brain dopamine—and receiving large quantities of an amino acid called L-dopa, which converts directly into dopamine.

When their urine was checked, it was discovered that levels of both types of TIQs were higher than in the first two subjects, but salsolinol was highest.

Knowing that alcohol promotes the formation of TIQs, they administered alcohol orally at intervals for two days, and then collected and tested the urine after four different intervals of time. They found the highest concentration of TIQs 12 hours after the alcohol was ingested, with salsolinol showing the highest concentration.[6]

Their conclusions were:

- Endogenous TIQs are present in the normal human.
- Raising the levels of dopamine increases the amount of TIQs in the urine.
- Alcohol raises the TIQ level even higher.

TIQ FORMATION "UNDER THE INFLUENCE"

Finding the opiate receptors, and identifying the specific narcotic antagonists, had given scientists increasing insight into the action of opiates in the brain. In the alcohol field, however, no such discoveries had been made. No alcohol receptors had been found; no natural substances that mimic the effect of alcohol had been found; no alcohol antagonists had been found. The mechanisms by which alcohol affects the brain were still puzzling.

The theory of the TIQs, suggested by Davis and Walsh, as well as Cohen and Collins, and supported by my own laboratory, held that the TIQs serve as a link between alcohol and opiates, but the theory still lacked confirmation. One major problem was that although TIQs had been found in human urine, they had not been identified in mammalian tissues in connection with alcohol intake.

An experiment conducted by Michael Collins in collaboration with M. G. Bigdeli at Loyola University of Chicago Stritch School of Medicine provided the first indication that TIQs are formed in animals during ethanol intoxication.

In preliminary experiments, they had not been able to find the TIQ salsolinol in mammalian brain tissue following short-term alcohol administration. Suspecting that the problem was a concentration of TIQ too low to be detected, they set up an experiment in which rat brain chemistry was modified to increase concentrations of dopamine and acetaldehyde prior to testing for salsolinol. Dopamine and acetaldehyde are sources from which TIQs are derived.

The experiment was too complex to describe fully here, but in summary they gave rats alcohol alone; in combination with a substance that builds up the supply of dopamine; in combination with a substance that prevents the breakdown of dopamine in the body; or in combination with a third substance that prevents the breakdown of dopamine and the alcohol by-product, acetaldehyde.[7]

Later, the rats were sacrificed and materials were extracted from their brains and analyzed. The results showed that when dopamine supplies are built up or protected *in the presence of alcohol,* the TIQ salsolinol is found in detectable quantities.[8]

Although he was unable to find salsolinol without this chemical manipulation, Collins felt that it was probable that long-term alcohol abuse would lead to vitamin deficiencies and liver damage, and that these deficiencies, in turn, would increase acetaldehyde levels—leading to the formation of TIQs.

In that context it is interesting to note that, at about this same time, Charles Lieber and his associates at the Veterans Administration Hospital, Bronx, New York, found that when chronic alcoholics are given alcohol their acetaldehyde blood levels are higher than those of normal individuals who are given alcohol. This indicates that the alcohol metabolism of chronic alcoholics is defective.[9]

The implications of these findings were that high concentrations of acetaldehyde in the alcoholic can lead to an abnormally high concentration of TIQs; and that this high concentration, in turn, may lead to alcohol addiction.

TIQS: A BIOCHEMICAL BRIDGE

The possibility that TIQs might be an active bridge between opiates and alcohol in the still-obscure workings of the brain was an intriguing idea, but to many scientists it seemed to be too speculative.

David Ross was one of the scientists who took the idea seriously. When he joined the Department of Pharmacology at the Health Science Center in the University of Texas at San Antonio, we had several discussions about the relationship between opiates and alcohol. He seemed particularly interested in my view that TIQs might be serving as a link between the two.

At the time, we knew there was a behavioral link between opiates and alcohol, but there was no scientific proof that they shared a biochemical linkage. Ross set up an experiment with Miguel A. Medina and H. Lee Cardenas to investigate the hypothesis. Their paper was originally rejected by *Science* as being too controversial, but was later published after revision.

Their experiment began with the known fact that calcium ions are involved in the regulation of neurotransmitter function, and that morphine produces a significant loss of brain calcium in experimental animals. They reasoned that if alcohol functions like morphine, it also should cause a loss of brain calcium. Further, if TIQs are formed as a by-product of alcohol consumption, they also should cause a loss of brain calcium.

In the essential part of the first phase of the experiment, they gave morphine to one group of male rats, alcohol to a second group, and salsolinol (a TIQ) to a third group. The animals were then sacrificed, and the content of brain materials in four specific areas was analyzed. They found that the concentration of calcium was significantly reduced in all of the specimens.

In the second phase of the experiment, they injected the opiate antagonist naloxone prior to the injection of these same substances. Brain calcium was then measured, and they found that there was no loss of calcium with either morphine, alcohol, or TIQs. Naloxone blocked their biochemical action.

The conclusion of the investigators was that since the opiate antagonist naloxone had prevented these substances from reducing calcium, the probability is that all three act through a common opiate receptor. This suggested that morphine and alcohol, and TIQs derived from alcohol, share a commonality. Furthermore, it suggested that TIQs possibly serve as a bridge between alcohol and the opiate receptor.

Ross had reservations, however. He stated that "until there is more conclusive evidence that these alkaloids (TIQs) are formed *in vivo* [in the body] after alcohol ingestion in mammalian systems, this idea must be regarded as highly speculative."[10] Despite his negative statement, however, his experiment moved the field further along a pathway that eventually would lead to proof of the involvement of TIQs in alcoholism.

ALCOHOL DEPENDENCE: MODIFICATION AT OPIATE RECEPTORS

During this period I was concerned with a simple question: If there is a link between alcohol and opiates, can a narcotic antagonist block or reduce alcohol-induced dependence in animals?

As I mentioned earlier, Avram Goldstein was maintaining that naloxone has no effect in altering alcohol withdrawal reaction in mice already addicted. This indicated to him that alcohol and opiates affect different sites in the brain. But I had seen Ross's evidence that alcohol works through the opiate receptors, and this finding was compatible with my earlier experiment on alcohol and sleep time. I decided to pursue the idea further.

J. Wallace, S. Futterman, and I designed an experiment to test the original hypothesis of Davis and Walsh that alcohol, TIQs, and opiates bind to common brain receptor sites. The technique we used was to place mice, in their cages, in an alcohol vapor chamber with access to food and water, and expose them to the vapor 24 hours a day for five days. The mice were divided into two groups. One control group was injected every six hours around the clock with a saline solution; the other was injected with the antagonist naloxone.

At the conclusion of the five-day experiment, we removed the animals from the vapor chamber and measured the intensity of their withdrawal convulsions. To our delight, the convulsions of the mice that had received naloxone were about half as severe as those of the control group that had received the saline solution.

We were excited by these results, but we wanted to check our conclusions further. We decided to investigate the effects of naloxone on a group of mice after they were in a state of severe dependence or withdrawal. In the midst of their convulsions we injected half of the group with saline, and the other half with naloxone. The saline group showed no diminution of their convulsions; the naloxone group showed a profound reduction.

We concluded that naloxone does alter alcohol-induced withdrawal symptoms, contrary to Goldstein; and that alcohol and opiates do share common receptor sites, as proposed by Davis and Walsh.[11]

These results also stimulated us to ask other questions. Are TIQs responsible for tremors in humans? For the tremor and convulsion symptoms of withdrawal found in animals? For "hangovers" in humans? If so, can they be blocked by a narcotic antagonist? We set out to try to answer the questions in an experiment with mice.

When we injected TIQs into a group of mice they went into convulsions (similar to tremors in humans.) But when we injected another group of mice with the narcotic antagonist naloxone before the injection of TIQs, the convulsions were blocked. Clearly, TIQ was a powerful convulsing agent, and its effects were largely blocked by naloxone, a narcotic antagonist.[12]

We were pleased by the results, but because of the pressure of work we did not publish until some years later when I received a letter soliciting papers for a meeting of the Committee on the Problems of Drug Dependence at the National Academy of Science in Washington. I remembered Goldstein's paper, and because I was young and brash—and not very politic—I entitled my submission: "Alcohol and Opiate Dependence: Evidence for Relationship in Mice."[13]

On the day of the meeting I had been assigned 15 minutes, but I was nervous and decided to take up 20 minutes so there could be no question period. I passed the 15 minute mark and kept going. Despite warnings from Chairman Louis Harris, I plowed ahead and ended at precisely 20 minutes. I had grabbed my papers and was leaving the stage when Harris stopped me.

"Dr. Blum," he said, "that was a fine paper, but because of the controversial nature of its contents I am going to interrupt the meeting for five minutes to give Dr. Goldstein time to comment."

Avram was a stately man bearing some resemblance to Abraham Lincoln. I knew he had strong opinions, and I expected the worst.

"Ken," he said, "I knew exactly what you were doing when you tried to talk through the question period. But, as you see, it didn't work. I'm going to have my say.

"Congratulations! I think you have made a significant contribution. Heretofore, we have not believed that a simple molecule like alcohol could have a cross-over effect on the opiate system. But your evidence that naloxone blocks alcohol effects under these conditions can only mean that it is acting through the opiate system. Therefore, I will reconsider my argument against a common mechanism between alcohol and opiates."

I have been forever grateful to Goldstein for his generosity and courtesy to an impetuous young man.

Later, he visited my laboratory in San Antonio and I discussed with him the naloxone evidence which indicated that TIQs, if formed from alcohol, would interact specifically with opiate receptors. If this could be proved, we would know that the behavioral actions of alcohol are linked to those of the opiates through the TIQs. Goldstein was far from convinced, but he did accept from me a vial containing a sample of a TIQ (if I remember correctly, it was salsolinol), and promised to test it in his lab where he was set up to do opiate receptor bio-assays.

He wrote me some two weeks later to say that the TIQ I sent did bind specifically to opiate receptors, but the binding was weak. He said that the binding was so "stereospecific" it had to be an opiate, like morphine, but because the binding was so weak he suspected that it might be due to the presence of a morphine contaminant in the sample.

I trusted my sample, which I had received from Gerald Cohen, and when I subjected it to a careful chemical analysis I found it was over 99 percent pure. However, because the binding was weak I decided not to publish the data.

THE DISCOVERY OF ENDORPHINS

At this point as I looked around the field I felt that substantial progress was being made. There was persuasive evidence that an opiate receptor had been isolated; that naturally occurring TIQs had been found in humans, and that their formation is enhanced by alcohol; that certain biochemical and behavioral actions of alcohol, opiates, and TIQs are shared; and that these shared actions are linked to specific brain receptors—probably opiate receptors.

It was now reasonable to assume that the existence of a specific receptor site in the brain indicates the probable existence of a specific substance to activate it. It was known, for example, that insulin interacts with specific membrane receptors to increase the body's utilization of glucose in muscles. Therefore, since opiate receptors had been identified, it seemed likely that there was some *naturally occurring* opiate or opiate-like substance in the brain that interacts with them.

John Hughes at the University of Aberdeen in Scotland was inspired by earlier work to initiate a serious search for such a substance. He knew that scientists had found (1) a substance originating in the pituitary glands of experimental animals that increased the painkilling effect of morphine, and another substance that, following chronic morphine treatment, could alter the brain's response to morphine; and (2) a naturally occurring, opiate-like material in neural tissues that might be linked to receptors.

He also knew of the work of J. J. Jacob and his colleagues in France who had found that the narcotic antagonist naloxone increased the effect of painful stimuli, leading to the assumption that it was blocking a naturally occurring, opiate-like substance in the brain, inhibiting its painkilling power. [14]

Hughes decided to try to find, extract, and identify this natural painkilling substance. His elaborate procedure illustrates how complex the extraction process can be. He took brains from rabbit, guinea pig, rat, and pig, processed the materials into a powder, mixed the powder with liquid chemicals, centrifuged the mixture for 30 minutes at high speed to extract the liquid, dried the liquid, redissolved it in methanol, and finally filtered it and evacuated the methanol, leaving a yellow, waxy residue. He then dissolved this material in distilled water and adjusted the pH to make it acid. He called this compound "X."

In the experiment, he took mouse vas deferens, a neuromuscular tissue that contains a high density of opiate receptors, applied an electrical current to make the neurons fire, and measured the resultant muscle contractions. With these measurements as a baseline, he applied normorphine to the tissues, and found that this morphine-like material reduced the intensity of the contractions, as expected.

After the opiate effect wore off, Hughes applied a small amount of "X" to the vas deferens tissues, and found that this natural compound was a much more powerful inhibitor of muscular contraction than normorphine had been. This suggested to him that the brain extract "X" had morphine-like properties.

In a test of his hypothesis, he found that the narcotic antagonist naloxone, applied either before or after the addition of "X" or normorphine, blocked or reversed the inhibitory action of both compounds.

Operating on a hunch, he assumed that "X" was a compound of linked amino acids called a peptide, and applied an enzyme known to destroy peptides. The result was that "X" was blocked, but normorphine was unaffected. This indicated that "X" is a peptide, and that normorphine is not a peptide.

His conclusion was that "X," found naturally in the brain, has the structure of a peptide, combines directly with opiate receptors, and has morphine-like effects.

Through further analysis he found that "X" is widely but unevenly distributed in the brain. The most surprising discovery was that it is found not only in areas associated with pain, but also in those associated with pleasure or well-being. As Hughes observed, "the substance described in this study is part of an as yet unknown neurotransmitter system. However, its wide distribution within the brain suggests that its action may not be entirely concerned with pain suppression."[15]

What was needed next was identification of the physical and chemical characteristics of the peptides in the brain extracts that activate the opiate receptors.

THE CHEMICAL NATURE OF ENDORPHINS

Papers presented at the International Narcotics Research Club Conference in 1975 at Airlie House in Virginia threw considerable light on opiate receptors and the natural materials that activate them. Some of the papers aroused heated debate, and opened up new pathways for future investigations.

- John Hughes and his associates reported that they had further purified the "X" material and determined its molecular weight. He also gave it a name: "enkephalin."[16]
- Lars Terenius and Agneta Wahlstrom stated that they had isolated a material with the same molecular weight from the cerebral spinal fluid of nonaddicted humans. They called this material "MLF" for "morphine-like factor."[17]
- Solomon H. Snyder and his associates reported that these opiate-like materials are found in brain areas where there is the highest density of opiate receptors. They called their material "MLS" for "morphine-like substance."[18]
- Avram Goldstein and his associates reported that they had extracted from bovine pituitary glands a substance with an opiate-like effect that could be blocked by naloxone. This extract had a molecular weight twice that of the extracts used by Hughes, Terenius, and

Snyder, but all were peptides made up from amino acids. The extract was named "POP," or "pituitary opioid peptide."[19]

The hottest discussions developed over the naming of the new materials that were being discovered. As recalled in a 1988 interview by Eric Simon, who was present at the Conference:

While all these names were being thrown around—"X" factor, en-kephalin, MLF, MLS, POP 1—Chairman Goldstein stood up and said "Can't we have a name that is general, that is generic for all of the substances in the body that have an opioid-like activity?"

"How about the term *endorphin?*," I asked. "That would be a simple contraction of *endogenous*, which means within, and *morphine.*"

Avram liked it, and immediately wrote a circular letter to all of the officers and to some of the more distinguished members of the International Narcotic Research Club who were present at the meeting, asking them if they would accept the name *endorphin*. The answer from most of them was yes. The principal objection came from Hughes and Kosterlitz, who preferred the term *enkephalin*.

It turned out to be good that they objected, because C. H. Li and his collaborators soon started using the terms *alpha-, beta-* and *gamma-endorphin* to describe three different types of endorphins they had discovered. Therefore, although it was unknown to us at the time, the term *endorphin* was no longer useful as a generic term as I had proposed. But the term caught on, the media picked it up, and we are stuck with it. And it is understandable. Who in his right mind would want to say on television or in a book "endogenous opioid peptide"?

Actually, it is not all that complex. We have threshed it out among ourselves over the years, and this is how we worked it out. The *class* of terms applied to the various opioid peptides is correctly *endorphins*. The subclasses include a variety of endorphins such as *alpha-, beta-,* and *gamma-*; two *enkephalins*; and *dynorphin*.

I'm delighted that the term *endorphin* is in the *Index Medicus*, and that one of my names stuck. Sometimes I get more mileage out of the name than I do out of my work!

The Conference had helped to characterize both the biological activity and the physical properties of these peptides; now the focus was on their chemical nature and identity.

CHEMICAL IDENTIFICATION OF ENKEPHALINS

In 1975, Hughes, with Kosterlitz and other colleagues, analyzed enkephalin extracted from the guinea pig brain and found the following amino acids in different amounts: glycine, methionine, tyrosine, phenylalanine, and leucine. Through the use of a process called "sequential degradation" coupled with electrophoresis, they identified the sequence of specific amino acids in the amino acid chain.

They found two different kinds of peptides, both of which had four common amino acids: tyrosine/glycine/glycine/phenylalanine, in that order. In addition to the four, one of the chains had leucine at the terminal end, and the other had methionine. Such a linkage of five amino acids is called a *pentapeptide*.[20]

CHEMICAL IDENTIFICATION OF ENDORPHINS

Roger Guillemin, who eventually would receive the Nobel Prize for his work on the neuropeptides, was carrying out a series of experiments at the Salk Institute in La Jolla, California, when he succeeded in isolating and identifying several large peptides from pig hypothalamus and pituitary. One of these peptides, called beta-lipotropin, was found to be composed of 91 amino acids. A fragment of this peptide consisting of 17 of these amino acids had an opiate-like action when tested. He named this fragment *alpha-endorphin*, with a nod to Eric Simon. This would prove to be an important contribution.

In later experiments he found that other fragments of this large peptide also exhibit opiate-like activity. He suggested that "beta-lipotropin could be a prohormone [precursor] for . . . endorphins and enkephalins." His work undoubtedly stimulated the search for prohormones that serve as precursors of opioid peptides and of the enzymes involved in their formation.[21]

In that same year, Choh H. Li and David Chung, working at the Hormone Research Laboratory at the University of California in San Francisco, isolated from camel pituitary a large fragment of beta-lipotropin consisting of 31 amino acids. They analyzed the material and identified its chemical nature.[22] Their colleague Avram Goldstein then tested the substance and found that it, too, had opiate-like characteristics. They named it *beta-endorphin*.[23]

The discovery and identification of the opiate-like substances, or opioids, such as enkephalins and endorphins raised profound questions.

What is the function and purpose of such substances in the brain? What happens when an opioid molecule attaches itself and interacts with an opiate receptor? Do these receptors constitute centers where we experience pain that can be alleviated by opioids? Do other receptors constitute pleasure centers that can be stimulated by opioids? Do imbalances of these substances result in abnormal behavior such as opiate addiction, depression, and psychosis?

THE RELATIONSHIP OF OPIATES AND ALCOHOL

While these questions were being asked by scientists in the opiate field, other questions about the role of opioids in alcohol and opiate addiction were concerning me. Can a deficiency of these materials be related to the craving that underlies addiction to alcohol? Is addiction to alcohol and opiates a result of endorphin deficiency?

With these questions in the air, it seemed to me to be a good time for a symposium on the subject, and Frank Seixas, medical scientific director of the National Council on Alcoholism, agreed with me.

The conference in New York was called "Neurochemical and Behavioral Mechanisms of Alcohol and Opiate Dependence." It brought together people like Eric Simon, Horace Loh, and Avram Goldstein, on the opiate side; and Gerald Cohen, Richard Dietrich, and Boris Tabakoff on the alcohol side. In addition to the symposium papers, there were lively discussions on and off the floor for two full days.

The proceedings of this Conference were published in a book I edited, called *Alcohol and Opiates*. Among the key contributions:

- Eric Simon reported that the greatest concentration of opiate receptors is found in the reward area of the brain called the limbic system.[24]
- Werner A. Klee reported that morphine and other opiates inhibit the activity of an enzyme called adenylate cyclase which regulates neurotransmitter release.[25] This tied in with an earlier experiment by L. Volicer and B. I. Gold who found that alcohol, too, inhibits this enzyme in brain tissue.[26]
- Andrew K. S. Ho showed that morphine sharply reduces ethanol selection in mice genetically predisposed to prefer alcohol over water.[27] The significance was that morphine fills the opiate receptor sites and blocks alcohol intake; and further, that in the presence of one euphoriant, another may be rejected.

I reported on a recent experiment showing that morphine administration greatly reduced the withdrawal symptoms of mice that were physically dependent on alcohol. Withdrawal symptoms were also reduced by low doses of TIQs. In other words, morphine as well as small doses of TIQs were acting as alcohol substitutes, working through the opiate receptors.[28]

My associates and I also showed that dopamine acts in the same way as morphine and TIQs, markedly reducing alcohol withdrawal symptoms. This suggested that both morphine and TIQs may operate through a dopaminergic pathway.[29]

I also made reference to research by S. Liljequist in Sweden who found that if alcohol is withdrawn after chronic intoxication, the sensitivity of response to dopamine at its receptors in the nucleus accumbens— a major reward area in the limbic system—increases tremendously.[30] This sensitivity may be a clue to the powerful craving that often develops after an alcoholic has been sober for a period of time, and is re-exposed to alcohol. The dopamine is gone, the receptors are supersensitive, and craving becomes suddenly overwhelming.

In the last session I stuck my neck out and said: "I believe that the bridge between the action of opiates and alcohol may lie in the neuropeptides, particularly the endorphins. When we understand the role of the endorphins in the physiology of the brain we will understand the action of alcohol."

The connection between the actions of alcohol, opiates, and opioids was gradually becoming clear. The discovery of opiate receptors and endogenous opioids (endorphins, enkephalins) clarified the action of the opiates; the discovery that the TIQs derived from alcohol also acted at opiate receptors established them as opiate-like substances. The finding that the biochemical actions and behavioral effects of alcohol, opiates, and TIQs are similar and mutually blocked by the opiate antagonist naloxone was a further indication that they share a common mechanism of action, with the TIQs serving as the linking factor.

SUGGESTED READING

Hamilton, M. G., and Hirst, M. Alcohol-related tetrahydroisoquinolines: Pharmacology and identification. *Substance and Alcohol Actions/Misuse* 1 (1980): 121–44.

Hunt, W. A., and Majchrowicz, E. Alterations in the turnover of brain norepinephrine and dopamine in alcohol-dependent rats. *Journal of Neurochemistry* 23 (1974): 549–52.

Tabakoff, B., and Boggan, W. O. Effects of ethanol on serotonin metabolism in brain. *Journal of Neurochemistry* 22 (1974): 759–64.

9

Poppies of the Brain

By the beginning of 1977, research into the causes and effects of alcoholism was concentrating in four principal areas: the effect of alcohol on brain function; the effect of alcohol withdrawal on brain function; the role of brain chemistry in determining the degree of response to alcohol; and the factors that go into the development of craving for alcohol. Questions were being generated more rapidly than answers, but there was no doubt that significant progress was being made.

There was a growing understanding of the interaction of alcohol, opiates, TIQs, enzymes, and neurotransmitters: that they act on specific receptor sites in the brain; that anomalies involving one or more of these factors are involved in alcoholism; and that these anomalies may be, at least in part, the result of genetic mutations.

But there were strong opposing views.

ALCOHOL AT THE NEURONAL MEMBRANE

Dora Goldstein and her associate J. H. Chin at Stanford University set up an experiment to test the hypothesis that alcohol acts as an anesthetic to disrupt neuronal function in a nonspecific manner at the membrane, rather than at specific receptor sites. Their rationale was that the alcohol molecule appears to be too simple in design to fit into a complex receptor site. Goldstein observed that "the simplicity of the chemical structure of ethanol suggests that its effects on membranes are similar to those of a large group of structurally unrelated anesthetic agents."

This idea appealed to them because alcohol appears to have an anesthetic effect when taken in sufficient quantities. In the days before anesthetics were invented, alcohol was used to deaden pain in operations ranging from tooth removal to amputation.

Anesthetics operate by changing the composition of neuronal membranes, blocking the passage of ions and preventing neurons from firing. Effectively, anesthetics "deaden" the neuron, prevent the release of neurotransmitters, and interfere with the movement of neurotransmitters across the synapse to the next neuron in the message transmission chain. The hypothesis was that ethanol acts in a similar way and achieves a similar effect.

In the experiment, Goldstein and Chin placed red blood cell membranes and neuronal membranes from mice in different test tubes, immersing the materials in what they described as "nonlethal" concentrations of alcohol. Using a technique called *electron paramagnetic resonance*, they measured the "fluidity" or disorder of the membranes.

They found that the addition of ethanol increased membrane disorder and reduced certain biological functions of the cell, including membrane permeability, enzyme activity, and the transport of neurotransmitters. These effects were similar to those induced by anaesthetic agents.

They concluded that the effect of alcohol on the nervous system is similar to that of general anesthetics. This suggested to them that alcohol acts by changing the state of the membrane, rather than by interfering with the action of neurotransmitters at specific receptor sites.[1]

When their paper appeared in 1977, it set off a major controversy. Some applauded the hypothesis and found evidence to confirm it, but others questioned it. Too much evidence had accumulated indicating a major role for receptors in alcohol response. The controversy was not to be resolved for over a decade.

THE PSYCHOGENETIC THEORY OF ALCOHOL CRAVING

In the summer of 1977 I spent eight weeks with Gerald McClearn at the Institute of Behavioral Genetics at the University of Colorado at Boulder. These weeks of sustained effort led to a concept that opened the way to all of my later work. The climax came on an evening at the end of August.

I had spent much of my time at the Institute reviewing the literature on the pharmacogenetics of addiction, and as I sat at my desk one evening my research and my reading came together suddenly in an integration that hit me like a "high." I reached for a scratch pad, and without quite understanding the significance of the formula, I first wrote out,

$$DCB = G + E$$

Translated, that simply meant that drug-craving behavior equals genetics plus environment. This formula, hardly world shaking, established a matrix that I gradually filled in as the night wore on. When I awoke the next morning I found that I had worked most of the night and was surrounded by crumpled papers.

After reading what I had written, I realized that I had developed an argument for a possible model of alcoholism:

- The gene that controls the synthesis and regulation of opioids can be involved in craving behavior.
- If a deficiency of opioids can lead to a craving for morphine, the same is probably true for alcohol, and people born with a genetic deficiency of opioids may be predisposed to become alcoholics. Environmental influences can delay or trigger this tendency.
- In people who are genetically sound, stress may cause a loss of opioids, and this deficiency may lead to alcohol craving.
- If an individual drinks too much alcohol over a period of time, a destructive feedback may occur that reduces the synthesis of naturally present opioids, leading to craving and addiction.

From these ideas I had derived three equations over which I had scrawled in block letters "The Psychogenetic Theory of Alcoholism." The equations were:

Type 1. Alcohol-craving behavior (ACB) = Genetic deficiency of internal opioids (G_{DIO}) + environment (E). This is the born alcoholic.

Type 2. ACB = Normal genetics of internal opioids (G_{NIO}) + stress-induced deficiency of internal opioids (S_{DIO}). This is the stress-related alcoholic.

Type 3. ACB = G_{NIO} + alcohol-induced deficiency of internal opioids (A_{DIO}). This is the chronic alcoholic.[2]

In the years since that morning, I have found no reason to change these basic equations, except to include deficits of other neurotransmitters along with those of the opioids, and to consider the possibility that a genetic anomaly may be present in all cases of true alcoholism. If the latter proves to be accurate, then stress and environment would be triggering factors.

INDUCTION OF ALCOHOL CRAVING BY TIQS

In his continuing investigation of TIQs, Robert Myers was now asking a provocative question: Do TIQs reduce drinking by acting like an opiate? The hypothesis underlying the question was that TIQs are addictive substances that should substitute for the need to drink. With his graduate student Christine Melchior he set up an experiment, with rats, to examine the hypothesis, injecting TIQs directly into the brains of the animals, and measuring the effect on their drinking behavior. Myers explained what happened next in a 1988 interview:

> I left shortly afterwards on a sabbatical leave to Australia to work at Latrobe University in Melbourne, and was just getting settled when I received a frantic telephone call from Christine. "Something weird is happening!" she said. "These rats are drinking enormous amounts of alcohol!"
>
> I said "That's impossible! The TIQs should fill their need for alcohol and stop them from drinking." But I couldn't deny the evidence. "It contradicts my theory," I told her, "but let's pursue it. Keep the rats on alcohol, see what happens, then take them off."
>
> She continued with the experiment, and reported that the rats drank more and more, and eventually had withdrawal symptoms similar to animals treated with morphine. So I told her to take pictures of them, and test them to see if they were going into seizures. She did, and they showed clear evidence of seizures.

These startling results raised two new questions. Can TIQs induce abnormal drinking behavior in animals that normally do not drink alcohol? In the absence of alcohol, will the animals become dependent on TIQs and show withdrawal symptoms similar to alcohol or morphine addiction? He set up an experiment with Melchior to seek answers.

They used his method to inject a TIQ called THP, which we have met before, directly into the brains of experimental rats. The injections came automatically, every 15 minutes for 12 days. The animals were given access to both water and alcohol and, although they normally preferred water, after three to six days of the injections they began to drink alcohol exclusively, and in increasingly large amounts. When alcohol was removed at the end of the period, the animals showed definite withdrawal symptoms.[3]

When the experiment was repeated with monkeys, and when other

TIQs were substituted for THP, the results were the same. Myers explained:

> We already knew that the brain produces TIQs following alcohol intake. We had now demonstrated that large amounts of TIQs injected directly into the brain stimulate an abnormal intake of alcohol. It seemed clear, therefore, that what we had done was simulate the overproduction of TIQs in the brain, as might be found in cases of chronic alcoholism.
>
> It seemed reasonable to conclude, therefore, that if TIQs are formed in sufficient quantities in certain crucial areas of the brain, they may induce changes in brain chemistry that will generate a pathological craving for alcohol, despite its bad aftereffects. This may well be the pattern that creates human alcoholism.[4]

Thus, although their role was surrounded by a continuing controversy, TIQs were emerging as a major factor in the etiology of alcoholism. If we accept Virginia Davis' earlier hypothesis, these by-products of alcohol are the source of opiate-like substances that act at the opiate receptor sites. It might be more than poetic license, then, to call the TIQs the "poppies of the brain."

TIQS AT OPIATE RECEPTORS

In a three-way collaboration, Maurice Hirst, his graduate student Murray Hamilton, and I designed an experiment to evaluate the interaction of TIQs and opiate receptors. The experiment was carried out in Hirst's laboratory in the University of Western Ontario.

Using nerve muscle strips from guinea pig ileum, rich in opiate receptors, we found that both morphine and TIQs reduced electrically stimulated muscular contractions. The inhibitory effect of morphine was stronger than that of the TIQs. When naloxone was administered before the morphine or TIQs, the inhibitory effect was blocked.[5]

These results suggested to us that, although morphine and the TIQ appeared to have similar actions at opiate receptor sites, the potency of the TIQ was lower. One explanation for this lower potency may be that, instead of acting directly on the opiate receptor, it may act first on an associated receptor which then influences the opiate receptor, itself.

This work raised two questions in the minds of R. H. Fertel and his associates at Ohio State: Can TIQs act directly on opiate receptors in the brain? Do they, like morphine, act as painkillers? They set up a series of experiments to seek answers. In the first experiment they looked at the direct interaction of naloxone and TIQs at isolated opiate receptors. They prepared rat brain material and added radioactive naloxone, followed by varying amounts of morphine and TIQs. Then, using scintillation spectrometry, they measured the amount of total radioactivity in each specimen.

The experiment was complex, but in essence what they found was that the morphine and the TIQs were knocking naloxone molecules out of the receptor sites and replacing them. Smaller amounts of morphine had the same effect, indicating its greater potency. This was the first published evidence that, like morphine, the TIQs can bind specifically to opiate receptor sites in brain tissue.

In the second experiment, Fertel and his colleagues tackled the question: Do TIQs, like morphine, act as painkillers? An ingenious technique was devised to answer the question. Small plastic tubes were implanted in the brains of four groups of rats, permitting direct injection of TIQs. The effect of these painkilling injections was determined by measuring the "tail flick" response of the animals to mild pain stimuli.[6]

In the first part of the experiment they found unmistakable evidence that TIQs dulled the pain. In the second part, they found that the opiate antagonist naloxone *blocked* this painkilling effect.[7] The evidence seemed unmistakable: TIQs were acting like opiates or endogenous opioids such as enkephalins at the opiate receptor sites.

When I heard about these results I was gratified because, not only did it support my work with Hamilton and Hirst, but it also confirmed an earlier experiment in which Alice Marshall had worked with Hirst and me to show that TIQs had painkilling effects and enhanced the painkilling effect of morphine.[8]

But what was particularly exciting to me was Fertel's conclusion: The potency of the painkilling effect of the TIQs is very close to that of the enkephalins. And metenkephalin is considered one of the most powerful natural painkillers.

SYMPOSIUM ON TIQS IN ALCOHOLISM

Interest in TIQs was focusing increasingly on the question of whether or not they are formed in the brain in sufficient quantities, following alcohol consumption, to play a major role in alcoholism. P. J. O'Neill and R. G. Rahwan at Ohio State University took a negative view. They were unable to find the TIQ salsolinol in mouse brain following chronic alcohol intake, but admitted the possibility that metabolic activity might be destroying the TIQs before they could be detected.[9]

Additional negative laboratory results followed, but positive evidence from other laboratories kept the controversy very much alive. So challenging was this situation that Frank Seixas and I decided to organize another symposium. It was held in San Diego in April 1978.

The participants represented half a dozen disciplines, all studying the effects of alcohol. Much of the material was highly technical, but the most salient points were:

- *Robert Myers.* Heavy doses of TIQs caused intense, permanent craving for alcohol in rats that normally prefer water. Repeated injections of TIQs in rats led to opiate-like withdrawal symptoms when the injections were suspended.[10]
- *Gerald Cohen.* TIQs are picked up by neurons and stored. In action, they regulate the release and metabolism of dopamine and norepinephrine at the synapse, and can mimic the action of these neurotransmitters at their receptors.[11]
- *Murray Hamilton.* In mice that had breathed alcohol vapors over an extended period of time, a metabolic by-product of TIQs called methyl salsalinol was found—the first time that this substance had been identified in the brain.[12]
- *David Ross.* TIQs and endorphins block the binding of calcium to its brain receptor sites, an action shared with opiates.[13]

Other reports were interesting and suggestive.[14]

For my part in the seminar, I delivered a paper on what I called the "link hypothesis," drawn from my own and related work in the field. If there is a connection between TIQs and the opiates, then the following statements constitute a reasonable hypothesis:

1. TIQs can be found in biological tissues following alcohol intake.
2. The effects of TIQs on the body are similar to those of alcohol and opiates.
3. The action of TIQs can be enhanced or inhibited by substances that enhance or inhibit alcohol and opiates.
4. The underlying biochemical mechanisms of TIQs, alcohol, and opiates are similar.
5. TIQs act upon opiate receptors to elicit neurochemical and behavioral responses.

6. With continued administration of TIQs, the response to each new application lessens. This resembles and is probably identical with the "tolerance" phenomenon found in the progression of alcoholism.

7. In the presence of alcohol or opiates, the response to each new application of TIQ is lessened. This is the phenomenon of "cross-tolerance."

8. TIQs create physical dependence leading to symptoms similar to those found in withdrawal from alcohol or opiates.[15]

The significance of the link hypothesis is that when alcohol is metabolized it produces TIQs which resemble opiates and act on opiate receptors. Due to this linkage, the effect of alcohol can be blocked by the same antagonists that block opiates.

We left the symposium with the feeling that progress was being made in understanding the role of TIQs in alcoholism.

BLOCKING HUMAN INTOXICATION WITH NALOXONE

When W. J. Jeffcoate decided to investigate the effect of the opiate antagonist naloxone on alcohol intoxication in humans, he was aware of our work demonstrating that naloxone can reduce the behavioral effects of alcohol on mice, as well as the experiment by G. K. Schenk and associates showing that large doses of naloxone reduced alcohol intoxication in human subjects.[16] He accepted the hypothesis that alcohol and its by-product TIQs were causing intoxication by stimulating opiate receptors, but he wanted to subject the hypothesis to a more rigorous and critical study.

Jeffcoate and his associates in Nottingham, England, carried out a double-blind, cross-over study of 20 male physician volunteers. After determining the average reaction time of the subjects, the researchers found that it increased slightly under stress, and increased still more after a drink of gin and tonic. When the subjects were given the narcotic antagonist naloxone, however, even though they were given additional alcohol, their reaction dropped back to near normal.[17]

The significance of the experiment was that in humans, as had been demonstrated in animals, naloxone blocks the intoxicating effects of alcohol.[18] Subsequent experiments have shown, however, that in humans the blocking effects of naloxone are too inconsistent to be used clinically as an antidote for alcohol intoxication.

SONS OF ALCOHOLICS:
DIFFERENCES IN ALCOHOL METABOLISM

In his investigations of alcoholism in humans, Marc A. Schuckit at the University of California at San Diego and San Diego Veterans Hospital was becoming increasingly convinced that it is a multifactored, genetically influenced disorder. Earlier studies had shown that:

- Alcohol preference can be bred into strains of animals.
- There is a 25–50 percent lifetime risk of alcoholism among sons and brothers of severely alcoholic men.
- There is a 55 percent or higher likelihood of alcoholism among identical twins from alcoholic parents, and a 28 percent likelihood of alcoholism among fraternal twins of the same sex.
- There is a fourfold or higher incidence of alcoholism among children of alcoholics than in children of nonalcoholics, even when they are separated from their biological parents at birth and reared by adopting parents who have no drinking problem.
- Children of nonalcoholic parents, adopted into alcoholic homes, have a low rate of alcoholism.

These findings strongly indicated a genetic factor, but although there were a number of "state markers," or blood tests, that seemed to correlate with heavy drinking, there was little evidence that any of them could be regarded as a genetic marker. Schuckit commented in a 1988 interview:

I was convinced that, although environmental factors play a role in alcoholism, the genetic factors may well determine the predisposition that environment triggers. These factors include, but are not limited to, a unique reaction to alcohol; differences in metabolism of alcohol; and different susceptibilities to the long-term consequences of heavy drinking.

To investigate the possibility of a genetic marker for alcoholism, Schuckit decided to evaluate acetaldehyde, a substance that not only is a breakdown product of alcohol, but also a direct precursor of TIQs. He mailed a questionnaire to 304 male students at the University of Washington. It covered their drinking and drug-use histories, their family history from the standpoint of alcohol and drug abuse, and their psychiatric difficulties. From these students he selected 40 who were well matched in age, race, sex, marital status, and drinking habits. None was alcoholic; their average intake was two to four drinks per drinking day. The primary difference was that 20 came from nonalcoholic families, and 20 had a parent who was alcoholic.

After fasting overnight, the individuals came to Schuckit's laboratory at 8:00 A.M. on a given morning. They were seated in a quiet, temperature-controlled room where their vital signs could be monitored and their blood tested. Each individual was asked to drink a sugar-free 7 UP spiked with alcohol. Blood samples were taken before the alcohol was given; 15 minutes after the alcohol; and at 30-minute intervals over the ensuing three hours.

When levels of acetaldehyde, a primary product of alcohol metabolism, were measured after alcohol consumption, the level among the 20 men from alcoholic families was more than 50 percent higher than that of the men from nonalcoholic families.[19]

The methodology of the experiment was challenged by C. J. P. Erikson and J. E. Peachey from Finland. They felt that if there is a genetic connection, the anomaly should show up in alcoholics as well as in the sons of alcoholics, and they failed to find a difference in blood acetaldehyde in alcoholics versus controls after alcohol ingestion.[20]

Despite the differences of opinion aroused by this study, and Schuckit's own reservations about the acetaldehyde assay method, my feeling at the time was that his findings fit in with other data to suggest that these higher levels of acetaldehyde are, indeed, found in the sons of alcoholics and are a genetic characteristic which favors the formation of TIQs when alcohol is ingested.[21]

When I added Myers' finding that TIQs are addictive substances and induce excessive drinking behavior, it seemed reasonable to conclude that there is a metabolic anomaly in the sons of alcoholics that puts them at risk of becoming, in their turn, alcoholics.

INCREASED FORMATION OF TIQS IN ALCOHOLICS

We have already seen in chapter 8 in the work of Sandler that TIQs form naturally in the human body, with or without alcohol. Now Michael Collins at Loyola's Stritch School of Medicine found evidence that TIQ production is increased in acutely intoxicated alcoholics. He and his associates tested urine samples for TIQs in two groups of subjects. One group consisted of heavily intoxicated alcoholics; the control group consisted of nonalcoholics who had not been drinking alcohol.

At the time of admission to the hospital, the alcoholics were deprived of alcohol, and urine samples of both groups were tested for the TIQ salsolinol. The tests were repeated at 24-hour intervals for the next three days. The concentration of TIQs in the alcoholic group was much higher in the beginning than in the control group, but dropped back almost to the level of the control group by the third day. During the three-day period the average TIQ concentration in the alcoholics was 28.8 micrograms, while that in the controls was 1.1 microgram.

The fact that the TIQs were much higher in the intoxicated alcoholics than in the nonalcoholics indicated that most of the TIQs were being formed from alcohol metabolism.

At the end of the first 24 hours, the two groups were tested for the metabolite of the TIQ salsolinol, a substance called salsoline (O-methylated salsolinol). The alcoholics showed a concentration of 111 micrograms of salsoline, compared to 21 micrograms for the controls. This level of metabolite was unexpected in the control group, because it had been assumed that salsolinol came only from the metabolism of alcohol.[22]

The fact that the concentration of salsoline in alcoholics was approximately four times higher than salsolinol, itself, indicates that the TIQ metabolizes at a very high rate. The amount of the metabolite in the controls also suggests that there may be a source of TIQs other than alcohol in the normal body. In an interview in 1988 Collins stated that "while the presence of TIQs in urine could be useful as a clinical measure of prior blood acetaldehyde levels in chronic alcoholics, caution should be exercised. Diet can alter TIQ concentration and lead to false measurements."[23]

ENKEPHALINS AND TIQS: SHARING COMMON RECEPTORS

George Siggins and Floyd E. Bloom at the Salk Institute were working on the relationship between neurotransmitters and the electrophysiological events that follow alcohol ingestion, seeking more information on three questions:

- Are the effects of alcohol and TIQs on the neuron similar to the effects of morphine or enkephalins?
- Does alcohol act on the neuron through opiate receptors?
- Do the TIQs interact *only* with the opiate receptors to affect the neuron?

They set up an experiment in which alcohol, morphine, three TIQs (THP, salsolinol, and its metabolite salsoline), and methionine enkephalin were applied to single neurons of rat brain, and their effects on neural firings measured and recorded. In the second stage the experiment was repeated in the presence of the antagonist naloxone which blocks opiate receptors, and the effect on neural firing was again measured and recorded. In the third stage, the experiment was repeated with the antagonist scopolamine which blocks the receptors for the neurotransmitter acetylcholine, but does not block receptors for opiates. Once again, the effect on neural firing was measured and recorded.[24]

The results of these experiments answered the questions that had been posed:

- Alcohol and TIQs mimic the effect of morphine and enkephalin on the neuron.
- The narcotic antagonist naloxone partially blocks the effects of TIQs, alcohol, morphine, and enkephalin.
- Scopolamine has a blocking effect on TIQs, but does not block the opioid enkephalin.

Although the effects of alcohol and TIQs on the brain appear to be similar to that of enkephalin, that is, they activate opiate receptors, it is probable that other neurotransmitters and other receptors are involved as well.

EVIDENCE AGAINST TIQ-INDUCED ALCOHOL CRAVING

Zalman Amit at Concordia University in Montreal, and his associates, Brian Smith and Zavie Brown, further stirred up the TIQ controversy when they repeated Myers' famous experiment. Whereas Myers had shown that when TIQs are infused into the brains of nonalcoholic rats the animals become permanently alcohol-preferring, Amit's group could not duplicate the results. They had initiated the experiment in the hope of verifying Myers' findings; instead, they raised questions that are still being debated.

In an attempt to help resolve this conflict, I invited both Amit and Myers to submit papers for the new journal *Substance and Alcohol Action/ Misuse* that I was launching with Ernest Noble. We felt that the papers would provide a critical evaluation of the two points of view. Both men agreed.

Amit's paper concluded:

We have hypothesized that acetaldehyde is responsible for the positive reinforcing effects of ethanol and perpetuates ethanol consumption, while TIQs signal satiety when they accumulate in the brain. However, the present data failed to show any effect of TIQ on ethanol intake, thereby raising the possibility that TIQs may simply be a by-product of consumed ethanol without any mediation role whatsoever. Nevertheless, further research is warranted to reconcile the differential results obtained by different laboratories on the possible involvement of TIQs in ethanol self-administration.[25]

Amit's suggestion that TIQs produce feelings of satiety was supported by the earlier work of Charles Duncan and Richard Dietrich at the University of Colorado. Unlike Myers, Duncan and Dietrich showed that the administration of THP (a TIQ) at a high dosage level almost completely stopped ethanol drinking in rats.

Myers reported in his paper that he had repeated his experiment and verified his results. He then listed possible areas of difference in his and Amit's approach—differences that could have caused the discrepancy in results.[26] Myers pointed out, for example, that results may be distorted if the animals used are not biologically sensitive to TIQs, or if the cannula (tube) is not inserted precisely at the site that controls drinking. In a telephone interview in 1988 he added:

Unlike Amit, I believe that TIQs have dual effects; that is, they can either increase or decrease drinking. These effects occur depending on the dose you use, the site in the brain into which you pump the material, and the particular animal species you are using in the experiment. TIQs can produce either a "need" state or a "satiety" state.

It is easy to understand how such controversies develop. Amit and Myers were working in an extraordinarily difficult and complex area of behavioral pharmacology. At times the work focuses on areas that are infinitesimal, with interactions that may involve billions of neurons and hundreds of different neurotransmitters, enzymes, and receptors affecting each other in complex patterns of excitation and inhibition. They raised questions that still have not been answered completely. From today's vantage point the role of the TIQs seems to some investigators to be well established, but the exact mechanisms and interactions are still being explored.

So the questions were well asked. Despite growing evidence favoring the involvement of TIQs in alcoholism, the jury was still out.

TOWARD VERIFICATION OF
THE PSYCHOGENETIC THEORY

Three experiments carried out in my laboratory partially verified the existence of the Type 1 and Type 3 alcoholics postulated in my psychogenetic theory, discussed earlier in this chapter. Type 1, if you remember, is the born alcoholic whose alcohol-craving behavior is genetic in origin. Type 3 is the alcoholic who develops the habit through the toxic effects of long-continued social drinking. Identification of Type 2, the alcoholic who develops the habit to offset the effects of stress, would come later. Inherent in the theory is the idea that all three types develop through the mechanism of opioid peptide (endorphin or enkephalin) deficiency or imbalance.

In a small preliminary study, my colleagues and I ordered 20 C57 black mice of the 6J substrain that prefers alcohol over water. When we gave them a choice of alcohol or water, they showed a preference for alcohol, confirming McClearn's earlier work on the C57 strain.

When we tried to order more of these special mice from Jackson Labs, we were told that they were temporarily out of stock. Since we were impatient to get our experiments under way, we decided to order mice of the same strain from Simonson Labs. To our surprise, when the mice came most of them stubbornly refused to drink alcohol. We couldn't understand it. These animals were *supposed* to drink alcohol! They were alcoholic mice!

Then an idea hit me that changed the experiment. We called Jackson, found that they now had stock, and ordered 40 mice. We also called Simonson and ordered 40 mice. All were C57s, and all were of the substrain that supposedly preferred alcohol. When they arrived we took 30 of the Jackson mice in one subgroup, and 30 of the Simonson mice in another subgroup, and gave them a choice of alcohol or water. As I more or less expected, the Jackson animals chose alcohol about 60 percent of the time; the Simonson group chose alcohol only about 20 percent of the time.

We then sacrificed the remaining alcohol-free animals—10 from Jackson, and 10 from Simonson—and checked the level of methionine enkephalin in whole brain samples. The alcohol-drinking Jackson animals had significantly less enkephalin in the brain than the Simonson animals.[27]

This showed, first, how precise the breeding selection has to be to preserve narrowly specific tendencies. Second, it offered preliminary support for the idea that animals who fit my Type 1 category drink—

in part, at least—because they have a genetic deficiency of enkephalins in their brain.

To further test this idea, we set up a second experiment in which we used four strains of mice: those that preferred water, those that showed a mild preference for water, and two that showed a preference for alcohol over water.[28] We checked their brains and found a striking correlation between enkephalin levels and drinking preference: The drinking animals, bred to prefer alcohol, were low in enkephalins, supporting the hypothesis of my Type 1 category of alcoholism.[29]

The question behind the third experiment was: What is the situation of the normal individual who is not, at first, an alcoholic, but develops into one through heavy social drinking? To answer the question, we placed two groups of Golden Syrian hamsters in cages for a period of one year. These animals have a natural preference for alcohol over water. One group was given water; the other was given a choice of water or a liquid containing 10 percent alcohol. We measured the total fluid intake of each animal for 365 days, and at the end of the year we found that the animals that had been exposed to alcohol had markedly reduced enkephalin levels in the reward area of the brain in comparison to the animals that had drunk only water.[30]

I theorized at the time that the cause of this depletion of enkephalins was, perhaps, the action of alcohol or its metabolite TIQ on the opiate receptor sites. The alcohol molecules or the TIQs may be saying to the receptors; "Hey, we're here, so you don't need enkephalins. Shut down the factory!" This provided a possible mechanism to explain Type 3 alcoholism.

THE ALCOHOL TOLERANCE FACTOR

While she was at the University of Illinois Medical Center, Paula Hoffman carried out a joint research project with Boris Tabakoff and associates to investigate the effect of a neuropeptide called arginine vasopressin on the response to alcohol, particularly on tolerance. Hoffman explained:

> The underlying hypothesis was that the initial response to alcohol is a pleasurable one, but as the alcohol level rises, it produces unpleasant (aversive) effects. If, after long exposure to alcohol, sensitivity to these unpleasant effects is lost, that is, if tolerance develops, the initial pleasurable effects become more pronounced, and this may lead to excessive drinking. If this tolerance could be reduced, it might help to solve the problem of excessive drinking.

There were reports that arginine vasopressin could affect memory processes, and there is a hypothesis that tolerance and memory may be the result of similar changes in the brain. We wondered whether arginine vasopressin might influence tolerance as it did memory.

In the experiment, Hoffman and her colleagues took an inbred strain of mice and placed them for seven days on a liquid diet containing alcohol. A control group received a liquid diet containing sucrose. On the eighth day, the alcohol group was switched to a sucrose diet and experienced withdrawal. Once this reaction was over, both groups were given an injection of alcohol, and the sedative-hypnotic response was measured. The group that had been on the alcohol liquid diet showed less tendency to sleep than the control group. This showed that they had become tolerant to alcohol.

Later, both groups were given alcohol injections, and their body temperature was measured. The body temperature of the animals that had been on the alcohol liquid diet was less affected than that of the mice in the control group. This, too, indicated an increasing tolerance for alcohol. The experiment was then repeated with four groups who received various controlled regimens. At the end of the eighth day, the four groups were tested with a large dose of alcohol, and the test was repeated every three days until the eighteenth day. The results showed:

- The group receiving sucrose and saline developed no tolerance.
- The group receiving sucrose and arginine vasopressin developed no tolerance.
- The group receiving an alcohol diet combined with saline developed tolerance, but for only a short time.
- The group receiving an alcohol diet combined with arginine vasopressin developed a lengthened period of tolerance.[31]

Hoffman commented:

It was interesting to see that arginine vasopressin did not *cause* tolerance—in conjunction with the control sucrose diet it had no effect at all. But when combined with alcohol it significantly increased the period of tolerance. We found this quite exciting, because there was a possibility that tolerance may be a factor in causing excessive alcohol drinking, and if arginine vasopressin can be manipulated it might prove to be a key to controlling tolerance.

Hoffman subsequently told me of an experiment in which she and her associates showed that if norepinephrine is chemically removed from the brain, arginine vasopressin loses its effect on alcohol tolerance. This indicated strongly that vasopressin acts *through* the norepinephrine system, and that if you block the effect of norepinephrine, you may remove a motivation toward excessive drinking.

An experiment by Steven Richardson and colleagues in Canada supported this idea. They found that when rats who have acquired a preference for alcohol are given brain injections of a substance that lowers norepinephrine levels, the free choice of alcohol is reduced.[32]

THE FIRST GORDON CONFERENCE ON ALCOHOLISM

The first Gordon Conference on Alcoholism, held in February 1979, in Santa Barbara, California, gave scientists working in the field a valuable overview of the progress that was being made and the problems that remained.[33] I am not permitted by the rules of the Conference to report on the actual proceedings, but I can give you my general impressions of the research pathways that were discussed, and the questions that were raised.

1. **When alcohol is ingested, it changes the chemical composition of neuronal membranes.**
   - What are the exact chemical changes that occur? Do membranes of animals bred to prefer alcohol react differently? What are the effects of membrane changes on neurotransmission? On cell metabolism? Do these changes affect future sensitivity to alcohol? Are these effects general, as in anesthesia, or specific, as in action on receptors?

2. **Short-term exposure to alcohol inhibits the binding of calcium to neuronal receptor sites in the membrane; long-term exposure stimulates binding.**
   - Does this calcium activity affect communication inside the cell— one of the "second messenger" effects? Does it affect the release of neurotransmitters, thereby affecting communication between neurons? Do these factors affect craving and withdrawal? Does in-bred sensitivity to alcohol affect calcium binding?

3. **Alcohol inhibits an enzyme that controls the flow of ions such as sodium and potassium across the membrane into the cell.**
   - What are the mechanisms involved? What are the receptor sites that are affected by this inhibition? After long-term alcohol exposure, what happens if the alcohol is withdrawn?

4. **At receptor sites, alcohol or its by-products can act like a neuro-transmitter: they can occupy the site and initiate activity in the neuron, or they can occupy the site and block the action of the natural neurotransmitter.**

   - Which neurotransmitter is alcohol mimicking? Which neuro-transmitter is being blocked? If alcohol is removed after long-term application, how is receptor sensitivity affected? Are these factors influenced by genetics?

5. **Alcohol, acetaldehyde, and TIQs, when applied directly to a neuron, either activate or inhibit electrical activity. The activity is similar to that caused by the opioids.**

   - Are these effects caused by nonspecific alterations of the chemical composition of the neuronal membrane, or by changes in the receptors themselves?

6. **Alcohol can stimulate or inhibit the enzymes that destroy it.**

   - Which enzymes are either increased or decreased in quantity in the presence of alcohol? Which enzymes are more active, and which are less active in the presence of alcohol? What is the role of acetaldehyde? Do genetic factors, alone, influence the synthesis and activity of these enzymes?

7. **The presence of alcohol stimulates or inhibits the production of enzymes that regulate neurotransmitter synthesis, storage, metabolism, release, and receptor activation.**

   - Which of these enzymes are increased or decreased in quantity in the presence of alcohol? Which enzymes are more active, and which are less active in the presence of alcohol? Do these enzymes influence reward? If so, what are the genetic influences on the reward process? What other proteins besides enzymes are stimulated or inhibited by alcohol?

8. **Alcohol affects sexual function; for example, it reduces the sexual hormones testosterone in males and estrogen in females.**

   - Through what mechanisms do these changes take place? Which neurotransmitters, including the natural opioids, are involved in the action of alcohol on hormones? Why does alcohol lead to feminization of some men and the defeminization of some women?

9. **Drinking during pregnancy poses a serious threat to the fetus.**

It can cause retardation of growth and development, and may cause brain damage.

- What are the amounts of alcohol needed to cause these changes during pregnancy? What are the mechanisms that produce the changes? What is the role of acetaldehyde and TIQs in these changes? What specific and nonspecific effects does alcohol have on the development of the nervous system in the fetus? Can it produce a predisposition to alcoholism?

Much of this research still was concerned with traditional goals of clarifying the effect of alcohol *as a poison* affecting tissues, muscles, and glands. I recognized its importance, but the investigations that interested me most were those that were pushing back the frontiers in pharmacology, neurology, and biophysics. Here, I felt, we were coming to view alcoholism as a progressive neurological disease, just as we would any other pathology of the central nervous system.

The scientist never "knows" anything, but at the end of the Gordon Conference, as I looked to the future, the "hunches" or hypotheses below seemed to comprise a reasonable integration of what we knew about addiction:

- Alcohol and opiates suppress the synthesis of certain natural opioids and other neurotransmitters, and affect the reward system through the endorphinergic receptors. Alcohol and opiates may have common mechanisms of action, and dependence on these substances may be due to a genetic factor.
- Alcohol, TIQs, and enkephalins directly act at opiate receptor sites.
- TIQs are natural components of the brain, but they can also be formed as metabolic by-products of alcohol. They induce long-term drinking in mammals.
- Alcoholics convert a higher percentage of alcohol into TIQs than do nonalcoholics.
- There is some evidence that genetic deficiencies of both neurotransmitters and opioids influence craving.
- There is stronger evidence that genetics is the determining factor that generates predisposition to alcoholism.

These hypotheses were not sufficiently complete to constitute a workable model of alcoholism, but unquestionably we were coming closer.

SUGGESTED READING

Blum, K., ed. *Alcohol and Opiates: Neurochemical and Behavioral Mechanisms.* New York: Academic Press, 1977.

Collins, M. A. *Aldehyde Adducts in Alcoholism.* New York: Alan Liss, 1985.

Crabbe, J. C., Jr., and Rigter, H. *Alcohol Tolerance and Dependence.* Amsterdam: Elsevier/North-Holland, 1980.

Goldstein, D. B. *Pharmacology of Alcohol.* New York: Oxford University Press, 1983.

Gross, M. M., ed. *Alcohol Intoxication and Withdrawal,* vols. 1 and 2. New York: Plenum Press, 1975.

Pattison, E. M., and Kaufman, E., eds. *Encyclopedic Handbook of Alcoholism.* New York: Gardner Press, 1982.

10

Malfunction of the Reward Messengers

Although the presence of natural opioids and opiate receptor sites in the reward areas of the brain seemed established, the idea that opioid imbalances or variations in receptor activity might cause addiction or abnormal drinking was no more than a hypothesis based on scanty evidence.

Furthermore, although individual differences had been observed in the amounts of opioids present, and in the number and activity of receptor sites in various parts of the brain, the cause or causes of these variations remained largely a mystery. The most likely hypothesis was that *genetic* differences, perhaps triggered by environmental phenomena, were responsible.

OPIATE RECEPTORS AND ALCOHOL CRAVING

In 1980, Harold Altschuler and his associates at the Texas Research Institute of Mental Health in Houston developed a unique method of determining the effect of opiate antagonists on the craving for alcohol in rats. Altschuler had read a paper by David Ross and associates in which they observed that morphine reduced the voluntary intake of alcohol in hamsters, probably through its action at the opiate receptor sites. Ross demonstrated this effect by showing that alcohol intake increases when the narcotic antagonist naltrexone is administered, blocking the opiate receptor.[1]

To carry this idea further, Altschuler devised a novel method of intravenous injection that enabled monkeys to self-administer alcohol over an extended period of time. Into a vein in each animal a catheter was inserted, connected to an infusion pump fed by a reservoir and controlled by a lever. When the animal pressed the lever, a measured amount of alcohol from the reservoir was delivered into the vein. Essentially what they found was that animals receiving a preliminary injection of naltrexone showed an initial *increase* of 15 percent in alcohol self-injection over a period of five days, followed by a progressive *decrease* until the animals no longer pressed the lever.

Altschuler suggested that the increase represented the animal's attempt to gain the same level of euphoria by injecting more alcohol to overcome the blocking effect of naltrexone. The decrease was a classic example of extinction of a conditioned reflex when there is no reinforcement; that is, when alcohol produced no good feeling, the animal abandoned the effort.[2]

When I read this paper I immediately called my colleague Ross, and we invited Altschuler to present a seminar in our department. At the conclusion of the seminar he summed up his interpretation of the findings:

> We hypothesize that . . . the pleasurable effects of alcohol are due to an interaction of alcohol with opiate systems, perhaps through the opioid peptides. An intriguing alternate hypothesis is that the opiate-like by-products of alcohol metabolism, the TIQs, may regulate ethanol-induced pleasure states through interactions with brain endogenous opiate systems.

GENETIC VARIATIONS IN OPIATE RECEPTORS AS A FACTOR IN ALCOHOL CRAVING

I first met Marco Trabucchi when I chaired a session on alcohol research at the First International Neurotoxicology Congress in Albino, Italy. I was familiar with his investigations of neurotransmitters and the pharmacology of receptors, and had a high regard for his work. We had a long talk, and he offered to send me his latest paper on the genetics of opiate receptors which, he said, might have a certain relevance to my work.[3]

His paper arrived soon after I returned to the United States, and it did, indeed, have a "certain relevance." I had reported earlier that in experiments with inbred animals:

- If the animal chooses water over alcohol it has a high level of opioid peptides.
- If the animal chooses alcohol over water it has a low level of opioid peptides.

In the paper, Trabucchi's group reported on the number of opiate receptor sites in the reward areas of the brain:

- If the animal chooses water over alcohol, it has a low level of opiate receptors.
- If the animal chooses alcohol over water it has a high level of opiate receptors.

Trabucchi and his associates did not speculate on the meaning of their findings in relation to alcohol-craving behavior, but I saw in them the basis for an intriguing hypothesis: When an animal is genetically equipped to produce a "normal" flow of enkephalins, the brain creates a "normal" number of receptor sites. If a genetic defect leads to an inadequate flow of enkephalins, the brain compensates by creating more receptor sites in an attempt to capture more of the available enkephalins.

On this hypothesis we can assume that alcohol-loving mice have a genetic anomaly that causes the neurons in their brain to produce an inadequate supply of enkephalins. To compensate, the brain increases the number of receptor sites until there are more sites than enkephalin molecules. This gap, in turn, as suggested by my Psychogenetic Theory discussed in chapter 9, leads to craving behavior.[4]

Breaking the sequence down into steps:

- A shortage of enkephalins leads to the formation of more opiate receptors.
- The excess of opiate receptors intensifies the brain's need for enkephalins.
- To restore balance, the brain seeks a substitute for enkephalins.
- If alcohol is taken into the system, the alcohol metabolizes to produce TIQs that have the ability to fill and stimulate the opiate receptors.
- The TIQs restore balance, but the effect is temporary, and more alcohol must be drunk to maintain the balance.

I knew that, even if true, this hypothesis could be only a partial explanation of alcohol craving, but it opened the door to intriguing possibilities.

CROSS-TOLERANCE BETWEEN ALCOHOL AND OPIATES

Earlier I mentioned a controversy in which Maurice Seevers questioned the Davis/Walsh hypothesis that alcohol and opiates share common mechanisms. Seevers stated that "no specific mutual cross-dependence or cross-tolerance exists between morphine-like drugs and . . . ethanol." That controversy was largely resolved by an experiment carried out by J. M. Khanna and H. Kalant with their associates at the University of Toronto.

The group set out to determine whether alcohol and morphine have a cross-tolerance relationship in their effect on opiate receptors in animal tissue; that is, whether alcohol modifies the effect of morphine, and vice versa. Using muscle tissue rich in opiate receptors, they subjected it to electrical stimulation and measured the resulting contractions. They found that previous exposure to morphine reduced the effect of subsequent morphine applications, and that the same held true for alcohol. Morphine, however, exerted the stronger influence.[5] This demonstrated a phenomenon that might be called "self-tolerance."

In the second phase of the experiment, alcohol was applied to tissues previously treated with morphine, and vice versa. After electrical stimulation, measurements of contractions showed that morphine inhibits the effects of alcohol and vice versa, with morphine having the stronger effect. Thus cross-tolerance appeared to be present, suggesting a biochemical commonality between alcohol and opiates.[6] In other words, this evidence appeared to indicate that Seevers was wrong and Davis and Walsh were right.

Later that year, 1980, we showed in our laboratory that the opiate antagonist naloxone blocked the action of alcohol on similar tissues, providing further support for the idea of cross-tolerance between alcohol and opiates.[7]

BINDING OF ALCOHOL AND TIQS
TO ENKEPHALIN RECEPTORS

The idea that the brain has more than one type of opiate receptor had received considerable attention since the discovery of the first opiate receptor and the first naturally occurring opiates in the early seventies. By 1981, at least three such receptors had been found: the *delta*, the *mu*, and the *kappa*, and the search was continuing for others. The delta receptor had been found primarily in connection with enkephalins and beta-endorphins, and the mu was involved primarily with heroin, morphine, codeine, and similar substances. Later, the kappa receptor was found to be associated with a naturally occurring substance called dynorphin.

Some work that I had done with Maurice Hirst suggested that alcohol or TIQs bind preferentially to enkephalin receptors rather than morphine receptors. We found that alcohol has more effect on tissues that are rich in delta receptors (associated with enkephalins) than on those that contain mostly mu receptors (associated with morphine).[8]

Eric Simon and his group accidentally provided the first confirmation for this idea. In an investigation of opiate receptors in rat brain, they began to get highly variable results. When they reviewed their procedure they found that the problem was that alcohol, which they were using as a solvent in some of the experiments, was strongly inhibiting the binding of enkephalins to the delta receptors. They investigated the effect and confirmed that morphine bound mostly to the mu receptors, and that enkephalin bound mostly to the delta receptors; and found that alcohol inhibited binding to the delta receptors much more strongly than to the mu receptors.[9] Simon commented, "We felt that these data strongly supported the idea of separate delta and mu receptors, and was the first demonstration of selective inhibition of one type of receptor by alcohol, a substance not naturally occurring in the brain."[10] I felt that the significance of this experiment was that alcohol, directly or indirectly, was interfering with the binding of natural enkephalins at these sites.

The finding by Simon's group that alcohol selectively inhibits the binding of enkephalin to delta receptors set off an interesting train of thought in my mind. Because of its structure, one might logically assume that a simple molecule like alcohol would not be selective in its binding to one receptor or another. But R. Greenwald had shown that certain TIQs have a complex, morphine-like structure, and generally bind to opiate receptors. Could it be, then, that it was not the alcohol molecules, but the TIQs derived from alcohol that were primarily responsible for the binding?

A possible affirmative answer to this question was suggested by the results of a new experiment in two parts conducted by M. Trabucchi and his group. In the first part, they used materials in a test tube to measure the effect of alcohol, acetaldehyde, salsolinol (TIQ), and enkephalin on the binding of natural enkephalin at its delta receptor sites. They found that:

- alcohol had only a slight inhibitory effect
- acetaldehyde had a somewhat greater effect
- TIQ had a still greater effect
- enkephalin had the greatest effect of all.

But when they administered alcohol orally to a group of rats, they found that alcohol and TIQs have an *equal* inhibitory effect on enkephalin binding at the delta site. This apparent increase in alcohol's inhibitory effect in the body may be due to the fact that it metabolizes into TIQs.[11]

This opened up another possibility: When opiate receptor sites become continuously occupied by TIQs, a feedback mechanism may interfere with the RNA message responsible for stimulating the manufacture of enkephalins in the neuron, further reducing the supply. Such a feedback mechanism would help to explain our earlier finding that enkephalins in the brain of hamsters were drastically reduced after a one-year consumption of alcohol.

ALCOHOL AND BRAIN OPIOID SYNTHESIS

The synthesis of proteins, including neurotransmitters and enzymes, is the principal manufacturing operation of the brain. As we saw in Chapter 7, Ernest Noble and Sujata Tewari pointed out in 1971 that chronic alcohol intake inhibits brain protein synthesis. Later, in a series of experiments, they provided additional insights:

1. Chronic alcohol intake *leads to a decrease in the incorporation of the amino acid leucine into the ribosomes in the neurons* where the coding for the manufacture of proteins takes place. Amino acids are the building blocks of protein. This reduction in protein synthesis may show up in individuals who are dependent on alcohol, or undergoing withdrawal.
2. Chronic alcohol intake *inhibits the incorporation of orotic acid into RNA.* Orotic acid is needed for the synthesis of RNA, which acts as the blueprint that controls production of proteins, including neurotransmitters and their regulatory enzymes.
3. Chronic alcohol intake *inhibits the incorporation of the amino acid phenylalanine into protein,* leading to a slowdown or halt in production of normal protein or the production of abnormal proteins.
4. Chronic alcohol intake *markedly reduces the activity of messenger RNA,* causing defects in the production of polypeptides which may, in turn, result in aberrant behavior.[12] Opioids are examples of polypeptides.

This work linked alcohol directly to interference with the most fundamental processes taking place in the neuron.

The next advance in understanding the effect of alcohol on brain opioid synthesis came in 1984 when Albert Herz and his group at the Max Planck Institute for Psychiatry in Munich reported on a further investigation of the effects of alcohol on opioid peptides. In their experiment they administered alcohol to rats as their only source of fluid over a period of three weeks. At the end of that time, the investigators found a 50 percent reduction in the amount and release of pituitary beta-endorphins in the test animals as compared to controls who had received no alcohol.

Furthermore, when they examined brain tissue from the alcohol-drinking animals and compared it to tissue from animals that had received no alcohol, they found that the alcohol-drinking animals showed a 30 percent decrease in the amino acid phenylalanine, an essential component of beta-endorphin. Thus, even the precursors and enzymes responsible for the synthesis of beta-endorphin were markedly reduced by alcohol. Herz explained, "Other investigators determined that alcohol interferes generally with the RNA-directed synthesis of protein and brain peptides. Combining this determination with our findings, we can suggest that alcohol interferes with messenger RNA, thereby interfering with the precursors and enzymes needed to make beta-endorphin, thereby reducing its output."[13] This finding helps to explain the mechanism whereby chronic alcoholism reduces the production of brain opioids.

INCREASING THE NUMBER OF OPIATE RECEPTORS

When the Ernest Gallo Clinic and Research Center was formed at the University of California in San Francisco, its missions were to understand how alcohol produces changes in nerve function; identify biological changes characteristic of alcohol abuse; and identify genetic markers in alcoholics and people at risk of becoming alcoholic. Among the Center's first appointments were clinical neurologist Ivan Diamond and biochemist Adrienne Gordon, both from the University. In association with Michael Charness, they set up an experiment using cultured neural cells that were known to have opiate receptors—but only delta receptors, which are the natural receptors for enkephalins.

In a series of experiments they found that:

- short-term exposure to alcohol significantly inhibits the binding of enkephalin to the delta receptors

- long-term exposure to alcohol increases the number of delta receptors.

They related long-term exposure to alcohol to the clinical phenomenon of tolerance, speculating that in time the neural membrane may undergo adaptive changes that cause an increase in the number of receptors in an effort to restore normal function.[14]

These findings partially fit into an earlier hypothesis I had considered regarding the role of TIQs in craving. Specifically, I had commented that "in short-term exposure, TIQs derived from alcohol occupy opioid sites and prevent binding of enkephalins, reducing craving. In long-term exposure, new receptor sites are created faster than the enkephalins or TIQs can fill them, generating craving anew."[15]

ENDORPHIN DEFICIENCY IN ALCOHOLICS

A press conference in Milan had an unexpected result. Luigi Manzo, of the University of Pavia, had called me in San Antonio to say that the Italian Society of Narcotics and the Italian Ministry of Health wanted me to meet with Italian journalists to explain current views of the biogenetic bases of alcohol-craving behavior, and the role of the endorphins. Would I come?

The conference took place in a castle in Milan, and I found myself besieged by 100 Italian journalists. They were warm and friendly, but some were outraged at the suggestion that alcoholism was anything other than a moral issue, and others had trouble with the idea that some alcoholics might be born with the disease.

It was an interesting day, but the most important outcome was an encounter with F. Facchinetti, a clinical pharmacologist from the University of Pavia. After I escaped from the journalists he joined me for lunch.

"We are working with investigators at the University of Calgary," he said, "to measure endorphin levels in the cerebral spinal fluid of a group of active human alcoholics. In view of your work on animals, do you think we'll find a deficiency?"

"I think the chances are good," I said. "And you know the work of Gianoulakis and her people at McGill showing that both morphine and alcohol reduce the brain synthesis of beta-endorphin in alcohol-preferring rats. This suggests a feedback mechanism. Maybe you can demonstrate it in humans."

I was pleased a year later to receive the paper reporting on the experiment. He and his associates took a group of people who had been active alcoholics for an average of 22 years, and compared them to a control group who had no history of alcoholism. They found that the beta-endorphin level in the spinal fluid of the active alcoholics was only one-third as high as that of the nonalcoholic control group.

The investigators suggested that this profound reduction may occur because TIQs occupy the opiate receptor sites, triggering a feedback mechanism that shuts off endorphin synthesis in humans as was seen earlier in animals.[16]

I think their suggestion was valid. Although in their experiment they had no opportunity to measure the endorphin levels of the subjects prior to long-term heavy drinking, it is unlikely that—even assuming a genetic predisposition—these subjects would have shown such a drastic beta-endorphin deficit at an early age. A reasonable hypothesis was that a genetic predisposition toward alcohol abuse can be triggered and made progressively worse by continued alcohol intake.

REDUCTION OF PAIN AND ALCOHOL CRAVING THROUGH ENKEPHALINASE INHIBITION

As I began looking deeper into the possible role of enkephalins in alcoholism, it would have been tempting to think of administering enkephalin as a therapy, except for one unfortunate fact: Enkephalin in itself is one of the most addictive substances known. Injected into the brain of a rat, it can induce addiction in 96 hours! In effect, its use would be similar to substituting morphine for alcohol—one craving for another. But could alcohol craving be safely controlled by using some *natural* means to increase the brain enkephalin supply, thereby stimulating the opiate receptors?

I was reminded of experiments on pain carried out by Seymour Ehrenpreis and his group at the University of Chicago Medical School. They showed that D-phenylalanine, an amino acid, can reduce pain in rodents in a manner similar to morphine in humans.

Their hypothesis was that enkephalins can regulate pain more effectively than morphine; that enkephalins are regulated by enzymes such as enkephalinase; that overregulation can reduce the supply of enkephalins and lead to increased pain; and that a possible way to reduce pain might be to inhibit the regulating enzyme, thereby increasing the enkephalin supply.

In a series of experiments they demonstrated the ability of D-phenylalanine to inhibit enkephalinase, resulting in a long-term painkilling effect in both animals and humans. Furthermore, they showed that this effect can be blocked by naloxone, indicating that the analgesic effect probably involves opiate receptors.[17]

These findings raised an intriguing question: Since the opiate receptors were involved, could this phenomenon be relevant to alcohol craving as well as pain?

Here is how the pieces of the puzzle looked to me:

- Genetically bred, alcohol-preferring mice have low enkephalin levels.
- Enkephalins reduce craving for alcohol in rats trained to drink.[18]
- Enkephalins are enormously addictive when injected into the brain of rats.
- D-phenylalanine seems to have the ability to increase enkephalin supply.

Early in 1981, I began to look for a natural means to control the enkephalin supply, avoiding substances that would be addictive. The most likely candidate was the nontoxic, nonaddictive amino acid D-phenylalanine. It was known to inhibit the enzyme enkephalinase which destroys enkephalin in the brain. Could we use this or some other natural substance to block or remove the enzyme, permitting more of the brain's output of enkephalin to reach the receptor sites, thereby reducing alcohol craving? When I discussed the experiment with Ehrenpreis he suggested that we begin by testing the effect of hydrocinnamic acid, a metabolite of D-phenylalanine thought to be a more potent inhibitor than D-phenylalanine, itself.

In my laboratory, my colleagues and I injected hydrocinnamic acid into the brains of alcohol-preferring mice whose alcohol intake had been measured under conditions in which they had a choice of alcohol or water. After the injection, their alcohol intake dropped significantly and remained low for approximately eight days, at the end of which time it returned to the original level. These results suggested that enkephalinase inhibition reduces, for the short-term, alcohol-seeking behavior in alcohol-preferring mice.[19]

We were now ready for the most exciting experiment I had ever carried out; an investigation of the use of a pharmacological agent to offset or reverse a genetic defect. In our C57 mice we knew that we had animals that, through genetic influences, had a predisposition to prefer alcohol over water, and a genetic deficiency of brain enkephalins. We knew, too, that in the light of present knowledge we could not alter their gene structure. But could we reduce or correct the deficiency by manipulating their brain chemistry?

In the first stage of the experiment, using a group of water-preferring and a group of alcohol-preferring animals, we removed their food and water for 24 hours, then presented both groups with a 10 percent alcohol solution and measured the amount each mouse drank over a period of one day. This established a baseline: The alcohol-preferring mice drank approximately 35 percent more alcohol than the water-preferring mice.

Over the next 18 days, we injected the alcohol-preferring mice with the enkephalinase inhibitor D-phenylalanine, and the water-preferring mice with a saline solution, then retested their one-day alcohol consumption. The water-preferring mice remained at their baseline; the alcohol-preferring mice not only significantly reduced their baseline alcohol consumption, but actually reduced it *below* that of the water-preferring mice.

We had successfully changed the genetically induced behavior of laboratory animals by pharmacogenetic manipulation!

I felt that there were profound implications in the anticraving effect of D-phenylalanine, but the mechanism was so obscure that I filed the data away and did not publish it for six years while I continued the investigation. Clearly, here were the makings of a useful treatment adjunct, but much animal work remained before I could consider its application to the problem of human alcoholism.

INACTIVATION OF OPIOIDS BY ALCOHOL

The role of opioids as a euphoriant had been well established by Larry Stein and James Belluzzi at the University of California at Irvine.[20] Furthermore, alcohol-craving behavior had been linked to deficiencies of the opioids. Now, in the culmination of a series of experiments that had begun in 1980, Michael Summers at the University of Pennsylvania threw new light on the role of acetaldehyde in alcoholism. He showed that this by-product of alcohol readily combines with opiate peptides such as the enkephalins to form compounds that are similar to TIQs, *but do not combine with opiate receptors.* Thus acetaldehyde may remove natural opioids that act as euphoriants—substances on which the body depends for feelings of well-being.[21]

Summers carried out his experiments in the test tube, and not in living bodies; but if this effect could be demonstrated in the body in the presence of alcohol, it would help to explain the intense, abnormal craving behavior that develops with long-term alcohol abuse.

OPIOID MODULATION OF ALCOHOL INTAKE

In the area of pharmacology, growing interest was focusing on the opioids. In one development, Larry D. Reid and his group at Rensselaer Polytechnic Institute made a highly controversial suggestion that problem drinking may be related to an *excess* of natural opioid activity, an idea in direct conflict with the belief of many scientists that abnormal alcohol craving is due to *reduced* opioid activity.

Reid's suggestion grew out of experiments with rats. In some experiments, the animals were given small doses of morphine sulfate, an opiate that has effects similar to those of natural opioids. The animals were then offered the opportunity to drink as much sweetened alcohol beverage as they wished over a short period of time. It was found that small doses of morphine increased the alcohol intake.

Later, they administered the opiate antagonist naloxone to see if it, taken alone, would interfere with the action of the natural opioids and alter alcohol intake. They found that naloxone decreased drinking. Reid said, "We speculate that any event that enhances the activity of the endogenous opioid systems may enhance rats' avidity toward palatable alcohol solutions."[22]

The experiments attracted wide attention, but findings of other investigators eventually provided a different explanation that seemed to resolve the conflict:

- Small doses of opiates or opioids act to prevent the natural flow of opioids out of the neuron. Thus Reid's injection of a small amount of opiates, rather than increasing the supply of opioids, may actually have created a deficiency at the receptor site, leading to an increase in alcohol intake.[23]
- Large doses of opiates activate opioid activity, and reduce alcohol intake.[24]

Simply, the main body of evidence indicates that a deficiency in natural opioids leads to an increase in alcohol intake, whereas an excess of opioid activity reduces alcohol intake.[25]

SLOWING OF NERVE IMPULSES IN ALCOHOLICS

By the early 1980s, researchers in the field had begun to recognize the need for looking beyond the individual neurotransmitter, such as an opioid, and considering the interaction of many neurotransmitters in some sort of pattern. Henri Begleiter and his associates made an important beginning by investigating the effect of alcohol on the overall rate of neurotransmission in a living system. By monitoring electrophysiological activity they demonstrated that the long-term abuse of alcohol can alter the speed of neurotransmission in the brain. The idea that continued use of alcohol could interfere with brain function had long been accepted by scientists, but this was the first time that electronic tools had been used to actually measure the rate of neurotransmission in alcoholics.

Their subjects in the experiment were 17 patients who had been active alcoholics for an average of 16 years. For a control group, they used a like number of patients who were occasional social drinkers. All were free from major medical problems.

Through earphones, each subject received auditory stimuli in the form of "clicks" that came at a rate of ten per second. Electrical responses of their brain to these clicks were recorded, and the delays between the signal and the response of alcoholics and controls were compared. In each case, the delay or "latency" of the response was significantly greater in the alcoholics than in the controls. Begleiter commented:

> The increase in neurotransmission time . . . may reflect a direct pathological process of demyelination [loss of nerve sheath]; this effect has been suspected in alcoholic patients, and observed in rats fed on alcohol for long periods. . . . The use of [this technique] may provide critical prognostic information about the progress of brain deficits in chronic alcoholics and their potential recovery with prolonged abstinence.[26]

Several other experiments tied alcohol to problems of neurotransmission, and some suggested a feedback phenomenon. For one example, alcohol reduces serotonin, which increases the desire for alcohol, leading to further reduction in the supply of serotonin.[27]

ALCOHOL AND GABA RECEPTORS

The neurotransmitters, in general, were now receiving increased attention. Investigations were under way on the opioids, serotonin, dopamine, norepinephrine, and acetylcholine, and on the enzymes that regulate them. Some work had also been done on GABA, a neurotransmitter that is responsible for probably 50 percent of the inhibition that takes place in the nervous system. As discussed in chapter 7, for example, Dora Goldstein had shown that GABA is involved in reducing alcohol withdrawal reactions in mice. I. Sutton and M. Simmonds had found that alcohol can alter the breakdown of GABA in the brain.[28] Other researchers had found that GABA influences response to alcohol.[29] No one, however, had investigated the effect of alcohol on GABA receptors.

Maharaj K. Ticku helped to fill that void when he joined us in the Department of Pharmacology at the University of Texas. He had discovered that barbiturates produce sleep by acting at GABA receptors. He knew that alcohol, too, induces sleep. He knew that, taken together, these substances reinforce each other, increasing their overall effect. So in his first investigation he set out to discover whether this reinforcing effect of alcohol was taking place at the GABA receptors, measuring changes in their sensitivity following alcohol intake.

In the first experiment in a series, Ticku injected laboratory rats with one-time shots of alcohol in varying amounts, and then measured the degree to which radioactive GABA bound to GABA receptor sites. He found that as the alcohol dosage rose, GABA binding rose as much as 20 percent. He suggested that this increased GABA binding offered a possible explanation for the tendency of alcohol to cause depression or sleep. As Ticku explained in a 1988 interview:

> My reasoning was simple. GABA is an inhibitory substance. In the normal brain, it regulates cell firing to prevent overstimulation. If alcohol raises receptor sensitivity to GABA, the response to GABA will increase, brain activity will be inhibited, and sleep or depression may result. Alcohol and barbiturates, apparently, do reinforce each other through the GABA system.

In his second experiment he investigated GABA involvement in tolerance to alcohol, and found that chronic or repeated exposure to alcohol appears to create a tolerance by decreasing the sensitivity of GABA receptors.

His third experiment was concerned with GABA involvement in the withdrawal response to alcohol; for example, in seizures and tremors. He administered alcohol to test animals over a period of three weeks. After he stopped the alcohol intake, he jingled keys near their ears and found that they went into seizure. At that point he analyzed their brain material and found that GABA receptor binding had declined well below normal. This suggested that GABA restrains the animal under normal conditions, but when alcohol removes the GABA brake, the animal gets the jitters. These findings supported the idea that GABA receptor activity is a significant factor in alcoholism and withdrawal.[30]

EFFECT OF GENETIC INFLUENCES AND ALCOHOL ON DOPAMINE RECEPTOR FUNCTION

Increasingly, now, scientists were coming to grips with fundamental problems of genetic and pharmacological interaction in alcoholism. One of the first significant experiments dealt with dopamine receptors.

Trabucchi and his group, whom we met in 1980, mounted an investigation of the effects of alcohol on dopamine function in alcohol-hating and alcohol-preferring laboratory mice. Their findings were:

1. When genetically alcohol-preferring mice were injected with an intoxicating dose of alcohol, there was an increase in dopamine metabolism, which indicated an overall increase in dopamine release. When alcohol-hating mice were injected with a similar dose of alcohol, there was no such change. This suggested that alcohol causes a greater release of dopamine in the neurons of alcohol-preferring mice than in those of alcohol-hating mice.

2. Following chronic alcohol ingestion over a three-week period, the brains of the alcohol-preferring mice were examined, and it was found that a 46 percent increase in dopamine binding had taken place at the dopamine receptors. Further investigation showed that this was the result of a 50 percent increase in the number of dopamine receptor sites. No such increase was found in the alcohol-hating mice. This suggested that chronic alcohol intake changes the dopamine receptor function in alcohol-preferring mice, but not in alcohol-hating mice.[31]

Up to this point, I had been using a simple model of alcohol craving in which alcohol-preferring mice have low levels of brain enkephalins as well as large numbers of enkephalin receptors; and alcohol-hating mice have high levels of brain enkephalins and smaller numbers of enkephalin receptors.[32] Now Trabucchi's work suggested an expansion of the model in which the dopaminergic system interacts with the enkephalin system. Thus, if one has a dysfunctional opiate receptor system as in the alcohol-preferring mice, the inference would be that:

• Alcohol interacts with the system to stimulate opiate receptors, causing dopamine release.

• This interaction affects the reward sites in the brain, and tends, temporarily, to reduce craving.

TIQS AND DOPAMINE RELEASE

Trabucchi's suggestion that alcohol or its metabolite TIQ causes dopamine release through activation of opiate receptors received confirmation through an experiment carried out by Irene Hoffman and Luigi Cubeddu at the University of Venezuela, Caracas. Into thinly sliced neural brain tissues from rabbits, electrodes were inserted to permit stimulation. After treatment with radioactive dopamine, the tissues were immersed in an electrolytic bath inside a glass chamber. As varying amounts of TIQs were added, the tissues were stimulated, causing them to release radioactive dopamine into the surrounding fluid. Readings from a scintillation counter showed the amount of dopamine released.

They found that as the level of TIQ increased, there was a corresponding increase in radioactive dopamine in the surrounding fluid.[33] This suggested that TIQ was facilitating dopamine release from the neural tissue, further confirming that TIQs are the link between alcohol and enkephalin receptors, indirectly leading to dopamine release.

THE DOPAMINE/GABA CONNECTION

We have seen that there is a relationship in the brain between alcohol, TIQs, enkephalins, and dopamine release. Now, Giampaolo Mereu and Gian Luigi Gessa at the University of Cagliari in Italy raised an interesting question: Can changes in dopamine activity result from a modification of GABA's inhibitory activity? The answer, based on their results, was positive. They found that low doses of alcohol cause a decrease in the firing of GABA-containing neurons. Since GABA inhibits dopamine release, they suggested that if alcohol reduces the GABA supply, the effect will be an increase in the availability of dopamine in the reward areas of the brain.[34]

TOWARD PHARMACOLOGICAL INTERVENTION: AGAINST INTOXICATION

Sobering Up Pill

A paper reported in *Science* by Stephen Paul's group at the National Institutes of Mental Health in Maryland caused an uproar in the popular press. The findings were interpreted to mean that the group had found a "sobering up" pill that would offset alcohol intoxication in humans. Unfortunately, the scientific data were misinterpreted.

What the paper showed was that RO15–4513, a unique substance produced by Hoffman-La Roche in Switzerland, alters the effect of alcohol in the brain. When alcohol is administered, it increases the movement of chloride ions into the neuron, causing a decrease in cell firing. This action takes place at the GABA-benzodiazepine receptor site. RO15–4513 markedly decreases this chloride ion movement, and the cell continues to fire at a normal rate. When this compound is given to mice before they ingest alcohol, they resist intoxication.[35] This suggested that the compound might help to explain the biochemical mechanism of alcohol intoxication.

In subsequent investigations by this group as well as others, it was found that when the compound is given to mice that have ingested sufficient alcohol to produce intoxication and sleep, within two minutes the animals wake up, and move about as though they had taken no alcohol.[36] These findings were blown out of all proportion by the popular media. The compound was reported to be not only a "sobering up" pill, but also an antidote for a lethal overdose of alcohol. Neither report was true. Scientists pointed out that while the compound temporarily blocks the behavioral effects of alcohol, rousing mice from their drunken sleep within two minutes, the drug rapidly metabolizes in the body, the effect wears off, and the mice relapse into their intoxicated state.[37]

Hoffman-La Roche decided not to develop and market the drug. Assuming that alcoholics drink in order to get drunk, if they took the drug beforehand they might drink so much alcohol to override the drug's effects that they would die from an alcohol overdose.

Stephen Paul, however, felt that a more powerful drug of this type might eventually help alcoholics avoid becoming drunk while learning to live without alcohol. This would be comparable to the use that is already being made of the opiate receptor antagonist naltrexone, marketed under the name Trexane, in the treatment of heroin addiction. Trexane blocks the mu receptors in the brain that accept heroin, thereby preventing or diminishing its euphoric effects. As Paul stated in an interview, "Alcohol addiction is a complex process that may involve some aspect of learning. An alcohol antagonist might help alcoholics 'unlearn.' "

In terms of immediate concrete results, however, the most important contribution of the experiments with RO15-4513 was that they helped to clarify the important role of the GABA-benzodiazepine receptors in intoxication, narrowing the search for an alcohol antidote.

Search for a Vaccine

Stephen Paul's findings stimulated Peter Sheridan and me to look for a vaccine that would directly attack and neutralize alcohol in the body. Sheridan, a molecular endocrinologist at the University of Texas in San Antonio, was interested in the role of immunology and the development of vaccines. We thought that if we could find a way to bypass the neurotransmitters and work directly on alcohol in the blood before it reached the receptors, we might solve the problem of a vaccine in the simplest way.

The approach we undertook was to couple alcohol molecules to protein molecules to form large molecules called *antigens*. It was our hope that the antigens would stimulate the creation of chemically specific antagonistic substances, or *antibodies*, that would neutralize the antigens. We hypothesized that if we could produce enough alcohol antibodies we might eliminate intoxication and euphoria, and remove the incentive to drink. In our experiment we immunized mice for three months with an alcohol-protein complex and then examined their blood for alcohol antibodies. We found them, but in concentrations too low to be useful.

At the height of our disappointment, we became aware of the work of Yedy Israel and his group, whom we discussed earlier. They first combined acetaldehyde with a large protein, and when they used the resulting material to immunize mice they found that a high concentration of specific aldehyde antibodies had been produced in the blood. Later, when they took blood from mice that had received alcohol for 45 days, and mixed it with antibodies from the first group, the resultant reaction indicated that similar antibodies had been created in the second group. This suggested that the body was creating its own antibodies to acetaldehyde, a by-product of alcohol.[38]

Israel saw this phenomenon as a potential test to see if a subject has been drinking—for example, in a treatment environment. In later discussions, however, we both agreed that there were deeper implications leading toward a possible vaccine. For example, by immunizing animals with an acetaldehyde-protein material, antibodies might be produced that would accentuate acetaldehyde, following alcohol consumption, and induce a natural disulfiram-like (Antabuse) aversive reaction. If this could be accomplished, a natural aversive vaccine might be developed that would reduce subsequent alcohol consumption, creating a powerful treatment adjunct.

TOWARD PHARMACOLOGICAL INTERVENTION: AGAINST CRAVING

Buprenorphine

While evidence was mounting that anomalies of genetics and neuro-transmission in animals play an important role in alcoholism, research activity was increasing in the pharmacology of alcohol craving. A new test of the hypothesis that alcohol craving is linked to opiate receptors was carried out by George Singer and his group at La Trobe University in Australia. Since it had been shown that morphine, enkephalins, and narcotic antagonists such as naltrexone can suppress alcohol consumption, they reasoned that it might be interesting to test the effects of buprenorphine, a peculiar drug that initially acts like morphine, but in the body changes and acts like a morphine antagonist. There was some evidence that it could reduce heroin dependence in humans without causing a secondary addiction.

Singer and his associates implanted catheters in 16 rats, giving them the ability to self-inject alcohol by pressing a lever. Half of the rats received an injection of buprenorphine, and the other half as a control group received a saline solution. When alcohol intake was measured over a three-day period, it was found that the animals receiving the drug showed a marked decrease in alcohol intake in comparison to the animals receiving saline.[39]

This was a significant development. We saw earlier that both morphine and enkephalin reduce alcohol intake, but cause secondary addiction, making them useless as therapeutic agents. Here was buprenorphine, however, reducing craving by means of the opiate mechanism, yet it was known to be nonaddictive.

Bromocriptine

A double-blind, placebo-controlled clinical study involving 50 human alcoholics was carried out by V. Borg and his group at the Blue Cross Clinic in Oslo, Norway, to investigate the effect of the drug bromocriptine on alcohol abuse. Their rationale was that the dopaminergic system was known to play an important role in alcohol-craving behavior, and bromocriptine activates dopamine receptors in the brain. The experiment involved people who, on the average, had been drinking heavily for 15 years. They were divided into two groups, half receiving bromocriptine and half receiving placebo capsules. The groups were studied over a six-month period from the standpoints of social functioning, social belonging, psychiatric status, craving, and alcohol abuse.

The investigators found that performance in social situations, motivations, personal insights, neurotic states, and depressive reactions were all significantly improved by bromocriptine compared to the placebo. Craving behavior was reduced from strong to very mild. At the end of the six months, there was a substantial reduction in the number of patients abusing alcohol. The conclusion of the investigators was that these positive results were due to the effect of bromocriptine on the dopaminergic system.[40] Borg commented that "the data do not explain the mechanism of bromocriptine's action, but they do suggest that the effect of alcohol may be mediated by dopaminergic mechanisms . . . Our data show that bromocriptine effectively betters the psychosocial situation of alcoholics, possibly by reducing their craving."

Zimelidine

From the 1950s on, there had been increasing evidence that brain serotonin is involved in intoxication, but some degree of controversy over its precise role in addiction and the craving process. The weight of the evidence, however, suggested that the lack of serotonin at the synapse in the brain may be a significant factor in the development of craving.[41]

A possible tool for correcting this specific lack had been found in the late 1960s by A. Carlsson and his group in Sweden. They discovered a class of substances that increase the availability of serotonin at the synapse by inhibiting its re-uptake into the neuron, leaving more serotonin outside the neuron where it can interact with adjacent cells.[42]

Some six years later, S. B. Ross and associates found a powerful member of this class of substances called zimelidine. They showed that it acts strongly to increase available serotonin by inhibiting re-uptake.[43] Later, Zalman Amit and his group in Canada demonstrated that this inhibitor significantly reduces alcohol consumption in rats.[44]

To explore zimelidine further, Claudio Naranjo and associates at the University of Toronto set up an experiment involving 13 human subjects who were all alcoholics. During the first two weeks, the subjects recorded their daily alcohol consumption on a self-reporting form, and mailed in daily urine samples for testing to see if they were using other drugs. At the end of the period the investigators selected subjects who were drinking a minimum of 28 drinks per week. Half of them were given zimelidine; half were given a placebo.

Those who received the placebo showed no decrease in alcohol consumption. Those who took zimelidine showed a small decrease in alcohol consumption, but a marked increase in the number of days of complete abstinence. Naranjo commented:

> There seem to be two possible explanations of this effect. The first is that zimelidine acts in the brain to reduce craving. The second is that it alters the taste of alcohol and makes it less palatable. My opinion is that the first is correct, since drugs of this class are known to reduce what we call "self-stimulation" behavior by increasing serotonin, stimulating "feel good" responses in the reward areas of the brain, and reducing craving.
>
> Although zimelidine appears to have possible applications as an anticraving agent, its side effects pose serious problems. For example, there is evidence that the drug may cause liver dysfunction in some subjects. But having identified the mechanism, we now may be able to find other similar agents without side effects that will be useful in the treatment of alcoholism.[45]

When I read this paper I was reminded of the commonality of the mechanisms underlying alcohol and drug addiction and other compulsive behavior. Working on zimelidine, for example, Zalman Amit's group had shown that it could reduce morphine consumption in rats, and others had shown that the drug could reduce excessive food intake in humans. Later, Naranjo would find a drug called citralopam that also increases the availability of serotonin at the synapse and reduces craving, with fewer side effects than zimelidine.

Antabuse: A New View

Aldehydes are the source of TIQs which, as we have seen, stimulate alcohol-craving behavior. In the body, the aldehydes are broken down by a family of enzymes called aldehyde dehydrogenases. Compounds that inhibit aldehyde dehydrogenase produce violent and sometimes fatal reactions in people who are drinking heavily. One such compound, oddly enough, is widely used in treatment for alcoholism to suppress the voluntary intake of alcohol by building up toxic amounts of the aldehyde. It is called Antabuse, or disulfiram. It is used for its aversive effect—those who take Antabuse and then drink become nauseated—but its long-term effect has been questioned. Patients often stop taking Antabuse because it does not reduce their craving.[46]

In a review of the clinical use of Antabuse, Peter Banys at the University of California in San Francisco stated:

> Although millions of doses of disulfiram (Antabuse) have been pre-scribed for the treatment of alcoholism since 1938, well-controlled studies have never demonstrated that it is more effective than a placebo in producing sustained abstinence. . . .
>
> . . . Indeed, most studies dealing with chronic alcoholics treated in outpatient settings reported very high early dropout rates. Typical programs [employing Antabuse as a sole therapeutic agent] can expect to keep only 20 percent of outpatients in treatment for a year.[46]

The explanation of the low compliance rate for Antabuse may have been found by R. D. Myers and E. C. Critcher in an experiment using cyanamide, a substance similar to Antabuse that inhibits the enzyme aldehyde dehydrogenase. They found that when nondrinking rats received low doses of cyanamide by injection, there was a significant increase in their later alcohol preference. This effect was still present after six weeks. Large doses reduced drinking because of aversive toxic effects.[47] Myers explained:

> These findings suggest that an increase in the level of one or more biogenic aldehydes (TIQs) induced endogenously by repeated injec-tions of cyanamide, both in the brain and in the periphery, can induce a prolonged enhancement of alcohol drinking. . . . This en-hanced alcohol drinking which persisted could have profound implica-tions for the abstinent alcoholic patient undergoing cyanamide or Antabuse therapy, because the treatment with either of these . . . inhibitors reportedly may result in a subsequent craving for alcohol.

However, these substances have a place in alcohol treatment programs, because clinicians have found them to be useful as an adjunct for selected alcoholic patients who are older, relapse-prone, socially stable, cogni-tively intact, not depressed or compulsive, and capable of following rules.

Such agents have not provided a medical solution to the problem of alcoholism, but they have opened valuable research pathways.

TOWARD AN INTEGRATED VIEW OF BRAIN REWARD MECHANISMS

In thinking about the causes of alcoholism and possible ways in which medical treatment might be improved, I found my attention turning more and more to the neurotransmitters and the enzymes that control them. We knew, for example, that GABA or GABA-like agents inhibit firing of dopamine-containing neurons; that inhibition of GABA leads to an increase in dopamine release; and that if there is an oversupply of GABA, dopamine release from the neuron is reduced. GABA, therefore, could be regarded as the "fine tuner" of dopamine, with highly evocative possibilities for treatment applications. Was it possible that similar interactions among other neurotransmitters and their controlling enzymes were involved in alcoholism and other addictive diseases?

By the mid-1980s, several neurotransmitters were being proposed as *the* agent responsible for alcohol-craving behavior. But although evidence was mounting for significant individual roles for serotonin, opioids, dopamine, norepinephrine, and GABA, it seemed more likely to me that several or all are involved in complex patterns of excitation and inhibition.

Sitting in my office one evening, I wrote down what I knew about neurotransmitters involved in craving.

Serotonin

- If the synthesis of brain serotonin is prevented, alcohol consumption increases.
- If serotonin brain receptors are blocked, alcohol consumption increases.
- If brain serotonin receptors are stimulated, alcohol consumption decreases.
- If the synaptic availability of serotonin is increased by preventing re-uptake, alcohol consumption decreases.

Opioids

- If there is a deficiency of brain opioids, alcohol consumption increases.
- If the number of opioid receptors in the brain is increased, alcohol consumption increases.

- If opioid receptors are blocked, alcohol consumption is initially increased; continued blocking leads to a decrease.
- If opioid activity is increased by inhibiting its metabolic breakdown, alcohol consumption decreases.
- If moderate doses of opioids are directly supplied, alcohol consumption decreases.

Norepinephrine

- If norepinephrine pathways in the brain are destroyed, alcohol consumption decreases.
- If the synthesis of norepinephrine is blocked, alcohol consumption decreases.

Dopamine

- If the breakdown of dopamine is increased, alcohol consumption increases.
- If the number of dopamine receptors is decreased, alcohol consumption increases.
- If dopamine receptors are blocked, alcohol consumption increases.
- If dopamine receptors are stimulated, alcohol consumption decreases.
- If the supply of dopamine is increased, alcohol consumption decreases.

GABA

- If the synthesis of GABA is accelerated or its activity is stimulated, dopamine release may be inhibited, causing an increase in alcohol consumption.
- If the supply of GABA is increased, benzodiazepine receptors (anti-anxiety) may be stimulated, causing a reduction in alcohol consumption.

When I read over this list of neurotransmitter functions, and realized that for each messenger known to be involved in craving behavior there may be five or ten more, and for each messenger there are controlling enzymes, and that governing them are the creative patterns—and often the distortions—of the genes, I felt a sense of awe at the complexity of the systems with which we were dealing. But beyond the awe I felt a growing sense of anticipation. We had come this far; now, perhaps, we could hope to go the rest of the way and adjust the malfunctions of the reward system, and change the genetic inheritance.

SUGGESTED READING

Belluzzi, J. D., and Stein, L. Enkephalin may mediate euphoria and drive-reduction reward. *Nature* 266 (1977): 556–58.

Blum, K., and Manzo L., eds. *Neurotoxicology.* New York: Marcel Dekker, 1985.

Petrakis, P. L. *Alcoholism: An Inherited Disease.* DHHS Publication No. (ADM) 85–1426 (1985).

Van Wolfswinkel, L., and Van Ree, J. M. Differential effect of naloxone on food and self-stimulation rewarded acquisition of a behavioral response pattern. *Pharmacological Biochemical Behavior* 23 (1985): 199–202.

Vereby, K., ed. *Opioids in Mental Illness: Theories, Clinical Observations, and Treatment Possibilities.* Annals of the New York Academy of Sciences, vol. 398, 1982.

Wise, R. A. Action of drugs of abuse on brain reward systems. *Pharmacological Biochemistry and Behavior* 13, suppl. 1 (1980): 213–23.

Wood, P. L. Multiple opiate receptors: support for unique mu, delta and kappa sites. *Neuropharmacology* 21 (1982): 487–97.

11

Toward a Craving Model

Despite my conviction that the ultimate solution to alcoholism lay in the gene, research along that pathway was still blocked for me by lack of a technical approach that offered promise. Despite the revelation of the double helix arrangement of the DNA, the structure and dynamics of chromosomes and genes in the early 1980s were still forbiddingly complex, mysterious, and remote. So I turned once more to the problem of neurotransmitter imbalance. Assuming that genetic anomalies result in neurotransmitter imbalance, what were the mechanisms? And, lacking a solution to the genetic problem, was there anything we could do that would help to restore balance?

At the functional level, it seemed clear that neurotransmitter imbalance was a problem of brain nutrition; more specifically, a deficiency or excess of amino acids. These fascinating substances are not only the building blocks from which proteins are made in the brain; they are the source of the neurotransmitters and the enzymes that regulate them. So the questions became, what could cause a deficiency or excess of amino acids? And, more importantly, what could be done about it?

BRAIN NUTRITION AND BEHAVIOR

As I tackled these questions in the laboratory, certain facts were known to me, established by my own research or that of others.

Amino Acids in the Brain

I knew that DNA and RNA in the nucleus carry the blueprint that controls linkages among amino acids as they unite to form neurotransmitters and enzymes. If DNA and RNA are impaired, proteins cannot be constructed properly, and abnormalities or deficiencies develop. In the healthy body, amino acids are in balance; if there is an excess or shortage, distortions of brain function can result.

The brain cannot synthesize all of the amino acids involved in the formation of neurotransmitters; some are derived from food metabolism, and come to the brain via the blood supply. Foods which contain high concentrations of amino acids include milk, eggs, meat, poultry and fish, and vegetables such as potatoes and greens. Unfortunately, the amino acid content of food is not uniform, and much of that content is lost through cooking. More importantly, some people have trouble metabolizing food, and cannot fully utilize the amino acids present.

There are two categories of amino acids: *essential* and *nonessential.* The essential amino acids are those that come from diet, and cannot be synthesized in the body. Of this essential group, five are necessary for the manufacture of neurotransmitters thought to play a role in alcoholism: methionine, leucine, phenylalanine, tyrosine, and tryptophan. Among the nonessential amino acids manufactured in the body, glutamine probably plays a significant role, because it is important in the manufacture of the neurotransmitter GABA.

Two forms of amino acids are found in nature. The L-form (as in L-phenylalanine) is found in living tissues. The amino acids in the brain that make up the neurotransmitters, and the enzymes that regulate them, are all derived from the L-form. The D-form (as in D-phenylalanine) is, chemically, a reversed image or variant of the L-form. D-form amino acids are found in a few types of microorganism, but otherwise can only be synthesized in a laboratory or chemical manufacturing facility.

Certain vitamins and minerals influence the conversion of amino acids into neurotransmitters and enzymes. For example, vitamin C assists in the conversion of dopamine to norepinephrine. Pyridoxal-5-phosphate, the active metabolite of vitamin B_6, is involved in the conversion of phenylalanine to dopamine, and tryptophan to serotonin. Calcium is involved in neurotransmitter release. Zinc influences neurotransmitter metabolism.

Amino Acids and Behavior

In their various modes, all of the amino acids involved in neurotransmitter synthesis exert a marked effect on behavior. For example, L-tryptophan acts as an antidepressant, and has been shown to have an anticraving effect in both rodents and humans. It is involved in the synthesis of serotonin in the brain, and serotonin, also, has an antidepressant and anticraving effect. For another example, L-phenylalanine is a precursor of brain norepinephrine, which aids in communication between neurons and enhances learning and memory.

Dietary Effects on Brain Nutrition

Food profoundly affects brain chemistry. A high fat diet, for example, increases the availability of tryptophan, a source of serotonin. Sucrose directly accelerates serotonin synthesis. When brain serotonin increases, craving has been found to diminish. Candy and junk foods with their high concentrations of sugar and fat are frequently used by alcoholics to relieve craving for alcohol.

The Blood/Brain Barrier

When food is digested, essential amino acids are freed and move from the gut into the bloodstream where they are transported to the brain. When they arrive they encounter a problem: the capillaries that carry the blood to the brain are difficult to penetrate and constitute a barrier. When amino acid molecules approach the barrier, special proteins expedite the passage through the brain capillaries with a kind of pumping action. This seems to work well unless too many amino acids seek to cross over at the same time, overloading the protein pumps. At any one moment, for example, tryptophan, phenylalanine, and tyrosine may be competing for the same transport system.

Diet, stress, alcohol, and drugs affect this system, sometimes in complex ways. A *carbohydrate* meal, for example, may increase the supply of insulin. Insulin promotes skeletal muscle utilization of essential amino acids such as valine and isoleucine from the blood. As these substances are removed from the blood, competition decreases, and tryptophan, phenylalanine, and tyrosine have easier access to the protein pump. As a result, neurotransmitter synthesis may increase. A *protein* meal reduces insulin flow, leaving more competitive amino acids in the blood. This condition may reduce penetration of amino acids into the brain, thereby decreasing neurotransmitter synthesis.

Stress tends to break down the blood/brain barrier, allowing a freer passage of amino acids. Drugs such as alcohol and cocaine also significantly increase the penetration of amino acids. After alcohol and cocaine intake, for example, concentrations of tryptophan and tyrosine in the blood plasma have been shown to decrease, indicating a transfer into the brain. Up to a point, this effect may act as a self-protecting bodily mechanism.

Easement of the blood/brain barrier does not solve the problems of neurotransmitter deficiencies and imbalances in the alcoholic, of course. The major causes of such anomalies lie beyond the barrier in the neuron, the synapse, and the receptor. But as will be seen later, an understanding of the barrier was crucial to the development of a formula, composed largely of amino acids, for improving neurotransmitter balance.

Single versus Multiple Amino Acid Neuronutrients

Up to this time, the use of amino acids in the treatment of behavioral disorders such as depression and alcoholism had been confined almost exclusively to single amino acids such as L-phenylalanine for depression, and L-glutamine for alcoholism. However, there were difficulties with this approach.

First, although a single amino acid may be involved in the formation of a given neurotransmitter, it does not act alone. It needs the help of co-factors such as vitamins and minerals before the formation can take place. For example, vitamin B_6 is needed for the manufacture of dopamine.

Second, alcoholism is the result of a complex of problems that involves processes taking place in the neuron, at the synapse, and at the receptor. Different neurotransmitters and enzymes may be involved at each step.

Third, we cannot yet determine the specific defect that is producing a particular part of the problem. Therefore, in the effort to offset neurotransmitter deficits, it is not feasible to depend on single amino acids.

Fourth, we do not as yet have specific behavioral or chemical tests to determine which neurotransmitter is deficient. Therefore, we cannot pinpoint the specific amino acid that is responsible for the deficit.

Fortunately, if a broad menu of amino acids is available in sufficient quantity, the brain appears to have the ability to choose from the menu the one or ones needed to manufacture more of the neurotransmitter that is deficient. This eliminates the need to choose a particular amino acid for the treatment process; if the menu is broad enough the brain makes the choice.

Fifth, an odd characteristic of the blood/brain barrier actually makes treatment easier. Stress, alcohol, and drugs weaken the barrier, facilitating the passage of restorative substances such as amino acids into the brain.

Alcohol and Brain Nutrition

In normal people, small amounts of alcohol increase feelings of well-being by augmenting the availability of dopamine and norepinephrine, the reward messengers of the brain. This takes place through the interaction of alcohol and its by-products with the neurotransmitters serotonin, opioid peptides, dopamine, and GABA. In the active alcoholic, however, there is a two-step process. First, alcohol causes a short-term feeling of relief or well-being—a "high"—as neurotransmitters are released at the reward sites. But this is followed by a "down" reaction as continued alcohol ingestion changes neurotransmitter synthesis and release, resulting in a deficiency of reward messengers. When research findings on alcohol-preferring animals are combined with what is known about human alcoholics, we can see that after chronic ingestion of alcohol the following pattern of deficiencies and imbalances emerges:

Serotonin. The activity of serotonin at the synapse is reduced. The metabolism of serotonin from its active to its nonactive form is accelerated. The amount of serotonin in the hypothalamus is reduced.

Opioid Peptides. The activity of enkephalin and beta-endorphin in the brain is reduced. The manufacture of opioid peptides is decreased; the manufacture of abnormal opioids having no biological activity is increased. The molecular structure and hydrogen bonding of enkephalins are altered. The amount of enkephalinase, the enzyme that metabolizes enkephalin, increases, thereby reducing the supply of this opioid at the synapse. The number of natural enkephalin receptors increases.

Dopamine. Dopamine release in the reward area is inhibited. At the same time, the metabolism of dopamine increases, thereby reducing its supply at the synapse. Furthermore, there is a decrease in the number of dopamine receptors, resulting in an increase in craving.

GABA. There is a decrease in the amount of GABA in the brain, which reduces its stimulatory effect on benzodiazepine receptors, thereby increasing anxiety and irritability. On the other hand, alcohol increases the transmission of GABA, which inhibits dopamine release, leading to increased craving.

Co-Factors. Vitamins which act as co-factors may be in short supply. A deficiency of thiamine, for example, may cause a decrease in the manufacture of glutamine needed for GABA synthesis, and a decrease in nerve conduction. A decrease in vitamin C may interfere with the conversion of dopamine to its metabolite norepinephrine. A deficiency of vitamin B_6 may interfere with the conversion of the amino acid phenylalanine to dopamine, and tryptophan to serotonin. Exacerbating this problem is the fact that the alcoholic cannot convert vitamin B_6 to its active by-product, pyridoxal-5-phosphate, which is essential to these conversion processes.

THE DEVELOPMENT OF AN AMINO ACID SUPPLEMENT

By 1983 I had begun tentative design work on a formula to reduce alcohol craving—a formula that could be used as an adjunct to therapy. I had ruled out the use of certain drugs known to reduce craving, because they were themselves addictive. I had also ruled out certain natural substances such as endorphins because they, too, were enormously addictive. What I sought were natural, non-habit-forming, anticraving materials that would work safely in the brain.

I had concluded that the most successful treatment adjunct for alcoholism would be a multiple amino acid formula that would "load" the brain with materials it needs to manufacture neurotransmitters in short supply, or to enhance utilization of neurotransmitters already present. This was, admittedly, a shotgun approach, but it had intriguing possibilities, for the brain seems to have the ability to select the materials it needs for a given purpose if they are present in adequate quantities.

My first step was to conduct a series of experiments with animals to evaluate the effect of imbalances or deficits of specific amino acids and neurotransmitters on alcohol craving and intoxication. By the end of 1984 I was able to begin exploring with others the effect of DL-phenylalanine (a combination of the D- and L-forms) on craving behavior in chronic human alcoholics. The results were inconclusive, but sufficiently interesting to encourage us to continue.

When we combined a small amount of L-tryptophan with DL-phenylalanine, the reduction of craving behavior was enhanced. We found, however, that the dosage of tryptophan was important. If the dosage was too small, the subjects had trouble sleeping; if it was too large, they tired easily.

We then added L-glutamine, vitamin B_6, and other vitamins and minerals, and lowered the amount of tryptophan. The following case history was typical of the effect of the resulting formula as an adjunct to therapy for alcoholics.

George R.

George R. was 54, divorced, and the father of five children. He had begun drinking beer when he was 13, and changed to whiskey when he went into the military. He drank heavily during his tour of duty, and by the time of his discharge he had accepted the fact that he was an alcoholic. Back in civilian life he switched back to beer. His average consumption was 18 cans per day, and up to 24 cans on a weekend day. He was never really sober. His wife eventually divorced him, his oldest son broke off all contact with him, and he was in and out of trouble with the police for driving while intoxicated. A brief rehabilitation program at a local alcohol treatment facility, using ANTABUSE, led to a temporary drying out, but when he was discharged he quickly returned to drinking.

He began using my early formula in 1984, and after two weeks reported that his craving for alcohol had decreased by 80 percent. After six months he decided to "try going it alone," but within a short period of time the craving returned and he resumed taking the formula in conjunction with therapy. At the end of the year he was still sober, was on friendly terms with his former wife, and had effected a reconciliation with his son. The only residue of his craving was a substitute desire for coffee at a level of seven or eight cups per day. He was certainly not "cured," but he was much more comfortable with himself, and better able to cope with the problems of daily living.

Early in 1985, encouraged by such preliminary results, I initiated talks with Matrix Technologies, Inc., in Houston, Texas, now a division of NeuroGenesis, Inc., seeking their assistance in moving forward with clinical studies. I knew that the formula was not a cure for alcoholism; that it could not work alone; that recovery would still depend in large part on the standard 28-day treatment program; and that such programs—inpatient or outpatient—in their turn, would continue to depend heavily on the Twelve-Step program of Alcoholics Anonymous. But I felt that as a nutritional adjunct to therapy the formula would help to make treatment easier in hospital, clinic, and treatment center environments.

During that year I worked closely with the company to develop field trials of the formula, including double-blind controlled studies in inpatient environments, and an open study in an outpatient setting. (In a double-blind study, neither the patient nor the counselor knows to whom the formula is being given; in the open study, both the counselor and the patient know when the formula is being given.)

The Ingredients of SAAVE

The formulation of this nutritional adjunct, now designated "SAAVE," consisted of the following:

1. D-phenylalanine, to inhibit enkephalinase, the enzyme that metabolizes or breaks down enkephalin, thereby increasing the availability of enkephalin and, presumably, making more dopamine available at the reward sites.
2. L-phenylalanine, to stimulate the production of dopamine, and/ or increase norepinephrine levels in the reward area of the brain.
3. L-tryptophan, to increase the amount of serotonin in the sleep-producing and reward areas in the brain.
4. L-glutamine, to increase brain GABA levels at receptors associated with anxiety.
5. Pyridoxal-5-phosphate, the active ingredient of vitamin B_6, to serve as a co-factor in the production of neurotransmitters and to enhance the gastrointestinal absorption of amino acids.

The amino acids have been studied extensively in both animals and humans since the 1930s, and the literature reports that they are safe and have few side effects in comparison to agents commonly used in therapy. It has been shown, for example, that DL-phenylalanine is less toxic than vitamin C, vitamin B_1, or pantothenic acid.[1]

EARLY TESTING OF SAAVE

My early clinical impressions were borne out by the results of a small clinical field test, a double-blind pilot evaluation of SAAVE using 22 patients enrolled in a 28-day, inpatient treatment program in San Antonio. As reported in the *International Journal of Addiction* in 1989, the SAAVE patients:

• had a 50 percent lower BUD score than the control group (the BUD test measures behavior indicating a "Building-Up-to-Drinking" pattern);

- made no requests for benzodiazepine tranquilizer medication, compared to 94 percent in the control group who requested it;
- were free of tremors 72 hours after withdrawal from alcohol, compared to 96 hours for the control group; and
- showed no signs of depression during the first seven days of treatment, compared to 24 percent of the control group who experienced depression during this period. No undesirable side effects were observed.[2]

The report concluded, "These preliminary data suggest that [the formula] is a valuable adjunct to the treatment of alcohol dependence by aiding the patient's physical adjustment to a detoxified state while facilitating a more positive response to behavioral therapy." These findings encouraged us to proceed with more sophisticated tests and evaluations.

Meanwhile, research on craving behavior and addiction was continuing, seeking to understand the nature and dynamics of neurotransmitters. Four questions of major importance were being asked: (1) How do genetic factors influence neurotransmitters to affect craving? (2) Can the number and sensitivity of receptors affect response to alcohol? (3) Which neurotransmitters are involved in behavioral responses such as anxiety and anger? (4) How do these emotions affect craving behavior?

THE ROLE OF NEUROTRANSMITTERS IN CRAVING BEHAVIOR

Genetics

Serotonin. Earlier, T.-K. Li and his research group had found ways to select high-alcohol-drinking (HAD) and low-alcohol-drinking (LAD) rats, segregate them, and breed them until the strains bred true. Now, in a series of experiments, they measured levels of serotonin, dopamine, and norepinephrine in the hypothalamus region of the brains of the two strains. Their findings indicated that (1) levels of dopamine and norepinephrine did not differ between the two strains, and (2) levels of serotonin were consistently lower in the high-alcohol drinkers than in the low-alcohol drinkers. Li commented, "The data suggest that there is an inverse relationship between the amount of serotonin in the hypothalamus and alcohol craving behavior; that is, the lower the level of serotonin the greater the inclination to drink."[3]

In a later experiment, the group showed that they could take the high-alcohol drinkers, inject them with fluoxetine, and reduce their drinking. The drug makes more serotonin available at the synapse by preventing its re-uptake into the neuron.[4]

At about this same time, D. A. Gorelick at UCLA carried out a double-blind, placebo-controlled study of 20 patients who were going through a 28-day treatment program for alcoholism. The patients were separated into two groups. One group received fluoxetine; the other group received a placebo. Both groups had free access to alcohol, hourly, for 12 hours each day. At the end of the experiment Gorelick found that the fluoxetine group had consumed significantly less alcohol than the control group: Gorelick concluded that "these results are consistent with Li's finding in rats, and suggest that serotonin is a possible controlling factor in human alcoholism."[5]

Endorphins. Although the role of opioid peptides was receiving considerable attention, the specific effect of individual peptides, endorphins, and enkephalins on alcohol-craving behavior was still unclear. Christina Gianoulakis and Alca Gupta at McGill in Canada, using animals and humans with a genetic history of alcoholism, shed important light on the subject.

Initially, they measured the amount of beta-endorphin in both brain and blood tissues in alcohol-preferring and alcohol-nonpreferring mice. They found:

- There was less tissue activity of beta-endorphin in the alcohol-nonpreferring mice.
- When alcohol was administered to both types of mice, beta-endorphin release at the synapse was greater at the hypothalamus in the alcohol-preferring mice.
- When the study was extended to high-risk humans (with a family history of alcoholism extending back for three generations), and to low-risk humans (no alcoholism in their family history) they found beta-endorphin release at the pituitary after alcohol administration was greater in the high-risk group.[6]

The significance of these findings was stated by Gianoulakis in a 1989 interview:

> We believe that endorphin release in these subjects is responsible for the reinforcing properties of alcohol. The lack of response to alcohol in either nondrinking animals or low-risk individuals, coupled

with a lowered beta-endorphin activity, may explain why these subjects do not like alcohol. Simply, if alcohol does not release endorphins, subjects cannot obtain positive reinforcement from it.

My laboratory later extended this work. We confirmed the finding that beta-endorphins are higher in the alcohol-preferring mice, but we found that when this is true, the levels of methionine enkephalins are low. The suggestion is that it is the *ratio* of endorphins to enkephalins that predisposes to alcohol craving, rather than the levels of either of these peptides alone.[7]

Two additional findings helped to clarify our picture of endorphin regulation in the nervous system. Diana Sapun-Malcolm and her associates at the Uniform Services University of the Health Sciences in Maryland found that serotonin stimulates the release of beta-endorphin in the pituitary, whereas dopamine inhibits the release.[8]

J. P. Schwartz and I. Mocchetti showed that treatment of rats with drugs that decreased the availability of serotonin at the synapse caused an increase in the levels of the peptides enkephalin and beta-endorphin in the hypothalamus. They also determined that this increase was not due to a change in the synthesis of the peptides, suggesting the probability that it was due to a reduction in the releases rate of the peptides from the neuron into the synapse.[9]

Dopamine D2 Receptors. When I first met David Sinclair he was working at the research laboratories of the Finnish State Alcohol Company in Helsinki, engaged in studies of biological factors in alcohol-craving behavior, particularly the effect of opioids on alcohol intake. Subsequently, he became interested in neurotransmitter regulation, and the genetics of alcohol-craving behavior. It was in this context that he and his group undertook an important experiment to investigate the role of dopamine in alcohol-preferring and alcohol-nonpreferring rats.

Since alcohol was known to cause dopamine release in the reward sites of the brain, producing feelings of well-being as Gessa of Italy proposed earlier, Sinclair and his colleagues reasoned that genetics may control craving behavior by influencing the strength of dopamine binding to its receptor sites.

Working with genetic lines of rats bred in Finland, Sinclair and his group, in a complex experiment, used a dopamine agonist and a radioactive dopamine antagonist to measure the number of D2 receptors in homogenized tissues in a reward area of the brain. They found that the number of dopamine D2 receptor sites in the alcohol-preferring rats was significantly lower than in the alcohol-nonpreferring rats.[10]

This finding added to the growing evidence that dopamine and the dopamine D2 receptor sites are of critical importance in the interaction of the neurotransmitters involved in alcohol craving. This suggested that individuals born with a dopamine D2 receptor defect may not respond normally to dopamine release, which goes on continuously in the brain. They may be inclined to attempt to increase dopamine activity by taking substances such as alcohol that stimulate dopamine release. These individuals would be at risk of becoming alcoholics.

Receptors

Dopamine Receptors and Reward. The next new insight came as a result of a series of experiments by Larry Stein and J. Belluzzi that began in 1977 and extended into 1986. They were exploring the effect of drugs on the neuronal activity (firing patterns) of the hippocampus in the brain, an area in the brain that is considered a center of memory and learning. They found that cocaine produced a specific pattern or "burst" of neuronal firings which they equated with "reward." The natural neurotransmitter dopamine produced the same pattern.

In their work they had to distinguish between two types of dopamine receptor: dopamine D1 and dopamine D2. They undertook to determine which receptor is involved in reward. When they used a known dopamine D1 receptor antagonist, SCH23390, they found no effect on neuronal dopamine-induced firing bursts associated with reward. However, when they used a substance called sulpiride, a known dopamine D2 receptor antagonist, it abolished neuronal dopamine-induced firing bursts associated with reward.[11]

Their conclusion was that dopamine acts through the dopamine D2 receptor to generate the feelings of well-being associated with reward.[12]

The Morphine Factory in Our Brain. Throughout 1986 and early 1987, five facts from earlier research had been dancing around in my mind:[13]

1. Chronic alcohol intake produces an unusual sensitivity in dopamine receptors in the reward sites of the brain. A similar sensitivity in these receptors can be observed when alcohol is withdrawn.
2. Dopamine administration in animals significantly suppresses alcohol withdrawal seizures.

3. Morphine administration also significantly suppresses alcohol withdrawal seizures. The pattern is similar to that of dopamine. This is not to suggest, however, that morphine is a useful substance to counter withdrawal from alcohol; it is too powerfully addictive.
4. Both morphine and dopamine-like substances such as bromocriptine reduce alcohol-craving behavior.
5. Morphine causes the release of dopamine in the reward centers.

Out of these facts came a question: Is it possible that a natural morphine, unrelated to opioid peptides such as endorphins, can be found in the brain?

A startling answer came in 1987 when Sidney Spector and his group at the Roche Institute of Molecular Biology announced the discovery of both morphine and codeine in the cerebral spinal fluid of nonaddicted humans.

The story had begun in 1975 with the discovery of natural opiate-like materials in the brain: the endorphins and enkephalins. The next chapter came in 1976 when A. Gintzler, A. Levy, and S. Spector reported that they had found a substance in the brain that was equal to morphine in potency as a painkiller, but was not an opioid peptide. Then in 1985 came Spector's announcement that morphine had been found in both toad skin and rat brain.[14]

In 1987, Spector's group extended the experiment to humans, using twelve nonaddicted hospital patients who had not taken morphine or codeine for the past two months. Since both of these substances metabolize completely in 24 hours, it was assumed that the subjects were free of the drugs from any external source. Their cerebral spinal fluid was analyzed, and both codeine and morphine were found in significant quantities.[15] It was interesting to note that the amounts were similar to those of endogenous endorphins and enkephalins that other investigators had found in human cerebral spinal fluid.

The discovery of endogenous morphine in mammalian brain tissue, extending the finding of Walsh and Davis that the brain manufactures its own TIQs which act like opiates and are precursors of morphine in the poppy plant, suggested a fascinating hypothesis: In the normal individual, the brain produces sufficient natural morphine to play a role in the reward system, providing a feeling of well-being. But if the production is insufficient, the individual experiences a feeling of need or craving, and may attempt to satisfy this craving by the use of external substances such as morphine, heroin, or alcohol.

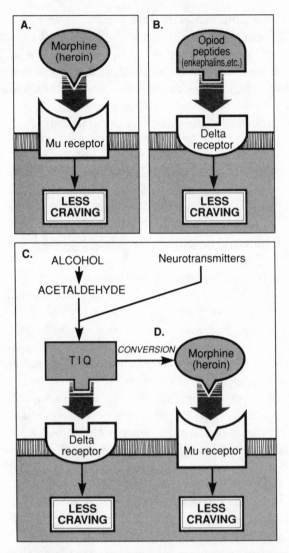

Figure 11–1 Endogenous Morphine Adequacy: A Suggested Model of *Short-Term* Craving Behavior. Schematic of endogenous morphine activity as a suggested model of short-term craving relief. When morphine, opioid peptides, and TIQ are sufficient to stimulate their respective receptors, craving behavior is lessened.

As can be seen in Figure 11–1:

- Morphine, or its derivative heroin, stimulates mu receptors, reducing craving (A).
- Opioid peptides, such as enkephalins, stimulate delta receptors, reducing craving (B).
- Alcohol converts to acetaldehyde, which combines with neuro-transmitters such as dopamine or serotonin to form TIQs which, in turn, stimulate delta receptors, reducing craving (C).
- Or TIQs convert to morphine, reducing craving (D).

Further, as can be seen in Figure 11–2:

- Morphine reduces the production of enkephalins, increasing craving (A).

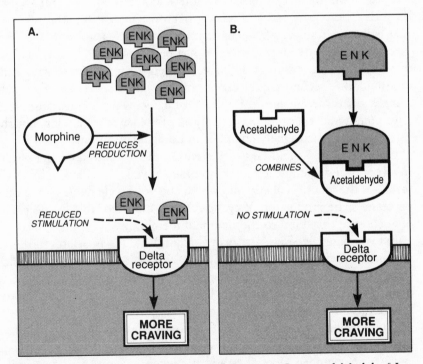

Figure 11–2 Endogenous Morphine Deficiency: A Suggested Model of *Long-Term* Craving Behavior. Schematic of endogenous morphine activity as a suggested model of long-term craving behavior. When the amounts of morphine or enkephalin are inadequate to activate their respective receptors, craving behavior increases.

- Acetaldehyde combines with enkephalins and makes them inactive; in their inactive state they lose their ability to stimulate delta recep-tors, increasing craving (B).

These models provide a possible explanation for the fact that, for the very short term, alcohol, morphine, and heroin appear to have beneficial effects. They ease stress and provide a euphoric "high." But this effect is short-lived. Very quickly the craving becomes uncontrollable and more and more of the drug must be taken to achieve less and less relief.

An odd side note is that chocolate contains a high content of TIQs which may explain the craving for chocolates in alcoholics and children of alcoholics.[16] An interesting treatment of the subject can be found in Andrew Weil's book, *From Chocolates to Morphine*. (See Suggested Reading.)

Cyclic AMP and the Alcoholic. While major interest was still focused on interactions between and among neurons, increasing attention was now being given to what happens inside the neuron—the area of "second-messenger" activity after a stimulus has been received. In a typical se-quence, a neurotransmitter activates a receptor in a neuron, inhibiting or stimulating second-messenger responses. The second-messenger sub-stances, in turn, regulate the release of a secondary neurotransmitter. This communication function is an important key to behavior, but the interactions are extremely complex and difficult to follow.

One of the most important subsystems in the second-messenger system involves cyclic adenosine monophosphate (cyclic AMP). Cyclic AMP regulates the function of enzymes which control a wide range of neuronal processes. The production of cyclic AMP is made possible by molecules of adenosine that bind to the neuronal membrane.

In two related experiments, Ivan Diamond and his associates furthered our understanding of the role of cyclic AMP in alcoholism. In the first experiment, they found that whereas short-term alcohol exposure of neuronal cells in culture stimulated the production of cyclic AMP, long-term exposure produced a 50 percent reduction.[17]

To determine if this reversal of response to alcohol also took place in the living human body, the researchers studied lymphocytes (blood cells) from matched alcoholics and nonalcoholics and found a similar effect of alcohol.[18] Diamond commented in a 1988 interview:

The reduced levels of cyclic AMP in lymphocytes from alcoholics may reflect an acquired membrane abnormality caused by chronic alcohol abuse. On the other hand, our findings could be related to genetically determined differences in the membrane response of cells from alcoholics. Studies of ethanol interactions with lymphocytes from alcoholics and controls maintained over long periods of time . . . may help to explain the molecular basis of this defect, and might identify individuals at risk of alcoholism.

It is interesting to speculate that cyclic AMP may be involved in the depression of cellular firing known to be caused by alcohol. The initial effect of alcohol is to increase cyclic AMP, which may reduce firing. However, if alcohol use continues, this increase in cyclic AMP does not take place, and cell firing is not interfered with. This may be one explanation of the mechanism of tolerance, in which the effects of alcohol are lessened.

Diamond's speculation that this phenomenon of reduced cyclic AMP activity may have genetic significance merits further testing in children of alcoholics who have never been exposed to alcohol. Such testing is necessary because alcohol may have a nonspecific effect on DNA.

INSIGHTS INTO THE MYSTERY OF ANXIETY

Natural Anxiety Agents

While it was becoming increasingly clear that alcoholism is due, at least in part, to a neurotransmitter imbalance or deficiency that affects the reward system, some investigators were exploring the possibility that, at the behavioral level, anxiety also plays an important role.

As early as 1975, Erminio Costa and Alessandro Guidotti at the National Institute of Mental Health in Bethesda had helped to establish the fact that when the benzodiazepines (Librium-like tranquilizers) exert their anti-anxiety effect, the action in some way involves the GABA receptor. They later pioneered the idea that benzodiazepine receptors and GABA receptors are linked and interact in a reciprocal manner; that is, the filling of one inhibits the filling of the other.[19]

An additional complexity arose in the late 1970s when they looked at the role of beta-carboline, a TIQ formed when acetaldehyde combines with brain serotonin. They found that this TIQ, too, acts on benzodiazepine receptors, but in an opposed manner. Whereas benzodiazepine reduces anxiety, beta-carboline induces it. When Costa and Guidotti examined this phenomenon closely, they found that the action of this substance at receptor sites was linked to the GABA system.[20]

In 1978, Costa and Guidotti reported on a new substance extracted from rat brain, a neuropeptide that also acted on benzodiazepine receptors. This substance they called a diazepam binding inhibitor, or DBI. When DBI binds to the receptor it acts like beta-carboline and interferes with GABA activity. They subsequently found the substance in human brain tissues.

Five years later, they found that DBI inhibits the binding of benzodiazepine to its receptors by competing for the sites. They suspected that, as a consequence, it would induce anxiety. They later found that, indeed, the injection of DBI increases conflict behavior in rats, a condition directly related to anxiety states. They found higher levels of DBI in the cerebral spinal fluid of males than in females, and higher levels in females who were menstruating than in those who were not.[21]

Their conclusion was that the TIQ beta-carboline and DBI are natural anxiety agents in the brain, and that GABA is a natural anti-anxiety agent.

Alcohol and Anxiety: The Role of Beta-Carboline

Robert Myers became a figure in this anxiety story when he showed that infusing the hippocampus of a rat with beta-carboline induces a profoundly fearful or anxious state. This observation led him to micro-inject small amounts of beta-carboline into the hippocampus of alcohol-nonpreferring rats over a period of three to six days, and monitor their subsequent alcohol intake to see if the injections changed their behavior.[22] He found that beta-carboline significantly increased alcohol consumption.[23] Myers commented in a 1988 interview:

Although the exact mechanism of action of beta-carboline is unknown, these findings suggest that this substance which antagonizes benzodiazepine receptors can induce an anxiety-like state which is counteracted by the anti-anxiety properties of alcohol ingested voluntarily. . . .

The phenomenon of beta-carboline-induced anxiety may not be the sole or even the main cause of drinking in the alcoholic, but it seems clear that in some cases alcohol drinking occurs because of long-term states of induced anxiety. It should be noted that in a reverse action alcohol has been found to cause an increase in beta-carbolines in rat brain tissue. In addition, the urinary concentration of beta-carboline in alcoholic patients at hospital admission is higher than in normal individuals, and then declines toward the norm as alcohol in the system is metabolized.

Alcohol and Anxiety: The Role of DBI

Further insights into the role of DBI in anxiety came when Guidotti collaborated with H. Alho and his group at the Research Laboratories of the Finnish State Alcohol Company. The first experiment was complex, but two results stand out: (1) when alcohol-preferring rats were allowed to drink alcohol at will for a period of three months, the amount of DBI in the cerebellum and hypothalamus rose significantly, and (2) when alcohol-nonpreferring rats were subjected to the same experiment, no such increase was obtained. Prior to the intake of alcohol, there was no difference in the DBI level in the brain.[24]

The results of this experiment may provide at least a partial answer to the question of why the genetically predisposed individual or the chronic alcoholic so often develops intense anxiety, or aggressive or even violent behavior after drinking. The answer may simply be the effect of DBI, which has been shown to have powerful emotional side effects.

Alcohol and Anxiety: The Role of Buspirone

Robert Myers and D. Collins, seeking further understanding of the role of anxiety in alcoholism, investigated the effects of buspirone, an agent known to reduce anxiety and aggressive behavior in monkeys. The researchers were interested in this substance because it appeared to act through the serotonin and dopamine systems, rather than through the GABA system.

Using monkeys that, normally, do not like alcohol, they injected them with cerebrospinal fluid from humans having one or more of the following: a primary diagnosis or a family history of alcoholism; loss of control during social drinking of alcohol; and/or elevated levels of TIQs. After seven days of injection of this material into their brains, the monkeys showed a strong preference for alcohol.[25] As Myers explained in a 1989 interview:

Conceivably, one or more components of the cerebrospinal fluid injected into the brain of the monkey may have induced a chronic state of anxiety. One such constituent could be beta-carboline, which not only induces anxiety and aggressiveness in the monkey, but also causes an intense craving for alcohol as well.

In the next phase of the experiment they injected the monkeys with buspirone twice daily, and found that their alcohol intake dropped significantly and their aggressive behavior was reduced.[26]

GABA/NOREPINEPHRINE REGULATION
OF ALCOHOL INTAKE

Myers' suggestion was partially corroborated by the work of M. Daoust and associates in the G.R.A.F. Laboratoire de Pharmacologie in France. In previous experiments this laboratory had shown that stimulation of GABA A receptors reduced alcohol intake in rats. Zalman Amit's group had shown that stimulation of norepinephrine receptors also reduced alcohol intake. Now the Daoust group showed that blocking of GABA receptors restored the craving in both instances. They concluded that GABA A receptors release norepinephrine, which in turn causes a reduction in alcohol-craving behavior.[27]

I could now see the opposing roles of GABA more clearly. As I viewed them, GABA at one receptor site *promotes* craving by inhibiting the release of dopamine in the nucleus accumbens, while GABA at another receptor site *suppresses* craving by stimulating the release of norepinephrine in the hippocampus.

Two of the active agents that influence GABA are beta-carboline and DBI. If they are present in abundance in the hippocampus they inhibit GABA. If this inhibition occurs, norepinephrine is reduced and alcohol craving increases. Other agents no doubt act on GABA in the nucleus accumbens.

ALCOHOL AND OPIATES:
A CONTINUING CONTROVERSY

Throughout the 1980s, doubts were still being expressed about the validity of the alcohol-opiate connection. Particularly controversial were experiments using naloxone to block opiate receptors. Some investigators found evidence to support the blocking action; others were unable to verify the effect.

To evaluate the pros and cons of this issue, our laboratory undertook an international survey of the literature. We cross-referenced all papers that studied the interaction of alcohol, opiates, and opioid peptides in both animals and humans, with a special focus on the interaction between narcotic antagonists and alcohol. The period covered was from 1970 to 1987. We found 103 papers that supported the alcohol-opiate connection, and 13 that questioned it. The survey results left little doubt in my mind that the alcohol-opiate connection is an important element of the puzzle.[28]

A MOTIVATIONAL MODEL OF ALCOHOL CRAVING

To simplify the complex of factors that enters into the initial urge to drink as well as the uncontrollable need to continue drinking, I developed a motivational model of alcohol craving. With a primary focus on the reward centers of the brain, the model involves both the genetic control of neurotransmission, and biochemical changes induced by alcohol itself. It assumes three basic phases: (1) setup; (2) substitution; and (3) destruction.

Setup

The individual who is genetically predisposed to alcoholism is born with a reduced supply of enkephalins or a reduced natural release of these neurotransmitters in the hypothalamus, the part of the brain associated with emotion. The amount of serotonin is lower in this region; there is an increase in the number of opioid receptors and a reduced number of dopamine D2 receptor binding sites; and there is an enhanced binding of GABA to its receptor sites.

The result of these anomalies is that this person under normal resting conditions cannot achieve feelings of well-being because not enough dopamine is being released, and not enough can bind to the dopamine D2 receptors in the reward part of the brain. Due to this deficiency of dopamine, a super-sensitivity develops in the nucleus accumbens, the major reward site of the brain. Anything that causes dopamine release— even small amounts of alcohol—can lead to strong feelings of well-being.

This is the setup phase.

Substitution

When first drinking alcohol, the alcohol-prone individual experiences pleasure and a marked sense of relaxation and is resistant to adverse effects such as loss of motor control, dizziness, and nausea. Thus alcohol makes this individual feel good without the penalty of feeling bad. Alcohol causes a release of dopamine, temporarily offsetting the genetic dopamine deficiency.

This is the substitution phase.

Destruction

The problem in the alcohol-prone individual worsens if alcohol intake increases either to counter stress (which also reduces natural opioid supply), or as the result of heavy social drinking. Such an increase may cause:

- a decrease in enkephalins and serotonin in the hypothalamus
- an increase in the number of enkephalin delta receptors
- a decrease in the number of dopamine receptors
- an increase in the breakdown of dopamine
- an increase in the binding capacity of dopamine D2 receptors
- an increase in the enkephalin-destroying enzymes
- a change in the molecular structure of enkephalins, making them inactive
- an increase in GABA transmission in the substantia nigra
- a decrease in dopamine release at the nucleus accumbens
- a decrease in cyclic AMP activity, and
- a general lowering of neurotransmission rates in the central nervous system.

The end result is a lowering of neurotransmitter activation of reward sites.

This is the destructive phase.

Under the assumptions of the model, as the person drinks more alcohol, its effect decreases and the damage to the reward centers increases, intensifying the need. It is a circular trap.

SUGGESTED READING

Anderson, G. H., and Johnston, J. L. Nutrient control of brain neurotransmitter synthesis and function. *Canadian Journal of Physiology and Pharmacology* 61 (1983): 271–80.

Cashaw, J. L., Geraghty, C. A., McLaughlin, B. R., and Davis, V. E. Effect of acute ethanol administration on brain levels of tetrahydropapaveroline in L-Dopa treated rats. *Journal of Neuroscience Research* 18 (1987): 497–503.

Davis, J. *Endorphins: New Waves in Brain Chemistry.* Garden City, N.Y.: Dale Press, 1984.

Diamond, I. The effects of alcohol on nerve cells. *California Society for the Treatment of Alcoholism and Other Drug Dependencies News* 14 (1987): 1–3.

Garrison, R. H., Jr., and Somer, E. *The Nutrition Desk Reference.* New Canaan, Conn.: Keats Publishing, 1985.

Madras, B. K., Cohen, E. L., Fernstrom, J. D., Larin, F., Munro, H. N., and Wurtman, R. J. Letter: Dietary carbohydrate increases brain tryptophan and decreases free plasma tryptophan. *Nature* 244 (1973): 34–35.

Marsa, L. Addiction and IQ. *OMNI* (March 1989).

McNichol, R. W., Ewing, J. A., and Faiman, M. D. *Disulfiram (Antabuse): A Unique Medical Aid to Sobriety.* Springfield, Ill.: Charles C Thomas, 1987.

Orrego, H., Blake, J. E., Blendis, L. M., Compton, K. V., and Israel, Y., Long-term treatment of alcoholic liver disease with propylthiouracil. *The New England Journal of Medicine* 317 (1987): 1421–27.

Phelps, J. K., and Nourse, A. E. *The Hidden Addiction and How to Get Free.* Boston: Little, Brown, 1986.

Shils, M. E., and Young, V. R. *Modern Nutrition in Health and Disease,* 7th edition. Philadelphia: Lee & Febiger, 1988.

Weil, A., and Rosen, W. *From Chocolates to Morphine: Understanding Mind-Active Drugs.* Boston: Houghton Mifflin, 1983.

12

The Reward Cascade

The motivational model of alcohol craving focused my interest on the concept of reward and pleasure, in the sense of brain dynamisms, and the factors that enhance or diminish them. These included endogenous factors such as the opioids and other neurotransmitters and their regulating enzymes, and external factors such as alcohol.

ENKEPHALINS AND THE PLEASURE RESPONSE IN THE BRAIN

Others were thinking along the same lines. To test the hypothesis that brain enkephalins enhance pleasure and reduce craving, B. Roques at the University of Descartes in Paris and an international group of associates set up an experiment using a substance that prevents the breakdown of enkephalins by enzymes. They surgically inserted cannulae (tiny plastic tubes) in the brain of rats to permit injections directly into the nucleus accumbens, a major reward area. They also implanted electrodes in the lateral hypothalamus, an area known to respond to electrical stimulation with intense sensations of pleasure. The rats were then trained to press a lever that sent an electrical stimulus through the electrodes into the brain, eliciting the pleasure response. The purpose of the experiment was to see if increasing the natural supply of enkephalins in the reward area of the brain, thereby increasing the level of pleasure, would reduce the rats' craving for the abnormal pleasure derived from electrical stimulation.

This form of "intracranial self-stimulation," developed three decades earlier by J. Olds, is highly addictive. In my own laboratory I have seen rats become so "hooked" on the pleasure feeling that they pressed the lever as many as 6,000 times in 30 minutes, leading to convulsion and death.

In the first experiment, kelatorphan, one of the most potent known inhibitors of the enkephalin-destroying enzyme, was injected into the nucleus accumbens, the major reward site in the brain. The result: After the injection, the lever pressing rate *decreased* by almost two-thirds. This result suggested that the injection of kelatorphin into the nucleus accumbens protected natural enkephalins from breakdown by enzymes, and the resulting rise in enkephalin activity increased the release of dopamine in the nucleus accumbens, leading to an increase in pleasure and a reduction in craving.

In a later part of the experiment kelatorphin was injected into the lateral ventricle, which distributed the drug widely throughout the brain, which meant a smaller concentration at any given point. In this case an opposite effect was obtained, and the rate of lever pressing *increased.* Thus the concentrated action of kelatorphin in the nucleus accumbens caused a release of dopamine and a reduction in lever pressing, indicating a reduction in craving; the dispersed action of kelatorphin through the lateral ventricle had a reverse effect.[1]

It was gratifying to read the report on Roques' experiment, because it helped to explain an earlier finding in my laboratory: that when D-phenylalanine is injected in alcohol-preferring mice to block the en-kephalin-destroying enzyme enkephalinase, alcohol consumption is reduced. This finding was later confirmed by Larry Grupp and associates at the University of Toronto when they showed that other types of enkephalinase inhibitors also reduce alcohol intake in rats.[2]

Additional experiments by others showed that alcohol can temporarily enhance pleasure directly by causing a release of dopamine in the nucleus accumbens.[3]

TRANSPORT OF OPIOID PEPTIDES: GENETIC ANOMALIES

An experiment carried out by William Banks and Abba Kastin at the Veterans' Affairs Medical Center and Tulane University in New Orleans provided new insight into the role of the blood/brain barrier in alcohol-seeking behavior. Their purpose was to investigate, in mice addicted to or genetically predisposed to drinking alcohol, the transport of enkephalins and other opioid peptides across the blood/brain barrier from the brain to the blood.

Earlier, these investigators had discovered a carrier system for this transport activity, the first significant insight into how peptides move through the barrier. It was an important finding, because researchers were beginning to understand that imbalances of neuropeptides are involved in such problems as dementia, mental retardation, depression, stress, sleep and food disorders, and alcoholism. The questions Banks and Kastin addressed were: How do the substances get into and out of the brain? In alcoholism, do genetic deficiencies of opioid peptides affect their movement from the brain to the blood, across the barrier?[4]

In their experiment, three types of mice were used: DBA alcohol-hating mice; and C57 and C58 alcohol-loving mice. Alcohol-loving mice were known to have a genetic deficiency of enkephalin in the brain. Using a radioactive tracer technique, they found that the transport of enkephalins from the brain to the blood is highest in alcohol-hating mice (representing a loss of enkephalin), and lowest in enkephalin-deficient alcohol-preferring mice (indicating preservation of enkephalin supplies). They suggested that the slowdown of transport in the alcohol-preferring mice was a mechanism developed by the brain to conserve its inadequate supply of enkephalins.[5]

In another experiment Banks and Kastin sought to evaluate the effect of alcohol on this *brain-to-blood* transport system. They divided ordinary mice into two groups, giving one group a liquid diet containing 5 percent alcohol, and the other an alcohol-free liquid diet containing sucrose. They found that the transport rate of enkephalins in the animals that received alcohol was only half that of the animals that received sucrose.

Since long-term alcohol intake is known to reduce brain enkephalin levels, it is exciting that the investigators found this slowed rate of enkephalin transport in the alcohol drinking mice. Banks commented:

> The decrease in transport may be in response to the decreased production and concentration of opioid peptides. This raises the possibility that the predisposition to drinking alcohol, which inversely correlates with brain enkephalin concentration and transport rate, might be affected by further inhibition of transport that would allow concentration of enkephalins in the brain to increase. . . .
> . . . the inhibition of this system that transports enkephalins out of the brain might offer a new approach to the control of drinking and withdrawal from alcohol.[6]

These findings showed that there is a direct relationship between the amount of enkephalins in the brain and the rate of their transport out of the brain into the blood. High concentrations of brain enkephalins lead to rapid rates of transport. Low concentrations lead to slow rates.

In a variation on this experiment, Banks and Kastin found that the neurotransmitter serotonin plays a dominant role in inhibiting the transport of enkephalins out of the brain into the blood. This supports the hypothesis that substances which inhibit the serotonin system could have therapeutic value in controlling alcohol-craving behavior.[7] It may also provide an explanation for the known anti-alcohol craving effects that occur when brain serotonin activity is increased.

SUPPRESSION OF DOPAMINE RECEPTORS BY ALCOHOL

Findings on the effect of alcohol, enkephalins, and serotonin on craving behavior seemed to have a common denominator: the release of dopamine, and its stimulation of receptors in the reward areas of the brain. As a consequence, a growing effort was being made to extend our knowledge of dopamine D1 and D2 receptors.

An experiment by L. Lucchi and his associates at the University of Milan and the Second University of Rome underlined the critical role of dopamine D2 receptors in reward. In a very complex experiment the group investigated the effect of long-term exposure to alcohol on dopamine D2 receptors in areas of rat brain rich in dopamine receptors. They found that long-term alcohol abuse had reduced the number of dopamine D2 receptor sites in the affected area.[8]

In an extension of this experiment, Lucchi's group used dopamine D1 receptor agonists and antagonists, and found that the number of the dopamine D1 receptor sites were also reduced by long-term alcohol intake. They also used other homogenized neuronal tissues from alcohol-drinking rats to study cyclic AMP, a substance involved in second-messenger response in the neuron, and found that when there is a reduction in the number of dopamine D1 binding sites there is a consequent reduction in cyclic AMP activity. Thus by interfering with both dopamine D1 and D2 receptors, alcohol has a powerful effect on second-messenger activity in the neuron and, as a consequence, on behavior.[9]

ON THE TRAIL OF THE SECOND MESSENGER

Research of this sort was now carrying many scientists in our field beyond the receptor, deep into the area of second-messenger interactions. Second-messenger activity includes the manufacture or destruction of neuronal materials, the activation or inactivation of neuronal chemical processes, and the transmission or blocking of messages within or between neurons.

Research in this field involves interactions and systems so complex that they are beyond the scope of this book, but the main thrust is to investigate stimulatory or inhibitory processes that lead to the release or suppression of neurotransmitters. In a typical sequence: A stimulatory process in a neuron may involve activation of proteins and enzymes that regulate the production of cyclic AMP and other substances; and these substances, in turn, open calcium ion channels leading to the release of neurotransmitters. In all likelihood there is an inhibitory process that prevents or controls this progression.

Alcohol affects second-messenger activity in a variety of ways. For one example, consider the effect of alcohol on the cyclic AMP system. In the short term, dopamine D1 receptors are activated, cyclic AMP production is increased, and neurotransmitter release is stimulated. In the long term, dopamine D1 receptors are impaired, cyclic AMP production is decreased, and neurotransmitter release is inhibited.[10]

DIAGNOSING ALCOHOLICS: A PROPOSED BLOOD TEST

A research finding that stimulated wide interest in newspapers and on radio and television was made by Boris Tabakoff and associates at NIAAA in Bethesda. Their research indicated that it might be possible to develop a blood test to identify alcoholics. The underlying rationale for their investigation was that:

- Alcohol *inhibits* an enzyme called monoamine oxidase, which regulates the breakdown of neurotransmitters such as serotonin and dopamine.
- Alcohol *stimulates* an enzyme called adenylate cyclase, which regulates the production of cyclic AMP.
- Long-term alcohol abuse alters the effect of alcohol on both of these enzymes.

The experiment involved 85 male alcoholics who were undergoing treatment, and 33 nonalcoholics as controls. In the first phase, a blood sample was taken from each subject and placed in a separate test tube, alcohol was added, and the activity of monoamine oxidase was measured. The researchers found that in the blood from alcoholics the activity of monoamine oxidase in the presence of alcohol was strongly inhibited; in that from controls, the inhibition was weak.

In the second phase, a drug called cesium fluoride, known to stimulate the enzyme adenylate cyclase, was added to the blood samples, and the activity of the enzyme was measured. In the blood from alcoholics, the activity of the enzyme in the presence of the drug was only weakly stimulated; in the controls, the stimulation was strong.

In the third phase, blood samples were taken from ten recovering alcoholics who had been abstinent one to four years, cesium fluoride was added, and the adenylate cyclase activity was measured. Tabakoff and his colleagues found that the activity of the enzyme in the blood of recovering alcoholics was weakly stimulated in comparison to that in the blood of the controls.

In computer analysis of both monoamine oxidase and adenylate cyclase in all the blood samples, the experimenters were able to identify 75 percent of the subjects who were alcoholic, and 73 percent of those who were not alcoholic. The former group included the recovering alcoholics who had been abstinent for one to four years.[11] Tabakoff observed:

> Both the differences in the inhibition of monamine oxidase activity by ethanol and the differences in adenylate cyclase activity may be interpreted either as reflecting a response to long-term consumption of alcohol, or an inherent characteristic of persons with alcoholism. The long-lasting nature of the changes and the lack of correlation with the time elapsed since the last alcoholic drink in alcoholics suggested that, if the changes in enzyme activity were the result of alcohol intake, they reversed quite slowly after cessation of alcohol consumption.
>
> Alternately . . . [these changes] could be a genetically influenced characteristic of the [blood] platelets of alcoholic subjects. . . .
>
> These measures [of enzyme activity] could be of value either as indexes of excessive alcohol consumption or as indications of a predisposition to alcoholism . . . but other experimental approaches will be necessary to reach a definitive conclusion.

Several other experimental findings held out the hope of developing biochemical markers for early identification of active alcohol abuse in patients. Under clinical evaluation none of the findings, alone, provided a base for a useful clinical marker for alcoholism, but together they showed encouraging movement in that direction.[12]

NATURAL TIQS AS A FACTOR IN ALCOHOL CRAVING

In earlier work, Robert Myers had shown that TIQs can induce abnormal alcohol-drinking behavior in rats that have a natural aversion to alcohol.

By injecting TIQs into their brains he produced a permanent craving. He suggested that an inborn predisposition to craving may involve the abnormal production of several types of endogenous TIQs in the brain. He called this the "multi-metabolite theory" of alcohol-craving behavior.

Myers' suggestion fitted in with my work on endorphins and aroused the interest of Helga Topel, a German psychologist working in the field of addiction. Topel and I wrote a paper on opioid peptides and alcoholism in which we tied the endogenous TIQs to a deficiency of endorphins. We proposed the idea that TIQs act on enkephalin receptors, in effect telling the brain to shut off the enkephalin supply. The resulting deficiency of endorphins leads to intensified craving behavior.[13]

This concept opened up three basic questions. Do TIQs form in greater quantities in the alcoholic than in the nonalcoholic? Where are they formed? What proof can we find that endogenous TIQs are formed in the brain?

Several findings by experimenters in the United States and abroad answered the first question in the affirmative. It was shown that: (1) the level of the TIQ salsolinol increases significantly in the urine of the moderate drinker of alcohol in comparison to the nondrinker;[14] and (2) following the ingestion of similar amounts of alcohol, the amount of urinary output of a variety of TIQs increases more in the alcoholic than in the nonalcoholic.[15]

In answer to the second question, it was found that in animals that had consumed alcohol in moderate amounts for ten months the concentration of TIQs rose in the hypothalamus, a region of the brain involved in reward.[16] It was also found that when rats are trained to self-inject acetaldehyde, a precursor of TIQs, the concentration of TIQs rises, mostly in the hypothalamus and striatum.[17]

To answer the third question, B. A. Faraj and associates at Emory University School of Medicine in Atlanta measured the amount of the TIQ salsolinol in chronic alcoholics who were recovering and not drinking, and compared it to the amount found in the blood of nonalcoholics. The method they used for measurement was highly complicated, involving radiographic analysis of a special metabolite of salsolinol, but their findings were simple: Recovering, nondrinking alcoholics had a higher level of salsalinol in their blood than the nonalcoholics.

In a still more significant experiment, they used alcoholic patients who had been abstinent for periods of two to ten years and compared them to chronic alcoholics in treatment who had been abstinent for only a few weeks. They found that the two groups secreted equally high levels of salsolinol. This suggested that the salsolinol was being produced from an endogenous source and not from alcohol.[18]

Since salsolinol production is dependent on the presence of dopamine and acetaldehyde, it would appear that in the alcoholic—and possibly in the individual predisposed to alcoholism but who has not yet formed the habit—the breakdown of dopamine is reduced, increasing the supply. Since this breakdown is regulated by the enzyme monoamine oxidase, it follows that the activity of this enzyme may be lower in the alcoholic, and those at risk of becoming alcoholic, than in the normal individual.[19] In an interview in his laboratory in Atlanta Faraj stated that "if our findings are correct, the measurement of plasma salsolinol may provide us with a specific biochemical test that may be helpful in screening subgroups of alcoholics, and identifying individuals at high risk, especially children of alcoholics before exposure to alcohol."

This is a novel and interesting idea, but before it can become a clinical procedure much more experimental work needs to be done. The first step might be to use a very large sample to determine the level of salsolinol in the normal individual as a baseline.

THE REWARD CASCADE: A NEUROCHEMICAL MODEL OF ALCOHOL CRAVING

I had become increasingly frustrated by the fragmented nature of the findings in the various fields of research into the causes of alcoholism. At one time the spotlight had fallen on the role of serotonin, at another on GABA or dopamine, and at still another on the opioid peptides; but there was no unifying, integrating thread.

As I considered one by one the factors known to be involved in alcoholism I realized that the cause could not be a single agent. The events we were observing were too complex. Furthermore, the relationship among several causal agents could not be simply *linear*; that is, the process could not be one in which independent agents acted in sequence. At the time, try as I might, I could not carry the thought further, and my feeling of frustration was intense.

During one of my attacks of insomnia when I was sitting in my living room, late at night, idly writing out, yet again, a list of the transmitters that had been shown to affect craving, I shut my eyes for a moment's rest and suddenly saw a behind-the-eyelids image of light flowing downward in a slow-moving cascade.

I sat up abruptly and over the next few hours wrote out a schematic model of a new theory. The basic idea is quite simple.

In the normal person, a single neurochemical agent produces a specific effect in a given subsystem known to be involved in reward. Other agents are similarly at work in related or parallel sequences. In patterns of stimulation or inhibition these subsystems interact and the effects branch and spread—like a cascade, leading to feelings of well-being: the ultimate reward.

This is the cascade theory of reward.

If a deficiency or imbalance interrupts or distorts the cascade, the result is a displacement of the feeling of well-being by anxiety or anger; or by craving for a substance that masks or relieves the bad feeling—for example, alcohol.

This is the cascade theory of alcoholism.

Although the neurotransmitter system is extremely complex and still not completely understood, Figure 12–1 helps us identify the central reward areas (Roman numerals). Figure 12–2 permits us to look with greater comprehension at the major interactions of the key players (Arabic numerals): serotonin, dopamine, norepinephrine, GABA, and enkepha-

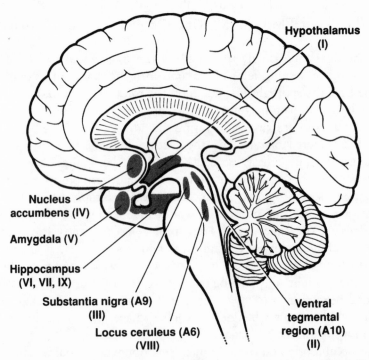

Figure 12–1 Schematic of the Brain's Meso-Limbic System. A simplified schematic representation of the structure of the brain's meso-limbic system, where the major reward activity takes place. Sites are indicated by roman numerals.

lins, and their enzymes and receptors. Other agents are certainly involved, but their identity and their interactions are still under study. Roman numerals are keyed to Figure 12–1. As I see the known activity of these agents in the reward areas, the following interactions take place:

- Serotonin (1) in the hypothalamus (I) indirectly activates opiate receptors (2) and causes a release of enkephalins in the ventral tegmental region A10 (II). The enkephalins inhibit the firing of GABA (3) which originates in the substantia nigra A9 region (III).
- GABA's normal role, acting through GABA B receptors (4), is to inhibit and control the amount of dopamine (5) released at the ventral tegmental region (II) for action at the nucleus accumbens (IV). When the dopamine is released in the nucleus accumbens it activates dopamine D2 receptors (6), a key reward site. This release is also regulated by enkephalins (7) acting through GABA (8). The supply of enkephalins is controlled by the amount of the neuro-peptidases (enzymes) (9) which destroy them.
- Dopamine may also be released into the amygdala (V). From the amygdala, dopamine (10) reaches the hippocampus (VI), and in CA1 cluster cells (VII) stimulates dopamine D2 receptors (11), another reward site.
- An alternate pathway involves norepinephrine (12) in the locus ceruleus A6 (VIII) whose fibers project into the hippocampus at a reward area centering around cluster cells which have not been precisely identified, but which I have designated as CAx (IX). When GABA A receptors (13) in the hippocampus are stimulated, they cause the release of norepinephrine (14) at the CAx site.[20]

In the cascade theory of reward, these interactions may be viewed as activities of subsystems of a larger system, taking place simultaneously or in sequence, merging in cascade fashion toward a specific effect in the reward areas of the brain: the generation of feelings of well-being.

In the cascade theory of alcoholism, genetic anomalies, long-continued stress, or long-term abuse of alcohol can lead to a self-sustaining pattern of abnormal craving.

TESTING THE CASCADE THEORY

Animals

Animal model support for the cascade theory can be derived from a series of experiments carried out by T.-K. Li and associates on their

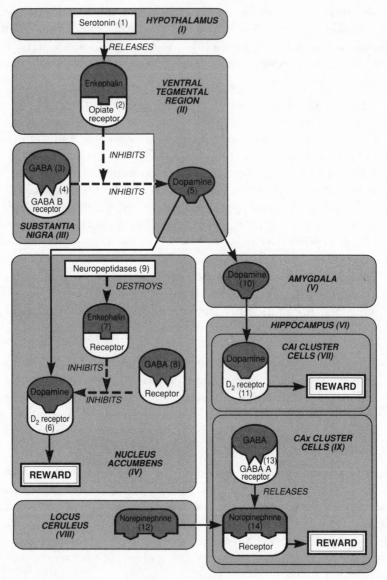

Figure 12–2 Detail from Reward Cascade Model. A schematic showing how neurotransmitters, enzymes, and receptors may interact to produce craving for alcohol. Individual elements of the "reward cascade model" are indicated by arabic numerals, keyed to roman numerals from Figure 12–1.

alcohol-preferring (P) and nonpreferring (NP) rat lines. They found that the P rats had:

- lower serotonin neurons in the hypothalamus
- higher levels of enkephalin in the hypothalamus
- increased serotonin receptors
- more GABA neurons in the nucleus accumbens
- reduced dopamine supply at the nucleus accumbens

This suggests a four-part cascade sequence leading to a reduction of net dopamine release in a key reward area. This was further confirmed when they found that by administering substances that increase the serotonin supply at the synapse, or by stimulating dopamine D2 receptors directly, they could reduce craving for alcohol.[21]

Humans

The results of further clinical tests on the formula SAAVE reported in 1988 and 1989 were promising, and provided a partial confirmation of the cascade theory. Because of multiple causes acting to distort reward, we had chosen to use the "amino acid loading technique" in our formula, combining key amino acids with an enkephalinase inhibitor with the goal of offsetting a wide range of neurotransmitter deficiencies. In effect, we were providing the raw materials, and letting the brain's natural mechanisms choose what to manufacture.

Two additional clinical tests yielding significant data on SAAVE's effect on alcoholics, and one clinical test of its effect on adult children of alcoholics, provided support for the basic assumptions underlying the theory.

STUDY ONE: INPATIENT, DOUBLE-BLIND, PLACEBO-CONTROLLED

Under the direction of Dr. Clyde Elliot, medical director of the Chemical Dependency Unit of Glenwood Regional Medical Center, West Monroe, Louisiana, a double-blind, placebo-controlled test was set up involving 62 inpatients undergoing a 28-day treatment program. Approximately half the patients were taking SAAVE, and half were taking a placebo. The results were as follows:

1. The SAAVE group showed only one-sixth as many AMAs (absences against medical advice) as the placebo group.

2. On the BESS test (behavioral, emotional, social, spiritual), the SAAVE group scored consistently higher than the placebo group.

3. Patients on SAAVE, in comparison to those on placebo, showed significantly reduced stress as measured by skin conductance using a device called an AUTOGEN 3000. This effect was most prominent at the seventh day of treatment, when patients tend to show the highest level of stress.

4. Analysis of withdrawal signs indicated that patients on SAAVE were in better physical condition at the tenth day, a time when patients tend to have the most somatic complaints.

5. Patients using SAAVE began to show significant positive results from the treatment program about one week before the placebo patients.[22]

Elliot said in a 1988 interview that "the study suggests that a formula such as SAAVE, based on the amino acid loading technique, may be an efficacious adjunct to treatment of alcoholics during detoxification and the initial recovery phase."

STUDY TWO: OUTPATIENT, OPEN TRIAL

Raymond J. Brown at the Cambridge Institute, San Francisco, carried out an open trial of 15 alcoholics who were using SAAVE plus vitamin B-complex and vitamin C in an outpatient environment over a ten-week period, with a ten-month follow-up. A control group of 15 alcoholics received the vitamins, but did not receive SAAVE. All of the patients had been intoxicated a minimum of twice weekly over the twelve months preceding the study.

The patients were seen twice each week in individual therapy sessions during the initial ten weeks of recovery. After this period, follow-up sessions were conducted at four-week intervals over the ten-month period.

While patients in both the SAAVE group and the control group were undergoing therapy they were asked to complete a "daily inventory" form which was later reviewed and analyzed. The form had two key sections:

1. The BUR (building up to relapse) score measured the extent of drug craving, stress, depression, irritability, paranoia, anxiety, and anger on a scale of 0 to 5.

2. The RS (recovery score) measured the subjective feelings of energy, self-confidence in the ability to remain abstinent, and feelings of well-being on a scale of 0 to 5.

In addition, Brown assessed and measured relapse. For the ten-week recovery period, he defined relapse as any use of alcohol or other psychoactive drug. For the ten-month period, he excused an occasional drink if there were general abstinence and a strong motivation to remain sober.

The ten-week inventory revealed:

1. The group receiving SAAVE had a significantly lower BUR score than the control.
2. The group receiving SAAVE had a significantly higher recovery score than the control group.

The ten-week relapse study revealed:

1. 53 percent of the control group relapsed;
2. only 13 percent of the group receiving SAAVE relapsed.

Over a ten-month period Brown carried out an extended study of the 87 percent of SAAVE patients who did not relapse, and found:

1. Their BUR score stayed virtually at zero.
2. Their RS score stayed at the highest level, near the top of the chart at five.

During this extended study of the 87 percent, only an additional 15.4 percent dropped out. This meant that 11 of the original 15 alcoholics on SAAVE, or 73 percent, remained sober after ten months.[23]

This was further evidence that SAAVE, based on the amino acid loading concept, may be useful as an adjunct to treatment and relapse prevention.

STUDY THREE:
ADULT CHILDREN OF ALCOHOLICS, OPEN TRIAL

Tommie Dahlmann, president of Dahlmann and Associates, San Antonio, carried out a clinical observation of adult children of alcoholics over a period of four years. This unpublished study involved over 200 patients who had one or more alcoholic parents, and were undergoing counseling for one or more problems of sleep, attention deficits, irritability, anger, poor self-esteem, high sensitivity to external stimuli, depression, or co-dependency. If they had two or more of these symptoms, they were put on SAAVE as therapy progressed, and assessed on a monthly basis for at least six months.

The clients were asked to report their own progress, and at the end

Dahlmann assessed their status. The assessment evaluated the effect of SAAVE in six categories:

1. *Emotional.* Lower anxiety level, less anger, less anxiety, increased feeling of well-being.
2. *Coping skills.* More resiliency, less desire to control, more spontaneity.
3. *Concentration.* Improved attention span, clearer thought processes, less dissociation.
4. *Memory.* Improved short-term memory, better recall, better retention.
5. *Learning.* More willingness to read, more interest in studying.
6. *Physical.* Improved sleep, higher energy level, improved sexual function, more able to relax.

Dahlmann observed that, in general, patients receiving SAAVE had more interest in exploring new behavior, were more willing to venture into self-disclosure, and were more receptive to change than those who were not receiving SAAVE. There was a longer attention span, more eye contact, and more willingness to trust. Where patients had been lacking in physiological resources, they began to feel better and more competent. Where they had been unable to make changes in their attitudes, they became more flexible and willing to explore new activities and new relationships.

Dahlmann's findings, added to the clinical tests, suggest that SAAVE, the first formula developed to apply the amino acid loading technique, can improve brain nutrition, have a reinforcing effect when used in conjunction with treatment procedures, and assist in reducing the frequency of relapse. The positive nature of the results merits further investigation and full-scale clinical testing of the concepts of amino acid loading and enkephalinase inhibition.

A question was raised in 1989 about the possible toxicity of one element of SAAVE, the amino acid tryptophan. The question arose because some circumstantial evidence had emerged linking certain health food products containing tryptophan to a blood disease called eosinophilia mialga syndrome (E-MS). The Food and Drug Administration quite properly issued an immediate recall of products containing tryptophan, although it was possible that the fault lay not with this amino acid, which has been in common use for many years, but with a contaminant introduced in the manufacturing or packaging process.[24]

L-tryptophan was immediately removed from the formula and replaced with chromium, a substance that assists in the transfer of natural tryptophan derived from food across the blood/brain barrier into the neuron. By freeing *natural* tryptophan, chromium eliminates the possibility of a problem without weakening the formula.

The more recent clinical results reported above seem to confirm my earlier evaluation. The formula is not a cure for alcoholism, but a useful adjunct that makes treatment easier in hospital, clinic, and treatment center environments, aided by the Twelve-Step program of Alcoholics Anonymous. The development of a cure for alcoholism remains a goal for the future.

Overall, however, I felt that scientists working in the field had reason for satisfaction. On the one hand, we now had unmistakable proof of the involvement of genetics in the etiology of alcoholism; we had a clearer picture of how the neurotransmitters are linked to reward; we were beginning to penetrate the complexities of the second-messenger systems; and in the cascade theories I saw suggestions for new directions in genetic and pharmacological research on craving for both alcohol and drugs.

But there were hundreds of frustrating questions remaining, and the ones dominating my thoughts were: Given that a genetic factor seems to predispose to alcoholism, awaiting the environmental trigger; and given the fact that human beings have upwards of 100,000 genes, what are the chances of finding the alcogene(s)? And, assuming the discovery of the alcogene(s), what can be done to alter the genetic legacy?

For a scientist who had devoted his life to neuropharmacology, these questions outside my field posed a major challenge.

SUGGESTED READING

Beasley, J. D. *Diagnosing and Managing Chemical Dependency.* Dallas: Essential Medical Information Systems, Inc., 1990.

Blum, K., and Briggs, A. H. Opioid peptides and genotypic responses to ethanol. *Biogenic Amines* 5 (1988): 527–33.

Blum, K., Briggs, A. H., and Trachtenberg, M. C. Ethanol ingestive behavior as a function of central neurotransmission. *Experientia* 45 (1989): 444–51.

Braverman, E. R., and Pfeiffer, C. C. *The Healing Nutrients Within.* New Canaan, Conn.: Keats Publishing, 1987.

Charness, M. E., Querimit, L. A., and Henteleff, M. Ethanol differentially regulates G proteins in neural cells, *Biochemical and Biophysical Research Communications.* 155 (1988): 138–43.

Cooper, J. R., Bloom, F. E., and Roth, R. H. *The Biochemical Basis of Neuropharmacology,* 5th edition. New York: Oxford University Press, 1986, p. 103.

Fadda, F., Mosca, E., Colombo, G., and Gessa, G. L. Effect of spontaneous ingestion of ethanol on brain dopamine metabolism. *Life Sciences*, 44 (1989): 281–87.

Gandhi, C. R., and Ross, D. H. Influence of ethanol on calcium, inositol phospholipids, and intracellular signalling mechanisms. *Experientia* 45 (1989): 407–12.

George, F. R. The role of arachidonic acid metabolites in mediating ethanol self-administration and intoxication. *Annals of the New York Academy of Science.* 559 (1989): 382–90.

Harris, R. A., Zaccaro, L. M., McQuilkin, S., and McClard, A. Effects of ethanol and calcium on lipid order of membranes from mice selected for genetic differences in ethanol intoxication. *Alcohol* 5 (1988): 251–57.

Hoffman, P. L., Moses, F., Luthin, G. R., and Tabakoff, B. Acute and chronic effects of ethanol on receptor-mediated phosphatidylinositol 4, 5-bisphosphate breakdown in mouse brain. *Molecular Pharmacology* 30 (1986): 13–18.

Myers, R. D. Isoquinolines, beta-carbolines and alcohol drinking: involvement of opioid and dopaminergic mechanisms. *Experientia* 45 (1989): 436–43.

Myers, R. D., and Privette, T. H. A neuroanatomical substrate for alcohol drinking: identification of tetrahydropapaveroline (THP)-reactive sites in the rat brain. *Brain Research Bulletin* 22 (1989): 899–911.

Ritchie, T., Kim, H.-S., Cole, R., DeVellis, J., and Noble, E. P. Alcohol-induced alterations in phosphoinositide hydrolysis in astrocytes. *Alcohol* 5 (1988): 183–87.

Svensson, L., Engel, J., and Hard, E. Effects of the 5-HT receptor agonist, 8-OH-DPAT, on ethanol preference in the rat. *Alcohol* 6 (1989): 17–21.

Takada, R., Saito, K., Matsuura, H., and Inoki, R. Effect of ethanol on hippocampal GABA receptors in the rat brain. *Alcohol* 6 (1989): 115–19.

Valverius, P., Hoffman, P. L., and Tabakoff, B. Hippocampal and cerebellar beta-adrenergic receptors and adenylate cyclase are differentially altered by chronic ethanol ingestion. *Journal of Neurochemistry*, 52 (1989): 492–97.

13

Alcogenes

Jack H. Mendelson of the Harvard Medical School laid down a broad challenge in 1975 to scientists investigating the causes of alcoholism:

> No specific biologic, psychologic, or social variable has been shown to have high predictive value for determining which individuals are at high risk to develop and sustain problem drinking behavior. There are no known psychological tests which can reliably differentiate alcohol abusers from normal drinkers. Many theories have purported to explain the causation of alcoholism in terms of psychodynamic factors, personality profiles, psychological developmental and growth characteristics, nutritional idiosyncracies, allergic disorders, and specific and non-specific metabolic derangements. To date, none of these theories of the causation of alcohol abuse or alcohol addiction have significant support from well-controlled laboratory and clinical investigations. . . . The contribution of specific genetic and environmental factors which may enhance the risk for development of alcohol-related problems has not been clarified.[1]

This statement questioned the accuracy of genetic, biological, psychological, and social theories of the causes of alcoholism and aroused new skepticism in the minds of treatment practitioners, but in the long run it helped to provide the impetus for an explosion of biogenetic research that led toward the discovery of suspect gene(s) linked to alcoholism.

ANIMAL MODELS OF ALCOHOLISM

Let us briefly review the progress that had been made by the beginning of 1990 in our understanding of the genetics of alcohol-craving behavior and the triggering effect of the environment. As we have already seen in chapter 6, McClearn—following up leads suggested by Williams and Mirone—had developed the C57 strain of mice as early as 1959 into a model that could be used as a powerful research tool for pharmacogenetics.

In 1977 T.-K. Li and his colleagues at the Indiana University School of Medicine developed the P (alcohol-preferring) and NP (nonpreferring) rat strains. The P rats met most of the requirements of an animal model of alcoholism. They voluntarily drank large quantities of an alcohol solution, and would actually work to obtain alcohol by pressing a lever. Eventually they became dependent on alcohol, developed a tolerance to it and, if it was withdrawn, experienced the withdrawal syndrome. These mouse and rat strains proved to be powerful tools for genetic research.[2]

FAMILIAL ALCOHOLISM: THE GENETIC FACTOR

But there was a troublesome question: Can findings from research in mice or rats be generalized to humans? Because alcoholic animals can be bred, can we assume that genetic influences are important factors in human alcoholism?

Affirmative answers began to emerge as early as 1972 when M. A. Schuckit, D. W. Goodwin, and G. Winokur at Washington University School of Medicine in St. Louis studied a group of individuals reared apart from their biological parents among which either a biological parent or a surrogate parent had a drinking problem. The subjects were significantly more likely to have a drinking problem if their biological parent was considered alcoholic than if their surrogate parent was alcoholic. This association occurred irrespective of personal contact with the alcoholic biological parent. For each comparison of genetic and environmental factors, the genetic factor seemed to be more closely associated with the development of alcoholism.[4]

In 1973, Goodwin, Winokur, and their colleagues at the Psykologisk Institut, Copenhagen, found further support for this thesis in a study based on a sample of 5,483 men in Denmark who had been adopted in early childhood. They found that the sons of alcoholics adopted by other families were over three times more likely to become alcoholics than were the adopted sons of nonalcoholics, and at an earlier age.[5]

Additional confirmation came in 1978 when Michael Bohman at Umea University in Sweden compared rates of alcohol abuse in 2,324 adoptees and their biological parents. The sample included 1,125 men and 1,199 women, adopted before the age of three years. The parents included 2,261 mothers and 1,902 fathers. Bohman found that adopted sons of alcoholic fathers were three times more likely to become alcoholic than adopted sons of nonalcoholic fathers. Adopted sons of alcoholic mothers were twice as likely to become alcoholic as those whose mothers were nonalcoholic.[6]

These earlier studies of sons of alcoholics were extended to include daughters in an important series of investigations of Swedish adoptees which was carried out by C. R. Cloninger and colleagues at the Washington University School of Medicine and at Umea.

They sought to answer four questions:

1. What characteristics of the biological parent influence the risk of alcohol abuse in the adoptees?
2. What characteristics of the adoptive parents influence the risk of alcohol abuse in the adoptees?
3. How do genetic and environmental factors interact in the development of alcohol abuse?
4. Is the genetic predisposition to alcoholism expressed in other psychopathological ways, depending on the environment experience and sex of the individual?

The investigators studied 862 men and 913 women of known parentage who had been adopted before the age of three by nonrelatives. A total of 35.3 percent of the adopted children had at least one biological parent known to abuse alcohol. A careful study was made of the subjects, categorized in terms of congenital background and postnatal home environment, and further divided into four subgroups according to their degree of alcoholism: none, mild, moderate, or severe. Characteristics of the biological parents were examined to identify those associated with a particular degree of alcoholism in the adoptees. To determine the effect of postnatal factors, the adoptive parents were also examined to identify influences that might be associated with particular degrees of alcoholism in the adoptees. Specific findings were:

- 22.8 percent of the sons of alcoholic biological fathers were alcoholic, compared to 14.7 percent of the sons who did not have an alcoholic biological parent.
- 28.1 percent of the sons of alcoholic biological mothers were alcohol abusers, compared to 14.7 percent of sons who did not have an alcoholic biological parent.

- 10.8 percent of the daughters of alcoholic biological mothers were alcohol abusers, compared to 2.8 percent of daughters who did not have an alcoholic biological parent.
- Alcoholism in the *adoptive* parents was not a factor in whether or not adoptees would become alcoholic, indicating that home environment and imitation of elders was not a determining factor.[7]

Investigators identified genetic predispositions to two distinct types of alcoholism:

- Type I, *milieu-limited* alcoholism. The investigators found this to be the most common type of alcoholism. Occurring in both males and females, this type of alcoholism requires both a genetic predisposition and triggering influences in the environment. Milieu-limited alcoholism is not likely to be severe and often goes untreated. It is usually associated with mild, untreated, adult-onset alcohol abuse in either biological parent. Typically, the alcoholic parent has not been a lawbreaker. Severity may be associated with low social status or unskilled occupation of the adoptive father. Milieu-limited alcohol abuse tends to have its onset after 25 years of age.
- Type II, *male-limited* alcoholism. The data suggested that this severe type of genetically driven alcoholism occurs only in men. It is less prevalent than milieu-limited alcoholism, and appears to be unaffected by environment. In families with male-limited susceptibility, alcohol abuse is found to be nine times greater in the adopted sons, regardless of the environment after their adoption.[8]

Male-limited susceptibility is related to severe alcoholism in the biological father, often severe enough to require treatment, and often involving lawbreaking; but is not associated with alcoholism in the biological mother. The onset of this particular type of alcoholism often comes early, before 25 years of age, and may be accompanied by serious encounters with the law. Postnatal influences in the adoptive family do not influence the development of alcoholism in the son, but may affect its severity. An interesting sidelight is that adoptees with male-limited alcoholism generally are not as severely afflicted as their fathers.[9]

These classifications represent an important contribution to our understanding of the interaction of genetics and environment, but some aspects relating to sex and age differences have proved to be controversial. When Marc Schuckit and his group, for example, attempted to correlate age of onset with Type I and Type II classification, they found that age of onset correlated not with types of alcoholism, but with antisocial personality disorder. Schuckit commented:

> These data emphasize the important association between early age at onset of alcoholism and more severe clinical characteristics, including the number of alcohol-related social complications, other drug use, and childhood criminality among primary alcoholics. The Type I-vs-Type II construct did not further contribute to the classification of alcoholic subtypes differing in clinical histories, suggesting that while this scheme is useful heuristically, further testing of its relevance is needed.[10]

Recently, NIAA has adopted Type III to designate alcoholics who have anti-social personality disorders. All of the human genetic studies discussed above helped to establish a strong role for genetic predisposition and to clarify the role of environmental factors in activating that predisposition.

ELECTROPHYSIOLOGICAL MARKERS OF INHERITED SUSCEPTIBILITY IN HUMANS

While some scientists were concentrating their attention on pharmacology, others were exploring a fascinating theory: that genetic susceptibility to alcoholism in humans may be accompanied by electrophysiological "markers" that can be detected and measured.

Henri Begleiter and B. Porjesz at New York State University in Brooklyn pioneered this research beginning in the late 1970s and have carried it forward in a series of highly innovative ongoing experiments.

The researchers attached electrodes to the scalps of their subjects to detect, amplify, and characterize electrical events in the brain resulting from incoming stimuli or accompanying specific mental processes. They made recordings of electrical activity in response to stimuli, with particular attention to a wave form designated P300 (P3).

They compared 25 boys aged 7–13 years who were sons of alcoholic fathers, with a control group of 25 boys who had no family history of alcoholism. None of the boys in either group used alcohol or drugs. The goal was to explore possible electrophysiological differences that might ultimately be used as a diagnostic tool, or "marker," to identify children at high risk. The investigators found that in response to visual stimuli the P3 wave had a markedly reduced amplitude in the sons of alcoholic fathers. They concluded, however, that the data were not sufficiently definitive for use as a clinical tool. Begleiter commented:

> Earlier, we reported P3 decrements in abstinent chronic alcoholics. The present study suggests that decrements in P3 activity are not a consequence of years of heavy drinking but are genetic antecedents of alcohol abuse. The present neurophysiological observations of boys at risk of alcoholism are striking in that they were obtained without the use of alcohol in sons of alcoholics not previously exposed to alcohol as a drug of abuse. However, our data do not allow us to infer that the observed P3 wave deficits in high risk male children represent a predisposing factor for subsequent alcohol abuse.
>
> Longitudinal studies to examine the relationship between the present neurological findings in male children and future patterns of alcohol intake are necessary.[11]

The results of these experiments suggested that differences in the P3 wave may be related more to genetics than to the pharmacological effects of alcohol.

GENETIC FACTORS IN SENSITIVITY TO ALCOHOL

By the mid-1980s, additional genetic questions were now beginning to be asked. For example: Assuming that children of alcoholics are at special risk of developing alcoholism, what are the specific genetic determinants of that risk? Are there other observable differences in bodily response to alcohol in animals and humans having a genetic predisposition?

In a meeting at Friends' Hospital in Philadelphia, I reported on a small experiment that produced an odd sidelight on genetic effects. I found that in alcohol-preferring mice it took a higher dose of alcohol to disturb their ability to balance on a bar than in water-preferring mice. This suggested that alcohol-preferring mice are, to some degree, protected from the early aversive effects of intoxication.[12]

Immediately after my presentation, I was excited to hear Marc Schuckit present data which indicated a similar reduction of sensitivity in humans. Schuckit had studied 23 nonalcoholic males who had close relatives who were alcoholics. He compared this set to a matched set of nonalcoholic males who had no family history of alcoholism.

All the subjects received, in rapid succession, three drinks of a sweetened, noncarbonated beverage to which alcohol had been added. They were then asked to describe their feelings, either positive ("talkative, elated, high") or negative ("dizzy, tired, sad") or both. The subjects who had close alcoholic relatives reported less intense *positive* and *negative* feelings following the beverage intake than those who had no alcoholic relatives.[13]

In a subsequent experiment with two similar groups, Schuckit found an objective way to measure physiological responses to alcohol, without reliance on self-reporting. He developed a "body sway" test in which the subjects were asked to wear a harness connected by a rope to a pulley. Any change of body position caused a movement of the pulley which was measured and recorded.

He found that, following the ingestion of alcohol, the degree of sway was significantly less in the nonalcoholic individuals who had close alcoholic relatives than in the nonalcoholic individuals who did not have close alcoholic relatives.[14] The fact that individuals from families with a history of alcoholism are less sensitive to the positive and negative effects of alcohol tends to encourage them to "take a chance" with heavier drinking, opening the way to alcohol abuse. The experiments were reported accurately by the press, and helped to correct the long-held myth that "he-men" and strong-willed women can "hold their liquor." On the contrary, the findings suggested that people who don't "get drunk" easily in the beginning may be the very ones who are at gravest risk of becoming alcoholics.

The nature of the trap for alcoholics was slowly becoming clearer, regardless of whether their problem was genetic or non-genetic in origin. As a hypothesis:

- The *genetically predisposed* alcoholic is born with a deficiency of opioid peptides, which leads to an increase in opioid receptor sites which, in turn, leads to an increased demand for opioid peptides, a biochemical imbalance that generates craving for alcohol.
- The initial effect of alcohol on this individual is a feeling of euphoria—an "up" feeling—caused by activation of opiate receptors by TIQs, leading to the release of dopamine.
- But continued excessive use of alcohol leads to dysphoria—a "down" feeling—caused by reduction of enkephalins, increased destruction of dopamine, a further increase in the number of opiate receptors, and the intensification of craving.
- The *nongenetic* alcoholic also experiences euphoria initially, although

less intensely, and continued drinking can lead to dysphoria. Over time, excessive drinking, particularly under conditions of continuing stress, may lead to biochemical abnormalities similar to those of the genetic alcoholic: deficiencies or imbalances that generate craving.

Thus the biochemical effects of long-term abuse of alcohol mirror the biochemical effects of genetic anomalies that lead to predisposition.

ELECTROPHYSIOLOGICAL MARKERS IN CHILDREN AT RISK

A Neurocognitive Profile

Following his appointment as Pike Professor of Alcohol Studies in the Neuropsychiatric Institute at UCLA, Ernest Noble teamed up with Stephen Whipple and Elizabeth Parker to use electrophysiological techniques to investigate cognitive functions in alcoholic fathers and their sons. Through newspaper ads they collected 45 father-son pairs, a total of 90 subjects, and divided them into three groups:

- Group A+, a high-risk group, had a strong family history of alcoholism. It consisted of 15 boys and their recovering alcoholic fathers. The fathers had at least one close alcoholic relative.
- Group NA+, an intermediate-risk group, had a strong family history of alcoholism. It consisted of 15 boys whose fathers were not alcoholic. The fathers had at least one alcoholic relative.
- Group NA−, a low-risk group, had no family history of alcoholism. It consisted of 15 boys and their nonalcoholic fathers. The fathers had *no* close alcoholic relatives.

In the experiment the subjects were hooked up to an electroencephalograph to monitor electrical activity in their brain following presentation of visual stimuli on a video monitor. The stimuli consisted of different shapes and colors, with a number from 0 to 9 located in the center of each shape. The task was to count, silently, the number of times that two consecutive stimuli matched in all three dimensions—shape, color, and number. Four runs of 200 stimuli each were presented, separated by five-minute rest periods.[15]

Noble's group found that:

- In the electrical tests, the A+ boys (high-risk) and their fathers showed the least ability to match sets of stimuli, and the lowest magnitude of electrical response as measured by the P3 waves. In the behavioral test, they showed the poorest visual perception and memory.
- The NA+ boys (intermediate-risk) and their fathers showed a somewhat better performance.
- The NA− boys (low-risk) and their fathers performed best of all.[16]

These findings confirmed and extended Begleiter's results in which he showed that boys at risk of developing alcoholism have a P3 wave deficit. Begleiter had raised the question of whether this deficit could be transferred from alcoholic father to son. Noble's answer was "yes," but he raised a further question: Is this deficit related to drug- and alcohol-seeking behavior in adult life? We will address this question later in the book by discussing his further experiments.

Some controversy still exists over the question of cognitive differences, however. Marc Schuckit, for example, working with relatively highly functioning young men, was unable to confirm neurocognitive behavioral differences between sons of alcoholics and sons of nonalcoholics.[17] But other research by Oscar Parsons and his group at the University of Oklahoma confirmed Noble's initial observations.[18]

HORMONAL RESPONSE TO ALCOHOL IN SONS OF ALCOHOLICS

Schuckit and his associates were also involved during this period in evaluating the effect of alcohol on levels of the hormone prolactin in the blood of sons of alcoholics. The researchers were aware of earlier findings that alcohol causes a profound increase of blood prolactin levels in humans; now they wanted to see whether alcohol causes a greater or lesser increase in sons of alcoholics in comparison to sons of nonalcoholics. They found little difference in prolactin levels between the two groups after administration of a low dose of alcohol, but when a higher dose was administered, the sons of alcoholics had significantly lower prolactin levels than the sons of nonalcoholics.[19]

Thus, in addition to seeing psychomotor and neuroelectrical differences in sons of alcoholics, we were now seeing hormonal differences as well. Such differences might well be a "window" into neurochemical anomalies in the brain. Since prolactin release is regulated in part by the dopa-

minergic system, and alcohol causes dopamine release, these differences
in prolactin levels may indicate a genetic defect in the brain of sons of
alcoholics that results in a predisposition toward alcohol-seeking behavior.

FINDING THE GENE(S) FOR ALCOHOLISM

Experiments with animals bred to prefer alcohol; twin studies involving
children of alcoholic parents; the observed frequency with which alcoholics come from alcoholic families; the electrophysiological patterns that
link alcoholic fathers and their sons; the differences in pharmacological
response to alcohol in adult children of alcoholics—all pointed to the
probability that genetic anomalies are time bombs waiting to explode.

Since I am not a molecular geneticist, and since the field is one of
bewildering complexity, I had not directly involved myself in this area
of research, but I felt a powerful—perhaps irrational—desire to become
involved. Several events pushed me in that direction. The first was a
talk in which Boris Tabakoff mentioned a new technique called *restriction fragment length polymorphisms* (RFLPs) that had proved effective in
associating specific genes with specific disease states. His suggestion that
this approach might enable scientists to discover and identify a gene
or genes responsible for alcohol-craving behavior aroused my interest.
I sought out my colleague Peter Sheridan who was working with RFLPs
and asked him for a briefing on the technique.

"RFLPs," he told me, "are used to identify variations in the DNA
of human chromosomes that can act as genetic landmarks for locating
defective genes responsible for a given disease. The technique was discovered by Ray White at the Howard Hughes School of Medicine in the
University of Utah. It was used by Gusella and his people at the Harvard
Medical School to identify a chromosomal marker for Huntington's disease."

Gusella's paper clarified the technique, and opened up a new avenue
of thought. If this tool could be used to discover a genetic marker for
Huntington's disease, a neurogenetic disorder, then it seemed to be
just the right one to use in searching for markers for other neurogenetic
diseases, such as alcoholism.

There are more than 3,000 known genetic diseases in the human
population, caused by defects in DNA and passed down from one generation to the next. As shown schematically in Figure 13–1 below, DNA
is a twisted ladder, each side rail a strand, and each rung a pair of
chemical bases connecting the strands. There are four bases: adenine,

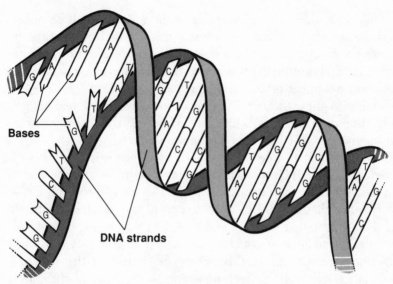

Figure 13–1 Structure of DNA. Simplified schematic of DNA, the structure of heredity. DNA is a twisted ladder, each side rail a DNA strand, and each rung a pair of chemical bases. Each of the four bases—adenine, guanine, cytosine, and thymine—can pair with only one of the other bases, that is, G with C, and T with A.

guanine, cytosine, and thymine. Each base can pair with only one of the other bases; that is, G *always* pairs with C, and T *always* pairs with A.

In the human body there are several billion cells, and each cell contains a billion pairs of DNA, stored in 46 packages called chromosomes. These chromosomal packages act in pairs, so there are 23 pairs in each cell. At conception, half of the chromosomes of each pair are derived from the egg of the mother, and half from the sperm of the father. Each chromosome is made up of many genes, with each containing the information necessary to control the generation of a specific protein or enzyme. Proteins and enzymes are the chemicals that carry out the basic functions of a living organism. These chemicals interact with one another, and if one or more of the chemicals necessary for a function is defective or missing the function may be carried out incorrectly or not at all, distorting behavior.

Since alcoholism is one of the genetic diseases, I could assume that somewhere among the 100,000 genes on 23 pairs of chromosomes in the child of an alcoholic parent one or more defects will be present. I knew the symptoms of the disease, and much of its biochemistry; but—assuming a genetic cause—how does one begin research to identify the specific gene(s) causing the trouble, so that diagnostic tests can be developed, and treatment procedures improved?

Coming to grips with that initial question took over a year of "getting ready" literature research before I could set up the first experiment. I will summarize what I learned during that year.

If we assume that a defect in one or more genes is responsible for a particular disease such as alcoholism, and want to identify that gene or genes, the task seems impossibly large. However, through the cascade theory I felt that I could identify several of the key neurotransmitters and their controlling enzymes and receptors that might be involved in alcoholism; and since it could be assumed that each was controlled by a specific candidate gene, this assumption narrowed the search. The combination of the RFLP technique and the identity of the candidate genes made the search practicable. For a rule of thumb, the first reduced the number of possible sites from billions to millions; the second reduced the figure to thousands.

The subject is too complex for treatment here, but the RFLP technique can be thought of in two parts: the cutting of the DNA, and the use of DNA probes to identify specific areas on the chromosome. Strands of DNA can be cut with great precision by using particular enzymes, called restriction enzymes, that act only at certain base pairs occurring in a specific sequence. For example, an enzyme called Msp1 will cut the DNA wherever the specific base pair sequence CCGG occurs. If this sequence occurs several times within the DNA, the cutting will take place several times. We then will have a batch of short pieces of DNA that contain the target gene.

We then use a fragment of DNA that matches the target DNA containing the gene thought to be defective. This is the probe. If the probe is made radioactive and inserted into a gel containing the target DNA that has been cut into lengths by an enzyme, it will bind to a complementary fragment, thereby "lighting up" the location of the gene on a photographic film.

THE SEARCH FOR ALCOGENES

To use this RFLP technique I needed three things: (1) a road map of DNA that would indicate likely sites for the alcogene(s); (2) a source of DNA specimens from a respectable sample of known alcoholics; and (3) sources of DNA probes that could be sent in like ferrets to locate the abnormal alcogene(s). I felt that there was a reasonable chance that the cascade theory would provide the roadmap, for there were strong indications that if there were a defective gene it would be among those responsible for the manufacture and utilization of such substances as enkephalins, serotonin, GABA, and dopamine which are known to play a role in alcoholism.

I knew exactly where to look for DNA specimens from known alcoholics. I had thought first of blood lymphocytes as a source of DNA, but I was aware that my friend and colleague Ernest Noble at UCLA had been doing extensive work on the brain electrophysiology of alcoholic fathers and their sons, with nonalcoholic fathers and their sons for controls, so I telephoned him. He was so enthusiastic about the project that he got on a plane and came to see Sheridan and me. He told us that he already had a large collection of brains of alcoholics and nonalcoholics, with complete medical records, obtained from the National Neurological Research Bank at the Veterans Administration Medical Center in Los Angeles. He said the brains would be a better DNA source than lymphocytes in our early experiments for two reasons. First, the brains were from alcoholics who had experienced multiple relapse from a virulent form of alcoholism, and died from alcohol-related pathologies. Since there are multiple forms of alcoholism, we wanted our sample to represent the purest or most extreme form. Second, the brain tissues would allow us to extend our study to *receptors* for neurotransmitters, enabling us to relate a gene defect to the impairment of a behavioral function—something that could not be done with white blood cells.

He suggested that the place to obtain money to support the project was the Seaver Institute of Los Angeles. The Institute had been funding his brain studies for the past five years, and he felt confident that they would be interested in supporting this pioneering effort. After several initial discussions with the Institute we put together a proposal, and within months the project was funded.

Meanwhile, we had tremendous good fortune in finding probes. A series of telephone calls and letters yielded over 50 candidate gene probes from all over the world to enable the study to get under way. The collection included probes for genes controlling a wide range of alcohol-related phenomena suggested by the road map, including alcohol metabolism, neurotransmitter metabolism, and receptors involved in reward.

The team we put together included Anne Montgomery, microbiologist; Arthur H. Briggs, clinical pharmacologist; Haruo Nogami, molecular endocrinologist; and Pudur Jagadeeswaran, molecular geneticist, all from the University of Texas Health Science Center; and Terry Richie, bio-chemical pharmacologist, and Jay B. Cohn, research psychiatrist, from the UCLA Neuropsychiatric Institute.

For an experiment so complex in its technical underpinnings, the actual procedures were fairly simple. What we were looking for was what we call a *polymorphism*—an unusual or abnormal form of a gene—that might prove to be associated with alcoholism. In other words, we were looking for *mutations* that had distorted the normal structure and/or function of genes, initiating changes in the organism leading to abnormal behavior.

The test samples for the experiments consisted of DNA derived from the brain tissues of deceased individuals, matched for age, sex, and race. We in my laboratory did not know it at the time, since this was a "blind" experiment, but half of the members of the sample had been alcoholic, and half had been nonalcoholic. Their medical records were completely documented. Noble kept secret the identity of the samples; that is, in our laboratory in the Health Science Center we did not know if a given brain came from an alcoholic or a nonalcoholic. We went only by numbers, and when we wanted to check data we called in these numbers to Noble and he correlated the numbers with the identities.

In the first experiment, as illustrated in Figure 13–2, we extracted from each brain paired DNA strands, used the restriction enzyme TAQ1 to cut them into smaller fragments (ABC), and placed the fragments in solution in small test tubes (ABC). Thus in each test tube we had DNA fragments from a single brain.

The solution containing the DNA fragments was placed in a gel (ABC), an electrical current was applied, and electrophoretic action sorted the fragments according to size. The paired strands of each fragment were then unraveled by chemical action.

A small pan was filled with buffer fluid; a porous filter was placed in the fluid; the gel with its DNA fragments was placed on top of the filter; and a nitrocellulose membrane was placed on top of the gel. The fluid, moving up through the filter and the gel, deposited on the membrane a layer of the DNA material (ABC) which was an exact replica of the material in the gel.

To this layer of material on the membrane we added a solution containing a radioactive, single stranded DNA probe that was known to be complementary to the gene that regulates the production of enkephalinase, the enzyme that causes the breakdown of enkephalins. The membrane was then washed thoroughly until only the radioactive probe

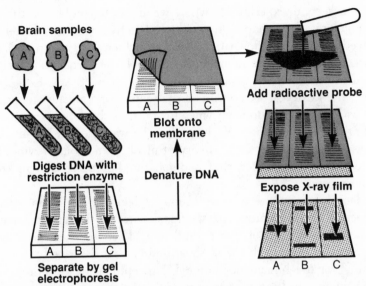

Brain samples

Digest DNA with restriction enzyme

Separate by gel electrophoresis

Blot onto membrane

Denature DNA

Add radioactive probe

Expose X-ray film

Figure 13–2 Schematic of the Restriction Length Polymorphisms (RFLPs) Method. Upon extracting the genetic code, or DNA, from brain matter or blood, researchers use enzymes to cut it into tiny pieces and place the pieces on a gel. When the samples are electrically charged, the gene material sorts itself into large and small pieces. When a radioactive gene probe is added to the sample, it bonds to other pieces of the DNA that are like itself. The sample and radioactive probe are then exposed to x-rays and photographed. The picture shows dark streaks, some only half visible, some thick, some thin, that indicate where the radioactive probe had bonded. The gene probe thus can look for specific genes in the brain samples.

material that had bound to a fragment of the target DNA was left. We then exposed an X-ray film to the membrane, and developed it. Wherever a radioactive DNA probe was located a black band appeared, indicating that the probe had bound to a DNA fragment—the gene, or a location close to it (ABC).

The pictures from the various samples were then compared to see if there were differences in the pattern. There were three possibilities: (1) the DNA patterns were all the same; (2) the patterns were different, but not linked to alcoholism; or (3) the patterns were different, and were linked to alcoholism. In the first experiment, with a proenkephalin probe, the patterns were all the same. This meant that there was no polymorphism; that is, there were no alternate gene forms.

In the second experiment, when we used the probe for the gene that regulates the production of alcohol dehydrogenase, the enzyme involved in the breakdown of alcohol, we found a pattern variation, but when we called the numbers in to Noble he found no association with alcoholism.

Over the next year we continued the search for a meaningful association, using a total of four enzymes for cutting the DNA strands, and eight probes for matching. Each gene probe was selected because of its potential role in the cascade theory of alcoholism. Four enzymes were selected because, together, they had generated 85 percent of all known polymorphisms.

In late July 1989, I was beginning to feel extremely impatient. I had been looking for a probe that would take me into the human dopamine system, but had been unable to find one. Then by sheer good luck I came across a story in the *Wall Street Journal* that described a successful "cloning" of the human dopamine D2 receptor gene on chromosome 11 by Olivier Civelli at the Oregon Health Sciences University in Portland. Since our studies could be done only with the aid of the proper DNA probe, I knew that he had what I needed. I called him that same day, and he agreed to send me the probe, suggesting that we try the restriction enzyme TAQ1 that he had used in his experiments on humans. Noble and Sheridan agreed, so we mounted the experiment.

When Anne Montgomery, my research associate, showed me the results of the first trial with the dopamine 2 receptor probe, I had trouble maintaining my professorial calm. In Figure 13–3, the DNA fragment on the left, showing two bands, represents one individual from the sample; the one on the right, showing three bands, represents another. In the total sample, alcoholics and nonalcoholics mixed:

- 27 of the 70 brains in the sample showed the 10.5 kb band, the 6.6 kb band, and the 3.7 kb band.
- 4 showed the 10.5 kb and the 6.6 kb band.
- 39 showed the 10.5 kb band, and the 3.7 kb band.

The exciting difference was the *presence* or *absence* of the 6.6 kb band, termed the A1 allele, and the 3.7 kb band, termed the A2 allele. The 10.5 kb band was constant. The A1 allele, and the A2 allele were polymorphisms, representing alternate gene forms.

"Run it again," I told Anne. We had to know if the results were accurate and the experiment repeatable.

When she brought in identical results at the end of two weeks, we decided to try this same probe with other restriction enzymes. We found no polymorphism.

We then ran the experiment a third time using TAQ1, the original enzyme, and again saw the polymorphisms.

On September 8, 1989, I called a meeting of team members at the Health Science Center, and we independently checked and agreed on the data. I then called Noble and read the numbers and the band patterns to him over the phone, then faxed a copy of the X-ray films.

He called me back in tremendous elation. His records showed:

- 80 percent of the *nonalcoholics* in the sample did not have the A1 allele.
- 69 percent of the *alcoholics* in the sample had the A1 allele.

Without knowing the identity of the subjects, working only from the DNA patterns in the brain tissues, we had correctly classified 72 percent of the alcoholics, and 77 percent of the nonalcoholics. This indicated a strong association between the A1 allele and alcoholism. Later statistical analysis showed that race and sex were not determining factors.

Since there are various subtypes of alcoholics, it would have been surprising if a 100 percent association had been found between the A1 allele and alcoholism. The fact that 31 percent of alcoholics in the sample did not have the A1 allele suggests that other genes may be

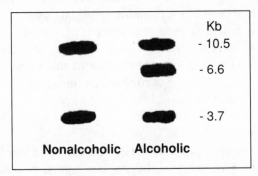

Figure 13–3 Human Dopamine D2 Receptor Gene Pattern. Banding pattern of the dopamine D2 receptor gene probe and DNA obtained from alcoholics and nonalcoholics. A 1.5-Kb fragment of this gene is shown here. The Blum, Noble, and Sheridan study found that the 6.6-Kb band was highly associated with the alcoholic compared to the nonalcoholic. The three bands are called the A_1 allele, and the two bands are called the A_2 allele. (*Reprinted from* The Journal of the American Medical Association [*1990; 263:2055–2067*], *Copyright © 1990, American Medical Association.*)

involved, or that in some cases environment may be the determining factor. We recognized our finding as the first in what is likely to be a long series of discoveries in the genetic linkage to compulsive disease.

After repeating our experiment again, we prepared a preliminary paper and submitted it for review by scientists working in the field. Their consensus confirmed our own feeling: *There was a high probability that we had found an unusual pattern, perhaps a defect, in the dopamine D2 receptor gene, or another gene close to it on the chromosome, associated with a virulent form of alcoholism!* The data from the experiment provide the most persuasive confirmation to date that genetic anomalies in the reward areas of the brain are responsible for at least one form of alcoholism.

We submitted the final paper to the *Journal of the American Medical Association* on January 12, 1990. It was published on April 18, 1990. We pointed out that this was an initial finding based on a limited sample; that other genes and other factors such as environment must be considered; and that future work must include DNA obtained from large groups of living alcoholics and their relatives.[20]

Enoch Gordis, director of NIAAA, reinforced these cautions in his editorial accompanying the article in *JAMA*:

> [The authors] . . . report a surprisingly strong association between an allele of the dopamine D2 receptor and alcoholism. This observation is provocative and promising but must be regarded with caution. . . . The dopamine receptor is a plausible candidate gene. It has been linked strongly with the neuromechanisms of reward. . . . This is the first candidate probe that has yielded results of such potential promise. . . . The need for confirmation of this work, however, is very evident. . . . This type of comparison [using DNA from deceased alcoholics compared to blood from living alcoholics] . . . although provocative, cannot substitute for . . . detailed . . . complex family studies . . .
>
> Success in research in the genetics of alcoholism would provide insight into the physiology of the disease, suggest new methods of prevention and treatment, and illuminate brain physiology far beyond the issue of alcoholism. Blum and his colleagues have added a promising new observation to current genetic research . . .

Among others, the findings raised a fascinating question. Does the presence of the A1 allele, which is associated with alcoholism, lead to an altered number of D2 receptors in the brain?

In a subsequent experiment using brain tissues that we had classified as having the A1 or A2 allele in the first study, we attempted to answer this question. We measured the number of dopamine D2 receptors in the tissues in an area called the caudate nucleus—an area that normally has the highest density of these receptors. We found that individuals having the A1 allele had approximately 30 percent fewer D2 receptors than those with the A2 allele. Since the dopamine D2 receptor gene controls the production of these receptors, this suggests that the A1 allele causes a reduction in the number of receptors.[21]

This finding suggests an interesting hypothesis. It is known that dopamine acts to reduce stress. When stress occurs in an individual with a normal number of dopamine receptors, dopamine is released, all of the receptors are filled, and equilibrium is restored. In an individual who has the A1 allele, however, the shortage of dopamine receptors interferes with this process and equilibrium is not restored. This person may seek alcohol or other substances or stimuli that release dopamine, in the attempt to find relief and pleasure. The desired effects do not come, however, because of the shortage of receptors, and the attempt is repeated, leading to aberrant pleasure-seeking behavior. I call this concept the *stress-dopamine-genotype hypothesis of craving.*

This hypothesis may explain why 20 percent of our nonalcoholic sample had the A1 allele which controls the production of dopamine D2 receptors. The nature of dopamine D2 receptor activity suggests a possible answer. Since this receptor may be involved with a wide range of pleasure-seeking behavior including compulsive alcohol and drug abuse, eating disorders, and abnormal sexual activity, it may well be that alcoholism is only one of the behavioral aberrations caused by a D2 defect. Further research is needed to explore other behaviors associated with the D2 receptor anomaly.

Currently, we are extending the experiment, using DNA derived from the blood of living alcoholics, and their offspring who have not used alcohol. By using living subjects, including offspring who may have the A1 allele but have not been exposed to alcohol, we will be able to prove or disprove the linkage of the dopamine D2 receptor gene or other nearby genes to alcoholism.

Another question raised by our experiment was: Is it possible that these genetic anomalies were consequences of alcohol abuse, rather than causes of alcoholism?

Fortunately, the question had already been addressed by Olivier Civelli and his group. They found the presence of the A1 allele of the dopamine D2 receptor gene in 39 children who had not been exposed to alcohol. This finding suggests that this polymorphism is genetically transmitted, and not the result of alcohol intake.

It would be premature to attempt to project future developments, but some possibilities suggest themselves:

1. It may be possible, eventually, to develop a DNA marker to identify potential alcoholics through a blood test; for example, children at risk in alcoholic families.
2. As we learn more about the role of genes in the development of alcoholism, it may be possible to design more effective treatment adjuncts that will counter the effects of genetic anomalies.

Several further questions growing out of the experiment need to be answered. Is the dopamine 2 receptor gene, itself, the true culprit in causing one or more forms of alcoholism? Or is it a gene nearby on the chromosome? Or is it two or more genes working in concert? Does the fact that one-third of the alcoholics in the sample did not show the A1 allele indicate that other, as yet undetected genes may be involved? Or that some forms of alcoholism can develop without genetic intervention? These questions point the way to interesting investigations in the future.

SUGGESTED READING

Blum, K. The alcoholic gene. *Professional Counselor* 5 (1990): 39–47.

Ollat, H., Parvez, S., and Parvez, H., eds. *Alcohol and Behavior*. Utrecht, Netherlands: VSP, 1990.

Petrakis, P. L. *Alcoholism: An Inherited Disease*. DHHS Publication No. (ADM) 85–1426, 1985.

Traynor v. Turnage, Administrator, Veterans Administration, *et al.* McKelvey v. Turnage, Administrator, Veterans Administration, *et al.* 108 SCT 1372, 99 (1988).

White, R., and Lalonel, J. R. Chromosome mapping with DNA markers. *Scientific American* 258 (1988): 40–48.

14

The Addictive Brain: Hope for a Cure

Forty years of research into the causes of alcoholism and other addictions have led to one conclusion: Irresistible craving is a malfunction of the reward centers of the brain involving the neurotransmitters and the enzymes that control them. Genetic research, including the experiments described in the last chapter, indicates that the malfunction begins in the gene. Psychological and sociological research indicates that the environment can trigger, worsen, or to some degree alleviate the genetic predisposition, but the determining factors are biogenetic and biochemical.

I am confident that the next forty years will bring cures not only for compulsive diseases such as alcoholism, drug addiction, and food disorders, but for all forms of disease and aberrant behavior arising from distortions of brain chemistry. I hope that I am not a foolish optimist.

I agree wholeheartedly with members of AA, and with most physicians and counselors that *as yet* there is no cure for alcoholism. Today, abstinence is the only permanent solution for the alcoholic. But in the entire record of experiments on animals and humans that I have carried out, observed, or read about, I have found no cause for pessimism.

THE CONTROVERSY OVER "CONTROLLED DRINKING"

There are, of course, those who disagree. Indeed, a replay of an old controversy about the underlying nature of alcoholism is now under way.[1] On one side are the scientists whose work I have described in this book. We hold and, I submit, have demonstrated that alcoholism is a biogenetic disease characterized by genetic anomalies leading to biochemical deficiencies or imbalances, and receptor malfunctions.

On the other side are a few psychologists and a philosopher, who ignore the vast body of research findings over the past four decades, reject the great mass of clinical data, reject even the disease concept, and advance three misleading hypotheses. In my view, these hypotheses are based on insufficient scientific knowledge, on misinterpretations, or on data compiled without true scientific rigor.

Hypothesis One. Total abstinence from alcohol and other psychoactive drugs is not necessary for recovery.

THE DAVIES REPORT

This hypothesis seems to have been derived, in part, from an early experiment in 1962 by D. L. Davies, who studied "normal drinking in recovered alcohol addicts." His findings were cited in the *American Psychologist* in 1983 by Alan Marlatt at the University of Seattle:

> Over two decades ago, Davies sent shock waves through the alcoholism field by publishing the result of a long-term follow-up of patients treated for alcoholism at the Maudsley Hospital in London. In his report, Davies (1962) challenged the traditional emphasis on total abstinence as the only viable "cure" for alcoholism by showing that of 93 male alcoholics who were followed up for a period of from 7 to 11 years after treatment, 7 reported a pattern of normal drinking.[2]

One problem with Marlatt's interpretation of this study is that it ignores the stated fact that seven out of 93 subjects is less than 8 percent, a tiny fraction. Furthermore, he seems to have overlooked Davies' own final conclusion at the end of his report: "It is suggested that such cases are more common than has hitherto been recognized, and that the generally accepted view that no alcohol addict can ever again drink normally should be modified, *although all patients should be advised to aim at total abstinence*" [Italics mine].[3]

THE GRIFFITH EDWARDS REPORT

The most important fallacy behind these data was revealed in 1985 when Griffith Edwards reported a follow-up study—three decades later—

of the seven subjects in Davies' sample who were supposed to have been able to drink normally. Edwards found that of the seven alcoholic men, five had resumed destructive drinking patterns; three of the five at some time had also used psychoactive drugs heavily; and three of the five had been using alcohol abnormally even during Davies' study. One of the seven eventually experienced Wernicke-Korsakoff syndrome, a form of alcohol-related brain damage; one was hospitalized for peptic ulcers; and one experienced liver enlargement as a result of heavy drinking.[4]

The data in support of controlled drinking have a way of disintegrating when they are examined closely.

Hypothesis Two. Alcoholism is not a disease, but merely a pattern of learned behavior.

THE SOBELLS' REPORT

This hypothesis was derived largely from the much-publicized work of Mark and Linda Sobell at Patton State Hospital in the California Department of Mental Hygiene in Patton, California. They attempted to prove that alcoholics could be *taught* controlled drinking skills, and that these skills would be effective outside the hospital environment. Again, the underlying thesis was that abstinence is not essential to recovery. The Sobells reported on a group of 20 alcoholic patients who had received behavioral therapy aimed at moderating their drinking patterns. In a follow-up study lasting two years, they claimed that 19 of the patients were successfully practicing controlled drinking.[5]

One of the leading proponents of the idea of controlled drinking is Herbert H. Fingarette in the Department of Philosophy at the University of California in Santa Barbara. In his book *Heavy Drinking: The Myth of Alcoholism as a Disease,* he referred to the Sobells' work in the following words, "In 1973, Mark Sobell and Linda Sobell issued their groundbreaking report detailing the successful result of their elaborate and carefully evaluated program of controlled drinking." Summing up his own views on the subject, he said, "Controlled drinking has become the umbrella term for the notion that abstinence may not be the only reasonable goal for the heavy drinker seeking help."[6]

Unfortunately for the proponents of controlled drinking, the Sobells' work did not stand up to closer scrutiny. On July 9, 1982, *Science* published a ten-year follow-up of the Sobells' evidence by M. L. Pendery,

I. M. Maltzman, and L. J. West in the Department of Psychiatry at UCLA. The study showed that 13 of the 20 Sobell subjects were hospitalized again within a year, and three others had used alcohol destructively during the period of the study. The other four subjects were found to be psychologically, though not physically, dependent on alcohol. Of these four, three had a record of repetitive arrests on drunk charges. Only one of them seemed to be able to indulge in controlled drinking, and this individual may not have been properly classed as an alcoholic. By 1983, five of the 20 subjects had suffered alcohol-related deaths— one-fourth of the sample. All were under the age of 42 at the time of death.[7]

Hypothesis Three. Alcoholism can be arrested, and often cured.

THE RAND REPORTS

To test this hypothesis, among others, the Rand Corporation, under contract from NIAAA, carried out two studies of alcoholics, one in 1976, and one in 1981. The first report evaluated 597 alcoholics 18 months after they had completed treatment. The authors found that 24 percent were abstaining, and 22 percent were drinking normally.[8]

This report was greeted with pleasure by adherents of the controlled drinking doctrine. For example, Morris Chafetz, former director of NIAAA, stated: "The Rand Report should make those interested in the plight of alcoholic people jump for joy."[9] Samuel B. Guze, head of the Department of Psychiatry at the Washington University School of Medicine, said: "What the data demonstrate is that remission is possible in many alcoholics, and that many of these are able to drink normally for an extended period." (See note 11.)

But the research methodology and conclusions of the first Rand Report were considered highly suspect by major scientists in the field. For two examples:

Ernest Noble, at that time director of the NIAAA, was particularly concerned about the effect of the Report on alcoholics and on the treatment community:

Until further definite scientific evidence exists to the contrary . . . I feel that abstinence must continue as the appropriate goal in the treatment of alcoholism. Furthermore, it would be extremely unwise for a recovered alcoholic to even try to experiment with controlled drinking.[10]

John Wallace, currently president of the Edgehill-Newport alcoholism treatment center, commented:

> The First Rand Report was so methodologically inadequate that nothing could be concluded from it. . . . The Report was seriously marred by an enormous "lost to follow-up" rate, sample bias on outcome, unreliable and invalid measurements of quantity and frequency of consumption, loss of entire treatment centers from the original sample of centers, shoddy data-gathering procedures by treatment staff, and a follow-up window of such short duration (30 days of drinking behavior) that it was an embarrassment.[11]

When the Second Rand Report was released, it claimed that nearly 40 percent of the subjects were drinking normally after four years. These results, like those in the First Report, appeared to indicate that alcoholism can, indeed, be arrested and perhaps cured. But the Second Report, too, came under strong attack, for example by John Wallace again:

> The Second Report was methodologically superior to the [First Report]. However, when the results are examined for sustained non-problem drinking over time and are corrected for invalid measurement of quantity/frequency [of drinking], the best estimate of the sustained non-problem drinking rate is around 3 percent to 4 percent. In short, at least 96 percent of the Second Rand Report subjects failed to give evidence of sustained non-problem drinking over the four-year follow-up period. This is hardly an advertisement for the success of controlled drinking in alcoholics.

In their efforts to discredit the disease concept, the proponents of controlled drinking resorted to some strange claims. For example, Stanton Peele, writing in *The Sciences*, said that the disease concept fosters irresponsibility, and provides an excuse for continued drinking.[12]

Anyone familiar with the modern treatment center would be excusably disturbed by this statement. John Wallace summed it up succinctly:

> At Edgehill-Newport, the disease model—including genetic, neurochemical, behavioral and cultural factors—is taught to patients to

help them understand the etiology of their illness. Among the 12,000 or so patients we have treated, there has been no tendency for them to lean on the disease model in order to avoid responsibility for their actions. In fact, accountability is stressed during treatment: a "graduation medallion" given to each patient on completion of our program is inscribed "I am responsible."[13]

A second strange claim by Peele in the same article in *The Sciences* was that people are put into treatment centers merely for getting drunk a few times after years of moderate drinking. Again Wallace remarked in response to Peele:

> In these days of stringent criteria for admission and continued stays (including extensive utilization reviews, third party payor, pre-certification of admissions, and rigorous managed-care patient audit), there is virtually no chance that a person would be admitted to treatment . . . in the absence of a significant prior history of drug or alcohol problems.

The efforts of the controlled drinking proponents are important only in that they mislead the alcoholic, and complicate the efforts of the treatment community. What the alcoholic who is resisting treatment wants to hear more than anything else is that he or she *can* drink in a controlled fashion without paying the penalty of relapse and eventual death.

TOWARD AN UNDERSTANDING OF COMPULSIVE DISEASE

Solutions to the problems of compulsive disease may not be impossible dreams. Pharmacological intervention on behalf of the alcoholic is already a reality. Treatment adjuncts are being used to improve the general physical condition, ease the discomfort of withdrawal, and help the recovering patient remain sober. Genetic engineering holds out the possibility that some day we will be able to adjust genetic anomalies and break the genetic link that predisposes to alcoholism.

Let us review where we have come and what we have learned in our effort to understand, prevent, control, and cure alcoholism; then let us look at the key disciplines that are seeking to advance our knowledge of craving and addiction, and see what the future is likely to bring.

As we have seen, alcohol in itself is a toxic substance that has a wide array of pharmacological actions. Once considered a simple anesthetic that caused general depression of brain neurons, alcohol is now seen as a substance that can cause specific changes in the biochemistry and electrophysiology of brain function.

Much of the early research on alcoholism focused on the aftereffects of alcohol as it acted on the body; for example, intoxication, tolerance, and withdrawal. The major benefit of such research was to provide the clinician with better agents to control anxiety, reduce the severity of withdrawal, and improve the patient's physical condition.

In the early 1970s when major advances were made, the research focus shifted to the mechanisms underlying craving behavior and its biophysiological and behavioral correlates. Out of an enormous and growing accumulation of data there began to emerge a new understanding of the role of neurotransmitters and receptors, and the enzymes that regulate their synthesis and breakdown. We began to see that their availability and balance, and the action at receptors, are keys to reward: pleasure, feelings of well-being, and euphoria.

We also saw growing evidence that any alteration or change in the neurochemistry of reward may lead to aberrant behavior; in particular, alcohol- or drug-seeking behavior.

The next step was the understanding that there is a blueprint that controls these neurochemical changes and interactions within the brain, and that this blueprint is laid down by the genes.

As the reality of these systems began to unfold, we felt a sense of awe at their complexity; yet we were soon able to begin making models of structure and function that gave us increasing insight into the mechanisms underlying reward. Alcoholism stood revealed as a biogenetic disease that may be triggered by environmental factors.

But we eventually learned that alcoholism is not unique; that it is one of a family of related diseases, all growing out of brain chemical deficiencies or imbalances, probably genetic in origin, accompanied by receptor anomalies. A significant demonstration of this fact was the finding by Ernest Noble and his group at UCLA that sons of recovering alcoholics have neurocognitive defects like their fathers. They showed that the sons at an early age are at serious risk of developing craving not only for alcohol, but for other addictive drugs such as nicotine and marijuana, also like their fathers.[14]

Such research findings suggest that genetic defects affecting brain reward sites may cause far broader anomalies than had been thought before. For example, animals bred to prefer alcohol over water may also show a preference for other drugs such as heroin or cocaine over water.

Research has begun to clarify the picture:

- Buprenorphine reduces the intake of alcohol, heroin, and cocaine.
- Bromocriptine reduces the craving for alcohol and cocaine.
- Drugs that increase the availability of serotonin at the synapse also reduce alcohol, drug, and food craving.
- Narcotic antagonists help to prevent relapse from alcoholism and food disorders, as well as from opiate addiction.
- SAAVE, a neuronutrient that reduces the breakdown of opioid peptides and may increase the supply of serotonin, dopamine, and GABA, has been found to be a useful adjunct in treatment and relapse prevention of alcohol and opiate addiction, and carbohydrate bingeing.
- Tropamine, a variant of SAAVE, increases the supply of dopamine, and has been found in early clinical tests to be a useful adjunct to therapy for cocaine addiction as well as alcoholism.

Literally hundreds of experiments have come together to suggest that craving for alcohol, drugs, and food share abnormal mechanisms involving a reward cascade in the mesolimbic area of the brain. These abnormalities create a compulsive behavioral syndrome involving alcohol and drugs, and the high probability is that many other abnormal behaviors, such as compulsive gambling and sexuality, share that syndrome.

If this view is correct, we can then derive a simple model: (1) genetic anomalies introduce defects into the structure of the reward cascade and (2) defects in the reward cascade cause behavioral distortions that we call compulsive diseases.

The defects in the reward cascade operate in three disruptive modes:

- They interfere with the normal, endogenous release of dopamine at critical receptor sites, particularly in the nucleus accumbens and hippocampus, the key reward sites of the brain. This interference is probably driven by a deficiency of opioid peptides.
- They distort the structure and function of the dopamine receptors, interfering with binding.
- They cause a reduction in the number of dopamine receptor sites, further interfering with binding.

Psychoactive drugs, like alcohol, morphine, and cocaine, temporarily offset or overcome such defects by artificially inducing the release of abnormal amounts of dopamine. Glucose probably has the same effect.

These substances act in different modes:

- Alcohol acts through TIQs to stimulate opiate receptors, inhibiting GABA and causing the release of dopamine at reward sites.
- Morphine acts directly to stimulate opiate receptors, inhibiting GABA, and causing the release of dopamine at reward sites.
- Cocaine acts directly to release dopamine at reward sites.
- Glucose acts indirectly by causing the release of opioid peptides which inhibit GABA and cause the release of dopamine at reward sites.

From both neurogenetics and pharmacology, there is now powerful evidence that we can go further and say that one of the root causes of compulsive disease may be a defect in the gene or genes which regulate the function of the dopamine D2 receptor, a critical reward site.

It is these anomalies leading to compulsive disease that characterize the addictive brain.

TOWARD THE PREVENTION AND CURE OF ADDICTION: LOOKING AHEAD

Dominating my thinking about the future of research on the addictive brain is a concept which I call the "neurogenetic theory of compulsive disease." It postulates a pleasure gene which I believe to be the gene that controls the dopamine D2 receptor. In the healthy individual, the normal D2 gene regulates pleasurable responses. In the addictive brain, a defective D2 gene initiates and regulates abnormal pleasure-seeking. Associated with it may be other defective genes that determine specific abnormal pleasure-seeking activity; for example, alcohol- or drug-seeking behavior. The pattern is illustrated in Figure 14–1. The abnormal D2 receptor gene creates a general need; other defective genes dictate the craving for a particular abusable substance. In applications of the theory to life situations, the alcogene may interfere with the synthesis of enkephalin or serotonin, leading to a craving for alcohol; the cocagene may interfere with the synthesis of a natural stimulant such as alpha-endorphin, leading to a craving for cocaine; the morphogene may interfere with the synthesis of natural brain morphine, leading to a craving for morphine or heroin; and the glucogene may interfere with the function of the glucose receptor, leading to a craving for sugar.

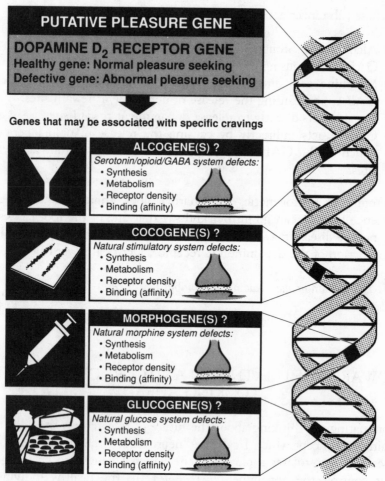

Figure 14–1 The Neurogenetic Theory of Compulsive Disease. This highly simplified schematic of the neurogenetic theory of compulsive disease suggests that the dopamine D2 receptor gene may be a putative pleasure gene, that a defective D2 gene may distort the pleasure response, and that other genes may determine specific types of abnormal pleasure-seeking behavior.

It seems certain that the search for these controlling genes will go forward in the decades ahead, and highly probable that new discoveries will alter our approach to the treatment of compulsive diseases.

Indeed, we may be entering a new phase in the search for answers to the ancient questions: What causes diseases? How can they be prevented? How can they be cured?

In the past century we have seen breakthroughs that led to an understanding of bacteria and infections; to extraordinary progress in the technology of diagnostics and the art of surgery; to a new understanding of the role of emotion in disease states; to an equally extraordinary expansion of the pharmacopeia; and to new understanding of the role of nutrition in brain function.

Now, we may be approaching the most exciting period in the history of the human sciences. On the one hand, we are watching the efforts of researchers as they push investigations of:

- viral infections responsible for afflictions such as AIDS and certain of the cancers;
- genetic anomalies that appear to be determining factors in neurological diseases such as cystic fibrosis, and compulsive diseases such as alcoholism;
- the design and synthesis of drugs that target specific receptor sites and enzymes;
- plants and organisms that manufacture natural substances with therapeutic value.

From earliest times individuals and sometimes whole societies have "self-medicated" with substances such as coca leaves, opium, and fermented sugars to relieve their fears or discomforts. Now, scientists are carrying out systematic searches to find natural substances in the forests and the oceans that will further enrich the pharmacopeia.

SOMATOPSYCHIC SYNDROMES

On the other hand, we are watching the development of a new orientation toward the interaction of brain, emotion, and behavior that may affect us even more profoundly. As in the years when we watched psychosomatic medicine clarifying the role of emotions in a variety of illnesses, we are now beginning to understand that genetic defects leading to deficiencies and imbalances in neurotransmitters, enzymes, and receptors may give rise to compulsive diseases and a wide range of behavioral disturbances. These *somatopsychic syndromes* constitute exciting new frontiers in medicine and treatment.

Just as emotional and mental disturbances cause organic disturbances leading to physical illness, so somatic predispositions, deficiencies, or imbalances may cause not only emotional and mental disturbances such as compulsive diseases, but also anxiety, hostility, depression, or reclusive or anti-social attitudes and responses. These may not be primary aberrations, but may represent, instead, the effort of the mind to adapt to the consequences of defects in genes.

FUTURE RESEARCH PATHWAYS

The somatopsychic model dictates certain research pathways:

- In the last chapter we saw, for the first time, a strong association between a severe form of alcoholism and an unusual DNA pattern in the area of the dopamine D2 receptor gene. Now we need to know the nature of the malfunction, and whether it leads to compulsive behavior.
- We need to extend the study to other genes and receptors to determine causal relationships, if any, to other forms of alcoholism; to other compulsive diseases such as cocaine abuse, food disorders, gambling, and sexual promiscuity; and to a wide range of severe behavioral aberrations.
- Out of these studies may come diagnostic tools that will make it possible to determine, for example, the degree of risk of alcoholic predisposition (1) in the prenatal period; (2) in young children; (3) in adults who may have the alcogene(s) but have not yet established a drinking habit; and (4) in alcoholics who enter treatment and want to know if their problem is genetic in origin.
- Since anxiety and anger—and often violence—may be manifestations of the somatopsychic syndrome, it may be useful to explore the relationship between genetic anomalies, neurotransmitter deficits and imbalances, and exaggerated "flight or fight" responses.

Farther into the future are two other ideas that hold promise, the first for prevention, the second, tantalizingly, for ultimate cure.

The approach to prevention that is most intriguing is the development of a vaccine against alcoholism. Such a vaccine would develop antibodies that bind to alcohol and neutralize it—in effect, reversing the biblical story of "water into wine" and turning alcohol into water. Since the euphoric effect of alcohol would be removed, the temptation to drink would be extinguished. The eventual development of a broad-spectrum vaccine might make it possible to manipulate neurotransmitters to offset generalized craving behavior.

Vis-à-vis cure, let us consider a brief scenario. A woman discovers that she carries an alcogene. She wants to conceive, but is reluctant to pass the gene along to her child. She goes to a genetic clinic while she is ovulating and has an egg removed and stored in the genetic bank. Her husband then donates sperm to fertilize the egg. The genetic engineer removes the defective gene chemically, and substitutes a healthy gene. The fertilized egg is then replaced in her fallopian tube at the time of her next ovulatory cycle, where it grows, and the child is born— free of any predisposition toward alcoholism.

At the present time we are not sure of the gene(s) involved in alcoholism or other compulsive diseases, but gene technology has been used with animals for other genetic disorders and seems readily adaptable to humans. The principal roadblock to this form of genetic engineering is the law against the use of recombinant DNA gene therapy to alter germ cell lines. However, as science makes gene therapy feasible for such killers as cancer, heart disease, and alcoholism, social policy in this area will surely be reexamined.

In the remainder of this century and the early decades of the century to come, I think that we will see neurobiology, neuropharmacology, biogenetics, psychiatry, and medicine moving forward in close coordination to reduce the devastating behavioral and social costs of faulty brain function. My vision of the future is a world in which the chemical and electrical functions of the brain are understood; the problem of chemical imbalances as they affect behavior has been solved; the role of genetic anomalies in defective brain chemistry is understood; pharmaceutical and nutritional intervention as an adjunct to Twelve-Step programs and professional treatment is precise and effective; and the technique of defective-gene replacement has been perfected, enabling us to break the genetic chain of inherited addiction. In this world, each individual will be able to enjoy the inborn legacy of reward and pleasure without having the need for addictive substances, without having to pay the price of addiction and pain.

Notes

Chapter 1
Introduction

1. *Seventh Special Report to the U.S. Congress on Alcohol and Health*, DHHS Publication No. (ADM) 90–1656 (1990), pp. ix, xxiv, 163, 261.

M. P. O'Donnell and T. H. Ainsworth, *Health Promotion in the Workplace* (New York: John Wiley, 1984), p. 481.

2. *Traynor v. Turnage, Administrator, Veterans Administration et al.* and *McKelvey v. Turnage, Administrator, Veterans Administration et al.* 108 SCt 1372, 99 (1988).

3. J. A. Ewing and B. A. Rouse eds., *Drinking, Alcohol in American Society: Issues and Current Research* (Chicago: Nelson-Hall, 1978); R. S. Shore and J. M. Luce, *To Your Health: The Pleasures, Problems and Politics of Alcohol* (New York: Seabury Press, 1976), pp. 29, 109.

4. E. M. Jellinek, *The Disease Concept of Alcoholism* (New Haven: College and University Press, 1960), 36–41; M. E. Lender and J. K. Martin, *Drinking in America: A History* (New York: Free Press, 1982), pp. 186–87.

5. *Seventh Special Report*, p. 261.

6. General Services Office of Alcoholics Anonymous, *A. A. Fact File* (New York: A. A. Publishing, 1989).

7. N. G. Hoffman and P. A. Harrison, *Treatment Outcome: Adult Patients Two Years Later.* CATOR Report (St. Paul: CATOR, 1988).

Chapter 2
Alcoholism: A Legacy of Pain for Alcoholics, Families, and Society

1. R. S. Shore and J. M. Luce, *To Your Health: The Pleasures, Problems and Politics of Alcohol* (New York: Seabury Press, 1976), pp. 3–33; G. A. Austin, *Alcohol in Western Society from Antiquity to 1800: A Chronological History* (Santa Barbara: ABC-Clio, 1985); J. A. Ewing and B. A. Rouse eds., *Drinking, Alcohol in American Society: Issues and Current Research* (Chicago: Nelson-Hall, 1978), pp. 6–36, 39–62; M. E. Lender and J. K. Martin, *Drinking in America: A History* (New York: Free Press, 1982).

251

2. B. Rush, *An Inquiry into the Effects of Ardent Spirits upon the Human Body and Mind*, 8th ed. (Bookfield: E. Merriam, 1814). Reprinted in *Quarterly Journal of Studies on Alcoholism* 4 (1943): 324–41.

3. *First Special Report to the U.S. Congress on Alcohol and Health*, DHEW Publication No. (ADM) 74–68 (1973).

4. The profile of the alcoholic below is drawn from my own observations as a visiting scientist in the Downstate Medical Center in Brooklyn, and in the Haight-Ashbury Free Medical Clinic in San Francisco; and from three principal sources in the literature: K. W. Fitzgerald, *Alcoholism: The Genetic Inheritance* (New York: Doubleday, 1988); D. W. Goodwin, *Is Alcoholism Hereditary?* (New York: Ballantine Books, 1988), pp. 63–82; D. M. Gallant, *Alcoholism: A Guide to Diagnosis, Intervention, and Treatment* (New York: W. W. Norton, 1987), pp. 86–98.

5. R. J. Frances, J. Franklin, D. K. Flavin, Suicide and alcoholism, *American Journal of Drug and Alcohol Abuse* 13 (1987): 327–41.

Chapter 3
Self-Help Approaches to Treatment: Alcoholics Anonymous

1. There is little doubt that part of their inspiration came from the Oxford Group which had been organized in 1921 at Christ Church, Oxford, England, by clergyman Frank Buchman. He envisioned a new world order in which individuals and whole societies would rebuild their lives through the practice of absolute honesty, purity, love, and unselfishness.

By 1935 the Oxford movement had spread throughout the world. Seeking help with his drinking problem, Bill W. had attended several meetings and had been impressed by the informality and fellowship. Members gathered together in homes, schools, and churches to share their religious experiences through personal confession and testimony. His concept of alcoholics helping alcoholics probably came from these meetings.

2. General Services Office of Alcoholics Anonymous, *A. A. Fact File* (New York: A. A. Publishing, 1989).

3. *Alcoholics Anonymous Comes of Age* (New York: Alcoholics Anonymous World Services, Inc., 1984).

4. *Alcoholics Anonymous* (New York: Alcoholics Anonymous World Services, Inc., 1976).

5. *Twelve Steps and Twelve Traditions* (New York: Alcoholics Anonymous World Services, Inc., 1987).

6. M. E. Chafetz and H. W. Demone, Jr., *Alcoholism and Society* (New York: Oxford University Press, 1962, pp. 148–65.

7. General Services Office of Alcoholics Anonymous, "Analysis of the 1983 Survey of the Membership of A. A." in *A. A. Fact File* (New York: A. A. Publishing, 1988).

8. Al-Anon Family Groups, *Al-Anon: Then and Now: A Brief History* (New York: Al-Anon Family Group Headquarters, Inc., 1986).

9. Al-Anon Family Groups, *Al-Anon Today* (New York: Al-Anon Family Group Headquarters, Inc., 1988).

Chapter 4
Biopsychic Approaches to Treatment: Frustration and Progress

1. Bill Pittman, *A. A.: The Way It Began* (Seattle: Glen Abbey Books, 1988), pp. 61–70.

2. M. E. Lender and J. K. Martin, *Drinking in America* (New York: Free Press, 1986), pp. 122–23.

3. James W. Smith, President, Schick Shadel Hospitals, Seattle. Unpublished interview, 1988.

4. Walter L. Voegtlin, The treatment of alcoholism by establishing a conditioned reflex, *American Journal of the Medical Sciences* 199 (1940): 802–10; Walter L. Voegtlin, Frederick Lemere, and William R. Broz, Conditioned reflex therapy of alcoholic addiction, III. An evelution of present results in the light of previous experiences with this method, *Quarterly Journal of Studies on Alcoholism* 1 (3) (Dec. 1940): 501–15; Ralph L. Elkins, Coordinator of Psychology Research, Veterans Administration Medical Center, Augusta. Unpublished paper, by permission.

5. Douglas M. Kerr and David H. Sumi, *Final Report: Alcohol Treatment Outcome Research,* for Schick Shadel Hospitals, Seattle, Washington. Report issued by Center for Law and Justice, University of Washington, Seattle, 1985.

6. R. S. Shore and J. M. Luce, *To Your Health: The Pleasures, Problems and Politics of Alcohol* (New York: Seabury Press, 1976); Donald M. Gallant, *Alcoholism: A Guide to Diagnosis, Intervention, and Treatment* (New York: W. W. Norton, 1987).

7. Norman G. Hoffman and Patricia Ann Harrison, *Treatment Outcome: Adult Patients Two Years Later. CATOR Report* St. Paul: CATOR, 1988), pp. 29–32.

8. D. J. Anderson, *Perspectives on Treatment: The Minnesota Experience* (Center City, Minn.: Hazelden, 1981).

9. Sidney Cahn, *The Treatment of Alcoholics* (New York: Oxford University Press, 1970), pp. 103–23.

10. R. L. Collins and G. A. Marlatt, Psychological correlates and explanations of alcohol use, in B. Tabakoff, P. Sutker, and C. Randall eds., *Medical and Social Aspects of Alcohol Abuse* (New York: Plenum Press, 1983), pp. 273–308; *First Special Report to the U.S. Congress on Alcohol & Health.* DHEW Publication No. (HSM) 72–9099, Revised Edition (1971), pp. 122–30.

11. Report from the Secretary of Health, Education, and Welfare, *Alcohol & Health* (New York: Charles Scribner's Sons, 1973), pp. 170–71.

Chapter 6
Science and the Disease Concept

1. E. M. Jellinek, *The Disease Concept of Alcoholism* (New Haven: College and University Press, 1960).

2. R. J. Mardones, On the relationship between deficiency of B vitamins and alcohol intake in rats, *Quarterly Journal of Studies on Alcoholism* 12 (1951): 563–75.

3. R. J. Mardones, M. N. Segovia, and D. A. Hederra, Heredity of experimental alcohol preference in rats, II. Coefficient of heredity, *Quarterly Journal of Studies on Alcoholism* 14 (1953): 1–2.

4. J. M. Ravel, B. Felsing, E. M. Lansford, R. H. Trubey, and W. Shive, Reversal of alcohol toxicity by glutamine, *Journal of Biological Chemistry* 214 (1955): 497–501.

5. L. L. Rogers, R. B. Pelton, and R. J. Williams, Voluntary alcohol consumption by rats following administration of glutamine, *Journal of Biological Chemistry* 214 (1955): 503–6.

6. R. J. Williams, L. J. Berry, and E. Beerstecher, Jr., Biochemical individuality, III. Genotropic factors in the etiology of alcoholism, *Archives of Biochemistry and Biophysics* 23 (1949): 235–90; H. Hakkinen and E. Kulonen, The effect of ethanol on the amino acids of the rat brain with a reference to the administration of glutamine, *Biochemical Journal* 78 (1961): 588–92. Williams' work was in part confirmed and extended by Hakkinen and Kulonen who found that, in the brains of intoxicated rats, ethanol reduced the amount of glutamine in their tissues, and increased the amount of the inhibitory neurotransmitter, GABA. If additional gluatamine was administered before ingestion of alcohol, these changes were prevented.

L. Sammalisto, Effect of glutamine on intoxication caused by ethyl alcohol, *Nature* 195 (1962): 185. Williams' work was further extended by Lasse Sammalisto who found that when glutamine is injected into intoxicated rats the level of intoxication is reduced.

The work of the Finnish scientists suggested that the intoxicating effect of alcohol may be due, in part, to its ability to increase the conversion of the amino acid glutamine into GABA.

7. L. Mirone, The effect of ethyl alcohol on growth, fecundity and voluntary consumption of alcohol by mice, *Quarterly Journal of Studies on Alcoholism* 13 (1952): 365–69.

8. L. Mirone, Dietary deficiency in mice in relation to voluntary alcohol consumption, *Quarterly Journal of Studies on Alcoholism* 18 (1957): 552–60.

9. G. E. McClearn and D. A. Rodgers, Differences in alcohol preference among inbred strains of mice, *Quarterly Journal of Studies on Alcoholism* 20 (1959): 691–95.

10. J. R. Nichols and S. Hsiao, Addiction liability of albino rats: breeding for quantitative differences in morphine drinking, *Science* 157 (1967): 561–63.

11. J. H. Masserman and K. S. Yum, An analysis of the influence of alcohol on experimental neuroses in cats, *Psychosomatic Medicine* 8(1946): 36–52.

12. J. J. Conger, Alcoholism: theory, problem and challenge, II: reinforcement theory and the dynamics of alcoholism. *Quarterly Journal of Studies on Alcoholism* 17 (1956): 296–305.

13. A. Casey, The effect of stress on the consumption of alcohol and reserpine, *Quarterly Journal of Studies on Alcoholism* 21 (1960): 208–16.

14. R. Kakihana, E. P. Noble, and J. C. Butte, Corticosterone response to ethanol in inbred strains of mice, *Nature* 218 (1968): 360–61.

15. R. D. Myers, Alcohol consumption in rats: effect of intracranial injections of ethanol, *Science* 142 (1963): 240–41.

Chapter 7
The Biochemistry of Alcoholism: Early Clues

1. J. N. Langley, On the stimulation and paralysis of nerve-cell and of nerve-endings, Part I, *Journal of Physiology (London)* 27 (1901): 224–36.

2. T. R. Elliott, The action of adrenalin, *Journal of Physiology (London)* 32 (1905): 401–67.

3. W. E. Dixon, On the mode of action of Drugs, *Medicine Magazine (London)* 16 (1907): 454–7.

4. O. Loewi, Über humorale Übertragbarkeit der Herznervenwirkung. *Pflügers Archiv für die Gesamte Physiologie des Menschen und der Tiere* 189 (1921): 239–42.

5. W. B. Cannon and J. E. Uridil, Studies on the conditions of activity in endocrine glands, VIII. Some effects on the denervated heart of stimulating the nerves of the liver, *American Journal of Physiology* 58 (1921): 353–64.

6. U. S. von Euler, A specific sympathomimetic ergone in adrenergic nerve fibers (sympathin) and its relations to adrenaline and nor-adrenaline, *Acta Physiologica Scandinavica* 12 (1946): 73–97.

7. D. Gursey and R. E. Olson, Depression of serotinin and norepinephrine levels in brain stem of rabbit by ethanol, *Proceedings of the Society for Experimental Biology and Medicine* 104 (1960): 280–81.

8. D. H. Efron and G. L. Gessa, Failure of ethanol and barbiturates to alter brain monoamine content, *Archives Internationales de Pharmacodynamie et de Thérapie* 142 (1963): 111–6.

9. G. Rosenfeld, Potentiation of the narcotic action and acute toxicity of alcohol by primary aromatic monoamines, *Quarterly Journal of Studies on Alcoholism* 21 (1960): 584–96.

10. R. D. Myers and W. L. Veale, Alcohol preference in the rat: reduction following depletion of brain serotonin, *Science* 160 (1968): 1469–71.

11. V. E. Davis and M. J. Walsh, Alcohol, amines, and alkaloids: a possible biochemical basis for alcohol addiction, *Science* 167 (1970): 1005–7.

12. M. H. Seevers, V. E. Davis, and M. J. Walsh, Morphine and ethanol physical dependence: a critique of a hypothesis, *Science* 170 (1970): 1113–15.

13. P. V. Halushka and P. C. Hoffmann, Alcohol addiction and tetrahydropapaveroline, *Science* 170 (1970): 1104–6.

14. G. Cohen and M. Collins, Alkaloids from catecholamines in adrenal tissue: possible role in alcoholism, *Science* 167 (1970): 1749–51.

15. G. Cohen, A biochemical basis for alcoholism as a disease, *Medical Counterpoint* 3 (1971): 11–15.

16. A. Goldstein and B. A. Judson, Alcohol dependence and opiate dependence: lack of relationship in mice, *Science* 172 (1971): 290–92.

17. I. Geller, N. D. Campbell, and K. Blum, Protection against acute alcoholic intoxication with diethanolamine-rutin, *Research Communications in Chemical Pathology and Pharmacology* 1 (1970): 383–94.

18. K. Blum, J. E. Wallace, R. S. Ryback, and I. Geller, Diethanolamine: a possible weak agonist-antagonist to ethanol, *European Journal of Pharmacology* 19 (1972): 218–22.

19. G. Duritz and E. B. Truitt, Jr., Importance of acetaldehyde in the action of ethanol on brain norepinephrine and 5-hydroxytryptamine, *Biochemical Pharmacology* 15 (1966): 711–21.

20. K. Blum, I. Geller, and J. E. Wallace, Interaction effects of ethanol and pyrazole in laboratory rodents, *British Journal of Pharmacology* 43 (1971): 67–73.

21. I. Geller, Ethanol preference in the rat as a function of photoperiod, *Science* 173 (1971): 456–59.

22. K. Blum, J. H. Merritt, R. J. Reiter, and J. E. Wallace, A possible relationship between the pineal gland and ethanol preference in the rat, *Current Therapeutic Research* 15 (1973): 25–30; R. J. Reiter, K. Blum, J. E. Wallace, and J. H. Merritt, Pineal gland: evidence for an influence on ethanol preference in male Syrian hamsters, *Comparative Biochemistry and Physiology* 47A (1974): 11–16.

In a subsequent experiment, we used Golden Syrian hamsters because they prefer alcohol over water in normal day-night conditions, and because their pineal glands were known to be very active in converting serotonin into melatonin.

We first placed all of the hamsters in a normal day-night environment for a three-week period, and found that they drank approximately two and a half times more alcohol than water. At the end of the third week these animals, too, were divided into two groups: a test group with pineal glands removed, and a control group with glands intact.

We then measured their alcohol preference over the next five weeks, and found that the animals in Group One—with pineal glands removed—were drinking 44 percent less alcohol than those in Group Two—with pineal glands intact.

At the beginning of the ninth week, we blinded the animals in both groups, to make an absolute determination about the effect of darkness, and measured their alcohol and water preference over the next five weeks. At the end of that period, the animals in Group Two—with pineal glands intact—were drinking almost two and a half times as much alcohol as those in Group One.

23. F. J. Reiter, K. Blum, J. E. Wallace, and J. H. Merritt, Effect of the pineal gland on alcohol consumption by congenitally blind male rats, *Quarterly Journal of Studies on Alcoholism* 34 (1973): 937–39.

24. I. Geller and R. Purdy, Alteration of ethanol preference in rats; effects of beta-carboline, in M. Gross ed., *Alcohol Intoxication and Withdrawal II* (New York: Plenum Press, 1975) pp. 295–302. (Advances in Experimental Medicine and Biology vol. 59.)

25. K. Blum, J. E. Wallace, J. D. Eubanks, and H. A. Schwertner, Effects of naloxone on ehtanol withdrawal, preference and narcosis, *Pharmacologist* 17 (1975): 197.

26. E. L. Way, H. H. Loh, and F. Shen, Morphine tolerance, physical dependence, and synthesis of brain 5-hydroxytryptamine, *Science* 162 (1968): 1290–92.

27. K. Kuriyama, G. E. Rauscher, and P. Y. Sze, Effect of acute and chronic administration of ethanol on the 5-hydroxytryptamine turnover and tryptophan hydroxylase activity of the mouse brain, *Brain Research* 26 (1971): 450–54.

28. A. Carlsson, T. Magnusson, T. H. Svensson, and B. Waldeck, Effect of ethanol on the metabolism of brain catecholamines, *Psychopharmacologia (Berlin)* 30 (1973): 27–36.

29. I. Sutton and M. A. Simmonds, Effects of acute and chronic ethanol on the gamma-aminobutyric system in rat brain, *Biochemical Pharmacology* 22 (1973): 1685–92.

30. D. B. Goldstein, Alcohol withdrawal reactions in mice: effects of drugs that modify neurotransmission, *Journal of Pharmacology and Experimental Therapeutics* 186 (1973): 1–9.

31. S. Tewari and E. P. Noble, Ethanol and brain protein synthesis, *Brain Research* 26 (1971): 560–74.

Chapter 8
The Opiate Connection

1. D. Van Praag and E. J. Simon, Studies on the intracellular distribution and tissue binding of dihydromorphine-7,8-H3 in the rat, *Proceedings of the Society for Experimental Biology and Medicine* 122 (1966): 6–11.

2. A. Goldstein, L. I. Lowney, and B. K. Pal, Stereospecific and nonspecific interactions of the morphine congener levorphanol in subcellular fractions of mouse brain, *Proceedings of the National Academy of Sciences of the United States of America* 58 (1971): 1742–47.

3. L. Terenius, Stereospecific interaction between narcotic analgesics and a synaptic plasma membrane fraction of rat cerebral cortex, *Acta Pharmacologica et Toxicologica* 32 (1973): 317–20.

4. Codeine, for example, which is about one-tenth as active as morphine, was found to bind only weakly to the opiate receptor. Levorphanol, which is five times more potent than morphine, binds three times more powerfully to the opiate receptor.

Later, they found that drugs such as phenobarbital and histamine, as well as common neurotransmitters such as serotonin and norepinephrine, had no effect on radioactive naloxone binding to the opiate receptor. The action seemed specific to the opiates.

5. C. B. Pert and S. H. Snyder, Opiate receptor: demonstration in nervous tissue, *Science* 179 (1973): 1011–14.

6. M. Sandler, S. B. Carter, K. R. Hunter, and G. M. Stern, Tetrahydroiso-quinoline alkaloids: in vivo metabolites of L-dopa in man, *Nature* 241 (1973): 439–43.

7. In Collins' experiment, the rats were given alcohol alone, or in various combinations with L-dopa, a substance that builds up the supply of dopamine; pargyline, a substance that prevents the breakdown of dopamine; or pyrogallol, which prevents the breakdown of dopamine and acetaldehyde. These substances were included because they interact with enzymes in the body to build up TIQs.

Seven hours into the experiment, the rats were sacrificed, and materials were extracted from their brains and analyzed. The results were:

- Alcohol alone, pyrogallol alone, and pargyline alone did not produce detectable TIQ.
- Pyrogallol and pargyline in combination did not produce detectable TIQ.
- Pyrogallol in combination with alcohol produced a small amount of TIQ.
- Pargyline in combination with alcohol produced a comparable amount of TIQ.
- Pyrogallol and pargyline together with alcohol produced seven times that amount of TIQ.

These results tied TIQ production directly to the presence of substances that increased the concentration of dopamine and acetaldehyde, *and to the presence of alcohol*, which probably was the primary source of the acetaldehyde.

8. M. A. Collins and M. G. Bigdeli, Tetrahydroisoquinolines *in vivo*. I. Rat brain formation of salsolinol, a condensation product of dopamine and acetaldehyde, under certain conditions during ethanol intoxication, *Life Sciences* 16 (1975): 585–601.

9. M. A. Korsten, S. Matsuzaki, A. Feinman, and C. S. Lieber, High blood acetaldehyde levels after ethanol administration: difference between alcoholic and non-alcoholic subjects, *New England Journal of Medicine* 292 (1975): 386–89.

10. D. H. Ross, M. A. Medina, and H. L. Cardena, Morphine and ethanol: selective depletion of regional brain calcium, *Science* 186 (1974): 63–65.

11. K. Blum, S. Futterman, J. E. Wallace, and H. A. Schwertner, Naloxone-induced inhibition of ethanol dependence in mice, *Nature* 265 (1977): 49–51.

12. K. Blum, Narcotic antagonism of seizures induced by a dopamine-derived tetrahydroisoquinoline alkaloid, *Experientia* 44 (1988): 751–53.

13. K. Blum, J. D. Eubanks, and J. E. Wallace, Alcohol dependence and opiate dependence: evidence for a relationship in mice, *Committee on the Problems of Drug Dependence Proceedings* (1975): 551–60.

14. J. J. Jacob, E. C. Tremblay, and M. C. Colombel, Facilitation de réactions nociceptives par la naloxone chez la souris et chez le rat, *Psychopharmacologia* 37 (1974): 217–23.

15. J. Hughes, Isolation of an endogenous compound from the brain with pharmacological properties similar to morphine, *Brain Research* 88 (1975): 295–308.

16. J. Hughes, T. Smith, B. Morgan, and L. Fothergill, Purification and properties of enkephalin: the possible endogenous ligand for the morphine receptor, *Life Sciences* 16 (1975): 1753–58.

17. L. Terenius and A. Wahlstrom, Morphine-like ligand for opiate receptors in human CSF, *Life Sciences* 16 (1975): 1759–64.

18. G. W. Pasternak, R. Goodman, and S. H. Snyder, An endogenous morphine-like factor in mammalian brain, *Life Sciences* 16 (1975): 1765–69.

19. H. Teschemacher, K. E. Opheim, B. M. Cox, and A. Goldstein, A peptide-like substance from pituitary that acts like morphine, I. isolation, *Life Sciences* 16 (1975): 1771–75.

20. J. Hughes, T. W. Smith, H. W. Kosterlitz, L. A. Fothergill, B. A. Morgan, and H. R. Morris, Identification of two related pentapeptides from the brain with potent opiate agonist activity, *Nature* 258 (1975): 577–80.

In the final phase of the experiment, knowing the specific amino acids contained in one of the natural peptides, and their linkage, they made a synthetic peptide and compared the biological activity of the synthetic product to the natural one. They found no significant difference between them. This was simple proof that they had correctly determined the chemical nature of the natural peptide in the brain which stimulates the opiate receptors.

21. L. H. Lazarus, N. Ling, and R. Guillemin, Beta-lipotropin as a prohormone for the morphinomimetic peptides, endorphins and enkephalins, *Proceedings of the National Academy of Sciences of the United States of America* 73 (1976): 2156–59.

22. C. H. Li and D. Chung, Isolation and structure of an untriakontapeptide with opiate activity from camel pituitary glands, *Proceedings of the National Academy of Sciences of the United States of America* 73 (1976): 1145–48.

23. B. M. Cox, A. Goldstein, and C. H. Li, Opioid activity of a peptide, beta-lipotropin-(61–91), derived from beta-lipotropin, *Proceedings of the National Academy of Sciences of the United States of America* 73 (1976): 1821–23.

24. E. J. Simon, Opiate receptors: isolation and mechanisms, in K. Blum ed., *Alcohol and Opiates: Neurochemical and Behavior Mechanisms* (New York: Academic Press, 1977), pp. 255–64.

25. W. A. Klee, Opiates and cyclic AMP, in K. Blum ed., *Alcohol and Opiates: Neurochemical and Behavioral Mechanisms* (New York: Academic Press, 1977), pp. 299–308.

26. L. Volicer and B. I. Gold, Effect of ethanol on cyclic AMP levels in rat brain, *Life Sciences* 13 (1973): 269–80.

27. A. K. S. Ho, R. C. A. Chen, and J. M. Morrison, Opiate-ethanol interaction studies, in K. Blum ed., *Alcohol and Opiates: Neurochemical and Behavioral Mechanisms* (New York: Academic Press, 1977), pp. 189–202.

28. K. Blum, Neurochemical and behavioral considerations on the relationship between ethanol and opiate dependence, in J. H. Lowinson ed., *Critical Concerns in the Field of Drug Abuse: Proceedings of the Third National Drug Abuse Conference, Inc., New York, 1976* (New York: Marcel Decker, 1978), 1144–49.

29. K. Blum, M. G. Hamilton, and J. E. Wallace, Alcohol and opiates: a review of common neurochemical and behavioral mechanisms, in K. Blum ed., *Alcohol and Opiates: Neurochemical and Behavioral Mechanisms* (New York: Academic Press, 1977), pp. 203–36.

30. S. Liljequist, Changes in the sensitivity of dopamine receptors in the nucleus accumbens and in the striatum induced by chronic ehtanol administration, *Acta Pharmacologica et Toxicologica* 43 (1978): 19–28.

Chapter 9
Poppies of the Brain

1. J. H. Chin and D. B. Goldstein, Effects of low concentrations of ethanol on the fluidity of spin-labeled erythrocyte and brain membranes, *Molecular Pharmacology* 13 (1977): 435–41.

2. K. Blum, A. H. Briggs, S. F. Elston, and L. DeLallo, Psychogenetics of drug seeking behavior, *Substance and Alcohol Actions/Misuse* 1 (1980): 255–57.

3. R. D. Myers and C. L. Melchior, Alcohol drinking: abnormal intake caused by tetrahydropapaveroline in brain, *Science* 196 (1977): 554–56.

4. This was a daring conclusion, but it was compatible with other findings. From his experiments he knew that acetaldehyde—a by-product of alcohol—stimulates abnormal alcohol drinking. And acetaldehyde is involved in the production of TIQs. Furthermore, if neurons containing serotonin, dopamine, and norepinephrine are destroyed in certain animals, abnormal drinking is stimulated.

From the work of Davis and Walsh, as well as that of Cohen and Collins, he knew that when serotonin, dopamine, and norepinephrine combine with aldehydes they cease to be neurotransmitters and become TIQs. This combination creates an artificial neurotransmitter deficiency, and stimulates abnormal drinking.

5. M. G. Hamilton, M. Hirst, and K. Blum, Opiate-like activity of salsolinol on the electrically stimulated guinea pig ileum, *Life Sciences* 25 (1979): 2205–10.

6. In the tail flick procedure to measure response to pain, the test apparatus consisted of an adjustable heat source which was brought into contact with the tail of the rat. Voltage applied to the heat source activated a highly accurate timer which shut off the current when the tail "flicked" or passed between the heat source and a photocell. The time between application of the heat source and the flicking of the tial was the index of the animal's pain perception.

7. R. H. Fertel, J. E. Greenwald, R. Schwarz, L. Wong, and J. Bianchine, Opiate receptor binding and analgesic effects of the tetrahydroisoquinolines salsolinol and tetrahydropapaveroline, *Research Communications in Chemical Pathology and Pharmacology* 27 (1980): 3–16.

8. A. Marshall, M. Hirst, and K. Blum, Analgesic effects of 3-carboxysalsolinol alone and in combination with morphine, *Experientia* 33 (1976): 754–55.

9. P. J. O'Neill and R. G. Rahwan, Absence of formation of brain salsolinol in ethanol-dependent mice, *Journal of Pharmacology and Experimental Therapeutics* 200 (1977): 306–13.

10. R. D. Myers, Tetrahydroisoquinolines in the brain: the basis of an animal model of alcoholism, *Alcoholism: Clinical and Experimental Research* 2 (1978): 145–54.

11. G. Cohen, The synaptic properties of some tetrahydroisoquinoline alkaloids, *Alcoholism: Clinical and Experimental Research* 2 (1978): 121–25.

12. M. G. Hamilton, K. Blum, and M. Hirst, Identification of an isoquinoline alkaloid after chronic exposure to ethanol, *Alcoholism: Clinical and Experimental Research* 2 (1978): 133–37.

13. D. H. Ross, Inhibition of high affinity calcium binding by salsolinol, *Alcoholism: Clinical and Experimental Research* 2 (1978): 139–43.

14. *Robert Myers* reported on an experiment in which test animals had been given heavy doses of TIQs, resulting in intense craving for alcohol. After six months, though the animals had received no more TIQs, the craving remained in full effect. This suggested that the TIQs had permanently altered the biochemical balance in the brain, supporting his earlier finding that infusions of acetaldehyde (which makes TIQs) had the same effect. A later experiment showed that when chronic injections of TIQs in rats were suspended, physical symptoms developed that were identical with those of morphine withdrawal.

Myers' paper had a big impact on me. Everything was adding up. I had been excited by Virginia Davis' theory that alcohol addiction and opiate addiction have the same biochemical base; excited to learn that alcohol-produced TIQs are the same as those involved in producing morphine in the poppy plant; and excited to hear her suggestion that TIQs might prove to be addictive. Now Myers' results indicated that this theory might be right.

Boris Tabakoff from the University of Illinois Medical School questioned the idea that there are specific receptors for TIQs in the brain, saying:

> To the best of my recollection, I do not think that TIQs affect specific
> receptor sites, particularly opiate receptors, as Dr. Myers suggests in his
> remarks on withdrawal. TIQs are likely to be formed wherever sufficient
> quantities of aldehydes and neurotransmitters are present in the brain, and
> not preferentially in areas which contain opiate receptors.

Later research was to provide evidence that TIQs *are* formed preferentially in reward areas that are rich in opiate receptor sites, but at the time the question was challenging, and aroused considerable discussion.

Gerald Cohen reported that when TIQ molecules are picked up by the neuron, some are stored, and some act as a kind of traffic cop, regulating the transmission of dopamine and norepinephrine across the synapse between an originating and a receiving neuron. TIQs also act to release norepinephrine from the neuron, and interact with dopamine and norepinephrine receptors to mimic neurotransmitter response. For example, an injection of TIQ in the nucleus accumbens, a brain area involved in reward, will have an energizing effect. The result is the same as with an injection of dopamine. These actions stimulate the reward system, producing a "feel good" response. Later in the year, Christine Melchior in Robert Myers' laboratory found that TIQs cause the release of dopamine from the neurons in the reward area of the brain.

Cohen's findings further supported the TIQ theory, and precipitated wide-ranging discussion. One of the exchanges following Cohen's paper included the following statement and response:

> *Statement:* It is difficult to detect TIQs in the brain following alcohol ingestion.
> This as been explained by the fact that TIQs are so rapidly metabolized
> that detection is difficult. If this is true, it raises a question. When a substance

is metabolized it is changed into something else, and loses its characteristic biological activity. Therefore, how could the TIQs be affecting neuronal activity at low concentrations?

Response: Research since the 1940s has shown that TIQs do not lose their potency when they are metabolized. For example, when Fasset and associates studied the effect of a TIQ and one of its metabolites on blood pressure in animals, they found the TIQ and its metabolite to be of equal potency.

Murray G. Hamilton discussed an experiment involving Hirst and me in which we exposed mice to alcohol vapor for ten days. At the end of that time we used gas chromatography to measure the amount of the TIQ salsolinol and its metabolite, methyl salsolinol, in the brain. We found no salsolinol, but we did find significant amounts of methyl salsolinol in a dopamine-rich area of the brain called the striatum, a part of the reward system. We concluded from our results that TIQs are formed in the brain following alcohol intake, and that their presence can be detected, without chemical manipulation, by measuring the metabolite.

David Ross, reporting on new work at his laboratory at the University of Texas at San Antonio, was the first to show that TIQs and opioid peptides share common biochemical mechanisms. In measuring the degree to which calcium binds to calcium receptors in the synaptic neurons of rats, he found that:

- An opiate, Levorphanol, inhibits calcium binding.
- Beta-endorphin and the TIQ salsolinol also inhibit calcium binding.
- When the opiate antagonist naloxone is administered before beta-endorphin or salsolinol, the inhibition is removed, and calcium binding resumes.

Even small amounts of Levorphanol, beta-endorphin, or salsolinol produce blocking at the calcium receptor site. The implication was, again, that the TIQs and the endorphins act in a manner similar to the opiates.

15. K. Blum, M. G. Hamilton, M. Hirst, and J. E. Wallace, Putative role of isoquinoline alkaloids in alcoholism: a link to opiates, *Alcoholism: Clinical and Experimental Research* 2 (1978): 113–20.

16. G. K. Schenk, M. P. Engelmeier, D. Matz, and J. Pach, High dosage naloxone treatment in acute alcohol intoxication, *Proceedings CINP* (Vienna, 1978): 386.

17. In the first phase of the experiment, Jeffcoate and his associates determined that the average reaction time of the subjects was 504 milliseconds. Later, after experiencing mild stress, the subjects' average reaction time increased to 509.6 milliseconds. This latter figure was taken as the baseline reaction time.

In the second phase, each subject received an intravenous injection of saline, followed by a strong drink of gin and tonic. At the 40-minute mark, their average reaction time had increased to 520 milliseconds.

In the third phase, the subjects were given naloxone instead of saline, plus alcohol, and after a 40-minute period their reaction time was tested. The average reaction time had dropped back to 505 milliseconds, almost the basal level.

18. W. J. Jeffcoate, M. Herbert, M. H. Cullen, A. G. Hastings, and C. P. Walder, Prevention of effects of alcohol intoxication by naloxone, *Lancet* 2 (1979): 1157–59.

19. M. A. Schuckit and V. Rayses, Ethanol ingestion: differences in blood acetaldehyde concentrations in relatives of alcoholics and controls, *Science* 203 (1979): 54–55.

20. C. J. P. Eriksson and J. E. Peachey, Lack of difference in blood acetaldehyde of alcoholics and controls after ethanol ingestion, *Pharmacology, Biochemistry and Behavior* 13 (1980) Suppl. 1: 101–5.

21. In an August 28, 1989, letter that I received from Schuckit he stated:

While the sons of alcoholics and sons of non-alcoholics did, indeed, differ on levels of acetaldehyde and while all analyses were done blindly, the acetaldehyde assay method available at the time was subsequently shown to produce spurious amounts of acetaldehyde during the analysis. Of course, this does nothing to explain why "family history positives" (FHPs) and "family history negatives" (FHNs) should be different. On the other hand, it does question whether the differences between the two family history groups really reflect levels of acetaldehyde found in the blood stream and brain, rather than levels of this substance produced during processing of samples.

22. M. A. Collins, W. P. Nijm, G. F. Borge, G. Teas, and C. Goldfarb, Dopamine-related tetrahydroisoquinolines: significant urinary excretion by alcoholics after alcohol consumption, *Science* 206 (1979): 1184–86.

23. M. A. Collins, N. S. Ung-Chun, D. Pranger and B. Cheng, Ethanol, brain dopamine condensation products, and dopa in the diet, *Abstracts, Society of Neuroscience* 14 (1989): 195.

24. G. R. Siggins and F. E. Bloom, Alcohol-related electrophysiology, *Pharmacology, Biochemistry and Behavior* 13 (1980) Suppl. 1: 203–11; G. R. Siggins and E. French, Central neurons are depressed by iontophoretic and micropressure application of ethanol and tetrahydropapaveroline, *Drug and Alcohol Dependence* 4 (1979): 239–43.

25. B. R. Smith, Z. W. Brown, and Z. Amit, Chronic intraventricular administration of tetrahydroisoquinoline alkaloids: lack of effect on voluntary ethanol consumption in the rat, *Substance and Alcohol Actions/Misuse* 1 (1980): 209–21.

26. R. D. Myers, C. Melchior, and H. S. Swartzwelder, Amine-aldehyde metabolites and alcoholism: fact, myth, or uncertainty, *Substance and Alcohol Actions/Misuse* 1 (1980): 223–38.

27. K. Blum, A. H. Briggs, L. DeLallo S. F., Elston, and R Ochoa, Whole brain methionine-enkephalin of ethanol-avoiding and ethanol-preferring C57BL mice, *Experientia* 38 (1982): 1469–70.

28. K. Blum, A. H. Briggs, S. F. Elston, and L. DeLallo, Ethanol preference as a function of genotypic levels of whole brain enkephalin in mice, *Toxicological European Research* 3 (1981): 261–62.

29. In this second experiment we used four strains: DBA (preference for water); C3H (mild preference for water); and C57 and C58 (both of whom prefer alcohol over water). When we checked their brains for methionine enkephalin, we found the following levels in *picamoles* per gram of brain material:

Strain	Preference	Enkephalin Levels in Picamoles
DBA	water	339
C3H	water	314
C57	alcohol	304
C58	alcohol	268

If further verified, this high correlation would indicate a genetic linkage between low enkephalins and a tendency toward alcohol preference.

30. K. Blum, A. H. Briggs, S. F. Elston, L. DeLallo, P. J. Sheridan, and M. Sar, Reduced leucine-enkephalin-like immunoreactive substance in hamster basal ganglia after long-term ethanol exposure, *Science* 216 (1982): 1425–27. R. Schulz, M. Wuster, T. Duka, and A. Herz, Acute and chronic ethanol treatment changes endorphin levels in brain and pituitary, *Psychopharmacology* 68 (1980): 221–27. Their findings at the Max Planck Institute confirmed the work of Blum and associates mentioned above.

31. P. L. Hoffman, R. F. Ritzmann, R. Walter, and B. Tabakoff, Arginine vasopressin maintains ethanol tolerance, *Nature* 276 (1978): 614–16.

32. J. S. Richardson and D. M. Novakovski, Brain monoamines and free choice ethanol consumption in rats, *Drug and Alcohol Dependence* 3 (1978): 253–64.

33. First organized in 1931 by Dr. Neil Gordon, a chemist at Johns Hopkins University in Baltimore, the Gordon Conferences bring together leading scientists in chemistry and related fields in academia and industry from all over the world. They bring their latest unpublished work and open it to discussion and criticism. The proceedings, even the informal discussions, are private; there is no publicity, and no publication of papers. Gordon saw the Conference as a forum where the best minds in the various fields could interact freely without the restrictions usually imposed upon refereed papers, protected from the possible embarrassment of publicity. To maintain the quality of the participants, invitees at Gordon Confrences are limited to a maximum of 100.

Over the years I had seen the concept expand from chemistry into other disciplines until virtually every branch of science was covered, except for the psychosocial sciences. I had been increasingly frustrated by the fact that my field, addiction research, was not represented. Then, in the late seventies, a Conference on Opiates was organized, with sharp emphasis on the chemistry of opiate action. I immediately began discussions with Dr. Noble at the National Institute on Alcohol and Alcoholism. He and I decided to make a formal application to Gordon Conference officials to include alcohol research as a Conference topic.

The invitation came in August 1978, and when the Conference opened in February we had 94 participants representing the leading laboratories in the United States and seven foreign countries.

The effectiveness of the Conference philosophy and format quickly became apparent as the sessions developed. The papers were almost incidental to the discussions they touched off, lasting sometimes until two o'clock in the morning. At times the discussions involved the entire group; sometimes they were carried out in small groups or in one-on-one heated debates; but in either case the participants spoke their mind.

Chapter 10
Malfunction of the Reward Messengers

1. D. Ross, R. J. Hartmann, and I. Geller, Ethanol preference in the hamster: effects of morphine sulfate and naltrexone, a long-acting morphine antagonist, *Proceedings of the Western Pharmacology Society* 19 (1976): 326–30.

2. H. L. Altschuler, P. E. Phillips, and D. A. Feinhandler, Alteration of ethanol self-administration by naltrexone, *Life Sciences* 26 (1980): 679–88.

3. A. Reggiani, F. Battaini, H. Kobayashi, P. Spano, and M. Trabucchi, Genotype-dependent sensitivity to morphine: role of different opiate receptor populations, *Brain Research* 189 (1980): 289–94.

4. K. Blum, A. H. Briggs, S. F. Elston, and L. DeLallo, Psychogenetics of drug-seeking behavior, *Substance and Alcohol Actions/Misuse* 1 (1980): 255–57.

5. Using two sets of guinea pigs, Kalant's group removed the ileum and measured normal muscle contraction in response to an electrical stimulus. They then applied varying amounts of morphine to muscle tissue taken from one set of test animals until they determined the dosage needed to reduce muscle contractions by 50 percent. To muscle tissue from the other animal set they applied varying amounts of alcohol to determine the dosage needed to reduce contractions by 50 percent. These amounts of morphine and alcohol were then taken as baselines for the experiment.

They divided another group of guinea pigs into two sets. In one set they implanted slow-release morphine pellets for three days. In the other set they injected alcohol every three hours for two weeks. The ileum tissues were then removed, placed in a bath, and stimulated electrically. After contraction began:

- In the tissues that had been treated with morphine, they had to add 170 percent more morphine to achieve a 50 percent reduction in muscle contraction.
- In the tissues that had been treated with alcohol, they had to add 40 percent more alcohol to achieve the same 50 percent reduction.

This demonstrated that previous exposure to either morphine or alcohol reduces the effect of subsequent applications, with morphine exerting the stronger influence. This phenomenon might be called *self-tolerance.*

The experiment was then repeated, except that alcohol was applied to the tissues previously treated with morphine, and vice versa. The results were:

- In the tissues that had been treated with morphine, it was found that alcohol had to be increased by 73 percent to achieve a 50 percent reduction in muscle contraction.
- In the tissues that had been treated with alcohol, it was found that morphine had to be increased by 41 percent to achieve a 50 percent reduction.

This phenomenon might be called *cross-tolerance.* It was weaker than self-tolerance, but definitely present.

6. J. M. Mayer, J. M. Khanna, H. Kalant, and L. Spero, Cross-tolerance between ethanol and morphine in the guinea-pig ileum longitudinal-muscle/myenteric-plexus preparation, *European Journal of Pharmacology* 63 (1980): 223–27.

7. K. Blum, A. H. Briggs, L. DeLallo, S. F. Elston, and M. Hirst, Naloxone antagonizes the action of low ethanol concentrations on mouse vas deferens, *Substance and Alcohol Actions/Misuse* 1 (1980): 327–34.

8. K. Blum, Alcohol and opiates: a review of common mechanisms, in L. Manzo ed., *Advances in Neurotoxicology: Proceedings of the International Congress on Neurotoxicology, Varese, Italy, 27–30 September, 1979* (Oxford, New York: Pergamon Press, 1980), pp. 71–90.

9. In the first phase of their investigation, Eric Simon and his group extracted neuronal membranes from:

- rat brain, which contained *delta* and *mu* receptors
- toad brain, which contained *delta* and *mu* receptors
- neuro-tissue culture cells which contained *delta* receptors only.

In the second phase they determine the baseline binding of radioactive solutions of morphine and enkephalin to these receptors. This part of the experiment was complex, but essentially what they found was:

- morphine bound mostly to the mu receptors
- enkephalin bound mostly to the delta receptors.

In the third phase they added alcohol, and then added the radioactive materials to each sample. They found that:

- morphine binding was not affected by alcohol
- enkephalin binding was inhibited.

This indicated that alcohol was binding to the delta receptors, and interfering with the binding of natural enkephalins.

10. J. M. Hiller, L. M. Angel, and E. J. Simon, Multiple opiate receptors: alcohol selectively inhibits binding to delta receptors, *Science* 214 (1981): 468–69.

11. L. Lucchi, A. Bosio, P. F. Spano, and M. Trabucchi, Action of ethanol and salsolinol on opiate receptor function, *Brain Research* 232 (1981): 506–10.

12. E. P. Noble, and S. Tewari, Ethanol and brain ribosomes, *Federal Proceedings* 34 (1975): 1942–47.

13. B. R. Seizinger, V. Hollt, and A. Herz, Effects of chronic ethanol treatment on the *in vitro* biosynthesis of pro-opiomelanocortin and its posttranslational processing of beta-endorphin in the intermediate lobe of the rat pituitary, *Journal of Neurochemistry* 43 (1984): 607–13.

14. M. E. Charness, A. S. Gordon, and I. Diamond, Ethanol modulation of opiate receptors in cultured neural cells, *Science* 222 (1983): 1246–48; M. E. Charness, L. A. Querimit, and I. Diamond, Ethanol increases the expression of functional delta-opioid receptors in neuroblastoma X glioma NG108–15 hybrid cells, *Journal of Biological Chemistry* 261 (1986): 3164–69.

15. K. Blum, S. F. A. Elton, L. DeLallo, A. H. Briggs, and J. E. Wallace, Ethanol acceptance as a function of genotype amounts of brain MET-enkephalin, *Proceedings of the National Academy of Sciences of the United States of America* 80 (1983): 6510–12.

16. A. R. Genazzani, G. Nappi, F. Facchinetti, G. L. Mazzella, D. Parrini, E. Sinforiani, F. Petraglia, and F. Savoldi, Central deficiency of beta-endorphin in alcohol addicts, *Journal of Clinical Endocrinology and Metabolism* 55 (1982): 583–86.

17. S. Ehrenpreis, R. C. Balagot, J. E. Comaty, and S. B. Myles, Naloxone reversible analgesia in mice produced by D-phenylalanine and hydrocinnamic acid, inhibitors of carboxypeptidase A, in J. J. Bonica, J. C. Liebeskind, and D. G. Albe-Fessard eds., *Proceedings of the Second World Congress on Pain* (New York: Raven Press, 1979), pp. 479–88. (Advances in Pain Research and Therapy, vol 3.)

18. A. K. Ho and N. Rossi, Suppression of ethanol consumption by MET-enkephalin in rats, *Journal of Pharmacology* 34 (1982): 118–19. In support of our studies, Andrew K. Ho and Nello Rossi at the University of Illinois found experimental evidence that the opioid MET-enkephalin can directly reduce alcohol consumption in rats.

19. K. Blum, A. H. Briggs, M. C. Trachtenberg, L. DeLallo, and J. E. Wallace, Enkephalinase inhibition: regulation of ethanol intake in genetically predisposed mice, *Alcohol* 4 (1987): 449–56.

To find the reason for this encouraging effect, we then injected one group of alcohol-preferring mice with hydrocinnamic acid, and another similar group with a saline solution. When we measured the level of brain enkephalin in both groups, we found it to be significantly higher in the group that had received the hydrocinnamic acid. This meant that, with the inhibiting enzyme inactivated, the level of enkephalins had risen. This rise, in turn, was a probable explanation for the drop in alcohol-seeking behavior we´had seen earlier.

20. L. Stein and J. Belluzzi, Second messengers, natural rewards, and drugs of abuse, *Clinical Neuropharmacology* 9 (1986) Suppl. 4: 205–7.

21. M. C. Summers, Structural and biological studies of the acetaldehyde adducts of enkephalins and related peptides: a short review, in M. A. Collins, ed., *Aldehyde Adducts in Alcoholism* (New York: Alan R. Liss, 1985), pp. 39–49.

22. L. D. Reid and G. A. Hunter, Morphine and naloxone modulate intake of ethanol, *Alcohol* 1 (1984): 33–37.

23. J. D. Belluzzi and L. Stein, Brain endorphins: possible role in long-term memory, in K. Vereby ed., *Opioids in Mental Illness: Theories, Clinical Observations, and Treatment Possibilities, Annals of the New York Academy of Sciences* 398 (1982): 221–29.

24. A. K. Ho, R. C. Chen, and J. M. Morrison, Opiate-ethanol interaction studies, in K. Blum ed., *Alcohol and Opiates: Neurochemical and Behavioral Mechanisms* (New York: Academic Press, 1977), pp. 189–202.

25. Reid's controversial interpretation may have grown out of other experiments he and his group had conducted in which they found that morphine increased food consumption. Their findings suggested that the increased opioid activity caused by small doses of morphine was linked to an ingestive disorder in which the individual consumes pleasurable food or alcohol in excessive amounts beyond the body's normal intake.

They concluded that certain types of alcohol abuse may be biochemically similar to the eating disorder known as Bulimia or "binge eating" which, in turn, may be linked to increased opioid activity.

Reid probably knew, at this time, that certain mice and rats are born with abnormally high levels of natural opioids. These animals tend to be obese, and consume abnormal amounts of food during their life span. What he may not have taken into account was that although high levels of natural opioids do lead to excessive food intake, the food choice is for lipids and proteins, and the animals' carbohydrate intake may be lower than normal. *This is not the eating pattern of the bulimic patient or the alcoholic.* They prefer chocolate and sweets rather than butter and meat. In fact, it had been shown that if you reduce natural opioids in the brain, carbohydrate intake rises markedly.

26. H. Begleiter, B. Porjesz, and C. L. Chou, Auditory brainstem potentials in chronic alcoholics, *Science* 211 (1981): 1064–66.

27. Other experiments on neurotransmission included:

- Back in 1965, knowing that the transmission of a nerve impulse from one cell to another involves the movement of sodium and potassium ions back and forth through the cell membrane, and is controlled by the enzyme sodium-potassium ATPase, Yedy Israel and Harold Kalant had set up an experiment that showed that alcohol inhibits the activity of this enzyme and tends to "shut off" the cell. Later, Kalant's group would show that this effect is increased in the presence of norepinephrine, suggesting a role for this neurotransmitter in alcoholism.

- It was also known that a substance called myo-Inositol 1-Phosphate, in turn, regulates the action of this ATPase enzyme on the other side of the synapse at the second neuronal membrane. A deficiency of the phosphate compound decreases the activity of the enzyme.

- James H. Allison and Theodore J. Cicero also found that alcohol decreases the activity of this substance. These related findings suggested that problems of nerve transmission across the synapse might be involved in alcohol intoxication.

- The neurotransmitter serotonin reentered the alcohol picture when Ryuji Fukomori of Japan found that when intoxicating doses of alcohol were injected into rats, the conversion of serotonin into its nonactive metabolite increased, thus reducing serotonin activity in the brain. This observation supported and partially explained Robert Myers' earlier finding that alcohol stimulates alcohol drinking; and the finding of Irving Geller, that the reduction of serotonin increases drinking behavior.

28. I. Sutton and M. A. Simmonds, Effects of acute and chronic ethanol on the gamma-aminobutyric acid system in rat brain, *Biochemical Pharmacology* 22 (1973): 1685–92.

29. J. Cott, A. Carlsson, J. Engel, and M. Lindquist, Suppression of ethanol-induced locomotor stimulation by GABA-like drugs, *Naunyn-Schmiedebergs Archives of Pharmacology* 295 (1976): 203–9.

30. M. K. Ticku and T. Burch, Alterations in gamma-aminobutyric acid receptor sensitivity following acute and chronic ethanol treatments, *Journal of Neurochemistry* 34 (1980): 417–23.

M. K. Ticku, The effects of acute and chronic ethanol administration and its withdrawal on gamma-aminobutyric acid receptor binding in rat brain, *British Journal of Pharmacology* 70 (1980): 403–10.

31. M. L. Barbaccia, A. Reggiani, P. F. Spano, and M. Trabucchi, Ethanol-induced changes of dopaminergic function in three strains of mice characterized by a different population of opiate receptors, *Psychopharmacologia* (Berlin) 74 (1981): 260–62.

32. K. Blum, A. H. Briggs, S. F. Elston, M. Hirst, M. G. Hamilton, and K. Vereby, A common denominator theory of alcohol and opiate dependence: review of similarities and differences, in H. Rigter and J. Crabbe eds., *Alcohol*

Tolerance and Dependence (Amsterdam and New York: Elsevier/North-Holland Biomedical Press, 1980), pp. 371–91.

33. I. S. Hoffman and L. X. Cubeddu, Presynaptic effects of tetrahydropapaveroline on striatal dopaminergic neurons, *Journal of Pharmacology and Experimental Therapeutics* 220 (1982): 16–22.

34. G. Mereu and G. L. Gessa, Low doses of ethanol inhibit the firing of neurons in the substantia nigra, pars reticulata: a GABAergic effect? *Brain Research* 360 (1985): 325–30.

35. P. D. Suzdak, J. R. Glowa, J. N. Crawley, R. D. Schwartz, P. Skolnick, and S. M. Paul, A selective Imidazobenzodiazepine antagonist of ethanol in the rat, *Science* 234 (1986): 1243–47.

36. G. Kolata, New drug counters alcohol intoxication, *Science* 234 (1986): 1198–99.

37. A. K. Mehta and M. K. Ticku, Chronic ethanol treatment alters the behavioral effects of Ro 15–4513, a partially negative ligand for benzodiazepine binding sites, *Brain Research* 489 (1989): 93–100. A problem with the drug recently pointed out by M. K. Ticku, is that the drug is a proconvulsant. That is, as the alcohol metabolizes in the body, convulsions are likely to occur.

D. J. Nutt, R. G. Lister, D. Rusche, E. P. Bonetti, R. E. Reese, and R. Rufener, Ro 15–4513 does not protect rats against the lethal effects of ethanol, *European Journal of Pharmacology* 151 (1988): 127–29; C. K. Erickson, Reviews and comments on alcohol research, *Alcohol* 6 (1989): 179–80. Nutt and his group found that the drug does not protect rats against the lethal effects of ethanol; Erickson reviewed the literature and found mixed reactions.

38. Y. Israel, E. Hurwitz, O. Niemela, and R. Arnon, Monoclonal and polyclonal antibodies against acetaldehyde-containing epitopes in acetaldehyde-protein adducts, *Proceedings of the National Academy of Sciences of the United States of America* 83 (1986): 7923–27.

39. A. Martin, R. Pilotto, G. Singer, and T. P. Oei, The suppression of ethanol self-injection by buprenorphine, *Pharmacology, Biochemistry and Behavior* 19 (1983): 985–86.

40. V. Borg, Bromocriptine in the prevention of alcohol absue, *Acta Psychiatrica Scandinavica* 68 (1983): 100–110.

41. The major evidence is as follows:
- In relation to intoxication, we had shown in my laboratory that serotonin augments loss of motor coordination and increases alcohol-induced sleep time in rodents.
- In relation to withdrawal, Dora Goldstein had found no evidence that serotonin has any effect; but in a later experiment in my laboratory we found that if serotonin receptors are blocked, alcohol-induced withdrawal

seizures are augmented, indicating a major role for this neurotransmitter in the addictive process.

- In relation to alcohol intake in animals, Robert Myers had found earlier that when brain serotonin is lowered by blocking its synthesis with PCPA, alcohol consumption is reduced. This view had been questioned, however, by Irving Geller who showed the exact opposite: that reduction of serotonin increases alcohol craving. Geller's view was later confirmed by further work in his laboratory, and by Myers, himself.
- Shirley Hill at the University of Washington in Seattle found that if animals receive serotonin, or its natural precursor 5-hydroxytryptophan, alcohol consumption is reduced. (S. Y. Hill, Intraventricular injection of 5-hydroxytryptamine and alcohol consumption in rats, *Biological Psychiatry* 8 [1974]: 151–58.)

42. A. Carlsson, J. Jonason, M. Lindquist, and K. Fuxe, Demonstration of extraneuronal 5-hydroxytryptamine accumulation in brain following membrane-pump blockade by chlorimipramine, *Brain Research* 12 (1969): 456–60.

43. S. B. Ross, S. O. Ogren, and A. L. Renyi, (Z)-Dimethyl-amino-1-(4-bromophenyl)-1-(3-pyridyl) propene (H102/09), a new selective inhibitor of neuronal 5-hydroxytryptamine uptake, *Acta Pharmacologica et Toxicologica* 39 (1976): 152–66.

44. G. E. Rockman, Z. Amit, G. Carr, Z. W. Brown, and S. O. Ogren, Attenuation of ethanol intake by 5-hydroxytryptamine uptake blockade in laboratory rats. I. Involvement of brain 5-hydroxytryptamine in the mediation of the positive reinforcing properties of ethanol. *Archives Internationales de Pharmacodynamie et de Thérapie* 241 (1979): 245–59.

45. C. A. Naranjo, E. M. Sellers, C. A. Roach, D. V. Woodley, M. Sanchez-Craig, and K. Sykora, Zimelidine-induced variations in alcohol intake by non-depressed heavy drinkers, *Clinical Pharmacology and Therapeutics* 35 (1983): 374–81.

46. P. Banys, The clinical use of disilfuram (Antabuse): a review, *Journal of Psychoactive Drugs* 20 (1988): 243–61.

47. E. C. Critcher and R. D. Myers, Cyanamide given ICV or systematically to the rat alters subsequent alcohol drinking, *Alcohol* 4 (1987): 347–53.

Chapter 11
Toward a Craving Model

1. A. Fox and B. Fox, *DLPA: To End Chronic Pain and Depression* (New York: Long Shadow Books, 1985), pp. 175.

2. K. Blum, M. C. Trachtenberg, and J. C. Ramsay, Improvement of inpatient treatment of the alcoholic as a function of neurotransmitter restoration: a pilot study, *International Journal of Addiction* 23 (1988): 991–98.

3. J. M. Murphy, W. J. McBride, L. Lumeng, and T.-K. Li. Alcohol preference

in regional brain monamine contents of N/NIH heterogeneous stock rats, *Alcohol and Drug Research* 7 (1986): 33–39.

4. J. M. Murphy, M. B. Waller, G. J. Gatto, W. J. McBride, L. Lumeng, and T.-K. Li, Effects of fluoxetine on the intragastric self-administration of ethanol in the alcohol-preferring P line of rats, *Alcohol* 5 (1988): 283–86.

5. D. A. Gorelick, Effect of fluoxetine on alcohol consumption, *Alcoholism: Clinical and Experimental Research* 10 (1986): 113.

6. C. Gianoulakis and A. Gupta, Inbred strains of mice with variable sensitivity to ethanol exhibit differences in the content and processing of beta-endorphin, *Life Sciences* 39 (1986): 2315–25. They first measured the level of pituitary and brain beta-endorphin in two forms: the acetylated, nonactive form, and the nonacetylated, active form. They found that:

- the nondrinking animals had a higher amount of the nonactive form of endorphin, and
- the drinking animals had a higher amount of the active form of endorphin.

After administering alcohol to the animals, they measured the amount of endorphin in the hypothalamus and the blood serum. They found that:

- the alcohol-preferring animals showed a reduction in the amount of beta-endorphin in the hypothalamus, and an increase in the blood serum, and
- alcohol had no effect on the level of beta-endorphin in either the hypothalamus or blood of the non-alcohol-preferring animals.

This reduction of beta-endorphin in the hypothalamus of the alcohol-preferring animals, and the accompanying increase in their blood serum, indicated that alcohol was causing a neuronal release of endorphin from the hypothalamus into the blood.

C. Gianoulakis, J. Thavundayl, V. Tawar, M. Dumas, and L. Geller, Differences in the response of the pituitary beta-endorphin to an acute ethanol challenge in individuals with and without a family history of alcoholism, *Alcoholism: Clinical and Experimental Research* 11 (1987): 199. On the day of testing, blood samples were taken at 9:00 A.M., after which both groups were given alcohol. Blood samples were then taken at intervals, and the amount of beta-endorphin was measured.

- Before alcohol ingestion, blood tests showed that the high-risk group had a lower beta-endorphin level than the low-risk group.
- After alcohol ingestion, the high-risk group showed a 170 percent increase in beta-endorphin; the low-risk group showed just the opposite—a slight decrease.

This result in humans reinforced their findings in animals discussed above; that is, high-risk human beings with a family history of alcoholism react the same as black mice with a family history of alcoholism.

7. K. Blum and A. H. Briggs, Opioid peptides and genotypic responses to ethanol, *Biogenic Amines* 5 (1988): 527–33.

8. D. Sapun-Malcolm, J. M. Farah, Jr., and G. P. Mueller, Serotonin and dopamine independently regulate pituitary beta-endorphin release in vivo, *Neuroendocrinology* 42 (1986): 191–96.

9. J. P. Schwartz and I. Mocchetti, Pharmacological studies on the regulation of biosynthesis of enkephalin, in C. Shagass, R. C. Josiassen, R. H. Bridger, K. J. Weiss, D. Stoff, and G. M. Simpson, eds., *Biological Psychiatry 1985: Proceedings of the IVth World Congress of Biological Psychiatry held from September 8th through 13th, 1985, in Philadelphia, Pennsylvania, U.S.A.* (New York: Elsevier, 1986), pp. 284–86.

10. E. R. Korpi, J. D. Sinclair, and O. Malminen, Dopamine D2 receptor binding in striatal membranes of rat lines selected for differences in alcohol-related behaviours, *Pharmacology and Toxicology* 61 (1987): 94–97.

11. L. Stein and J. Belluzzi, Second messengers, natural reward and drugs of abuse, *Clinical Neuropharmacology* 9 (1986) Suppl. 4: 205–7.

12. These individual findings seem simple, but the complexity of their interactions is enormous. In a paper prepared for the 25th Anniversary Anthology of the American College of Neuropsychopharmacology, Stein reviewed the neurochemistry of reward. In a very brief summary, he said that reward is a series of events initially activated by dopamine at the dopamine 2 receptor, causing a burst of firing associated with strong calcium penetration into the neuron. The calcium then interacts with "second-messenger" chemicals which cause the release of a neurotransmitter into the synaptic fluid, ready to activate the receptor in the adjacent dendrite.

13. S. Liljequist, Changes in the sensitivity of dopamine receptors in the nucleus accumbens and in the striatum induced by chronic ethanol administration, *Acta Pharmacologica et Toxicologica* 43 (1978): 19–28; K. Blum, J. D. Eubanks, J. E. Wallace, and H. A. Schwertner, Suppression of ethanol withdrawal by dopamine, *Experientia* 32 (1976): 493–95; K. Blum, J. E. Wallace, H. A. Schwertner, and J. D. Eubanks, Morphine suppression of ethanol withdrawal in mice, *Experientia* 32 (1976): 79–82.

14. A. R. Gintzler, A. Levy, and S. Spector, Antibodies as a means of isolating and characterizing biologically active substances: presence of a non-peptide, morphine-like compound in the central nervous system, *Proceedings of the National Academy of Sciences of the United States of America* 73 (1976): 2132–36; K. Oka, J. D. Kantrowitz, and S. Spector, Isolation of morphine from toad skin, *Proceedings of the National Academy of Sciences of the United States of America* 82 (1985):1852–54.

15. G. J. Cardinale, J. Donnerer, A. D. Finck, J. D. Kantrowitz, K. Oka, and S. Spector, Morphine and codeine are endogenous components of human cerebrospinal fluid, *Life Sciences* 40 (1987): 301–6.

16. M. Hirst, D. R. Evans, and C. W. Gowdey, Salsolinol in urine following chocolate consumption by social drinkers, *Alcohol and Drug Research* 7 (1987):

493–501. This experiment by Maurice Hirst and his associates demonstrated a curious fact: the brain can produce TIQs not only from alcohol, but also from chocolate! They found that chocolate contains 6 micrograms of the TIQ salsolinol per gram of weight. They gave varying amounts of chocolate to human volunteers, and found that the amount of salsolinol in the urine varied in direct ratio to the amount of chocolate the individual had consumed.

Since it is known that morphine can be derived from TIQs, this finding provided a possible explanation of the commonly observed "chocaholic," the person who has an abnormal craving for chocolate; and for the tendency of many alcoholics to consume large quantities of chocolate between binges and during recovery. Adult children of alcoholics who have not developed a pattern of heavy drinking are also inclined to overindulge in chocolate.

17. A. S. Gordon, K. Collier, and I. Diamond, Ethanol regulation of adenosine receptor-stimulated cAMP levels in a clonal neural cell line: an in vitro model of cellular tolerance to ethanol, *Proceedings of the National Academy of Sciences of the United States of America* 83 (1986): 2105–8.

18. I. Diamond, B. Wrubel, W. Estrin, and A. Gordon, Basal and adenosine receptor-stimulated levels of cAMP are reduced in lymphocytes from alcoholic patients, *Proceedings of the National Academy of Sciences of the United States of America* 84 (1987): 1413–16. Diamond's group studied cyclic AMP levels in the lymphocytes of two groups of age- and sex-matched human subjects: one group made up of chronic alcoholics, the other of normal individuals. They looked at lymphocytes because these blood cells have the same characteristics as nerve cells.

They found that:

- lymphocytes from alcoholics showed nearly a fourfold reduction in the amount of cyclic AMP naturally present in comparison to normal subjects.
- a similar reduction was found when adenosine was added to the lymphocytes of the alcoholic subjects. This was in contrast to an increase in cyclic AMP production when adenosine was added to the lymphocytes of nonalcoholics.
- when alcohol was added to the lymphocytes of the alcoholics, cyclic AMP production was increased, but only 24 percent as much as in normal subjects.

19. E. Costa and A. Guidotti, Molecular mechanisms in the receptor action of benzodiazepines, *Annual Review of Pharmacology and Toxicology* 19 (1979): 531–45.

20. E. Costa, Future trends of research in benzodiazepine-beta carboline-3-carboxylate ester recognition sites and their endogenous ligands, in B. Biggio and E. Costa eds., *GABAergic Transmission and Anxiety* (New York: Raven Press, 1986), pp. 239–42. (Advances in Biochemical Psychopharmacology, vol.41.) When GABA binds to its receptor it increases chloride ion conductance

into the neuron, decreasing neuronal firing and reducing anxiety. They suggested that when beta-carboline binds to its receptors it decreases GABA's effect on chloride ion conductance, increasing neuronal firing and increasing anxiety. They suggested, also, that benzodiazepines such as Librium have the opposite effect; they increase GABA activity, which tends to open the chloride ion channels, decreasing neuronal firing, and reducing anxiety.

21. J. Bormann, P. Ferrero, A. Guidotti, and E. Costa, Neuropeptide modulation of GABA receptor Cl-channel, *Regulatory Peptides* (1985) Suppl. 4: 33–38; E. Costa and A. Guidotti, Neuropeptides are cotransmitters: modulatory effects of GABAergic synapses, in H. Y. Meltzer ed., *Psychopharmacology: The Third Generation of Progress* (New York: Raven Press, 1987), pp. 425–35; P. Ferrero, B. Conti-Tronconi, and A. Guidotti, DBI, an anxiogenic neuropeptide found in human brain, in G. Biggio and E. Costa eds., *GABAergic Transmission and Anxiety* (New York: Raven Press, 1986), 177–85. (Advances in Biochemical Psychopharmacology, vol. 41.)

22. P. Huttunen and R. D. Myers, Anatomical localization in hippocampus of tetrahydro-Beta-carboline-induced alcohol drinking in the rat, *Alcohol* 4 (1987): 181–87.

23. Myers found that the amount of the consumption varied widely, depending on the precise location of the injection in the hippocampus. Fifteen percent of the animals injected in one area of the hippocampus showed an increased intake over their pre-injection level, or baseline. Injections at another site caused an increase in 75 percent of the animals. So marked was this geographical distribution that Myers was able to pinpoint the area that produced the most profound result.

24. H. Alho, M. Miyata, E. Korpi, K. Kiianmaa and A. Guidotti, Studies of a brain polypeptide functioning as a putative endogenous ligand to benzodiazepine recognition sites in rats selectively bred for alcohol-related behavior, *Alcohol and Alcoholism* (1987) Suppl. 1:637–41.

25. D. M. Collins and R. D. Myers, Buspirone attenuates volitional alcohol intake in the chronically drinking monkey, *Alcohol* 4 (1987): 49–56.

26. At first glance, Myers' finding might make it appear that the reduction of anxiety and aggressiveness by buspirone is due to its direct stimulation of serotonin, dopamine, and norepinephrine. But a closer look suggests that the mechanism is more complex:

- In the hippocampus, under normal circumstances, norepinephrine is stimulated by GABA A receptors.
- When that occurs there is a feeling of well-being.
- If beta-carboline is present, it interferes with the action of GABA A receptors, resulting in reduced norepinephrine release and feelings of anxiety, aggression, and/or craving behavior.
- Buspirone overcomes the action of beta-carboline by directly stimulating

norepinephrine, bypassing the GABA A receptor, and restoring feelings of well-being.

These results suggest a direct link between buspirone and craving, and an indirect linkage between norepinephrine, GABA, and craving.

27. M. Daoust, J. P. Lhuintre, C. Saligaut, N. Moore, J. L. Flipo, and F. Boismare, Noradrenaline and GABA brain receptors are co-involved in the voluntary intake of ethanol by rats, *Alcohol and Alcoholism* (1987) Suppl. 1:319–22. The Daoust group first showed that calcium bis acetylhomotaurine, a GABA A receptor agonist, reduced alcohol craving, and that this effect could be blocked by the GABA antagonist bicuculline, restoring craving. They then used a substance called metapramine, known to release norepinephrine from its neuron, and showed that this substance, also, reduced alcohol intake. Finally, they showed that this second reaction could be blocked by bicuculline.

28. Typical of the negative reports we found on the effect of naloxone were:

In France, D. P. Miceli and associates reported failure of naloxone to influence alcohol-induced tolerance in rats. H. A. Jorgensen and K. Hole, at the University of Bergen, Norway, found that naloxone in rats failed to alter the effect of alcohol on body temperature and sleep. John Ewing and associates at the University of North Carolina reported that naloxone failed to alter the euphoric response of humans to alcohol.

Typical of the positive reports on the effect of naloxone were:

In England, R. Bruce Holman and associates at the University of Reading examined the effects of naloxone on the alcohol-induced increase in dopamine release in the striatum of the brain. They found that naloxone blocked this increase.

Peter S. Widdowson and R. Bruce Holman set up an experiment to see specifically where the narcotic blocking effect was taking place. Naloxone was known to block enkephalin at both the mu and delta sites, so they used a different antagonist—ICI 174864—that operates only at the delta enkephalin site. When they repeated the first experiment with the new antagonist and found that the alcohol-induced increase in dopamine was blocked, they knew that the effect was taking place specifically at the delta site. Holman said:

> We have proposed from these experiments that alcohol increases release not by a direct action on the dopamine neuron but through the release of an endogenous delta opioid agonist, possibly met-enkephalin, to modulate dopamine activity.

Joseph R. Volpicelli at the University of Pennsylvania found that alcohol drinking increases after laboratory animals are subjected to inescapable electrical shocks. When he injected the narcotic antagonist naltrexone, he found that the alcohol intake was completely blocked. His conclusion was that the shocks cause a depletion of endorphins which leads to craving behavior. The naltrexone blocks the reinforcing effects of alcohol-derived TIQs at the opiate receptor sites.

Chapter 12
The Reward Cascade

1. C. Heidbreder, B. Roques, J. J. Vanderhaeghen, and P. De Witte, Kelatorphan, a potent enkephalinase inhibitor, presents opposite properties when injected intracerebroventricularly or into the nucleus accumbens on intracranial
self-stimulation, *Neurochemistry International,* 12 (1988): 347–50. The results
of this experiment are reminiscent of the experiment by Reid mentioned earlier
in which he found that small doses of morphine injected into peripheral parts
of the body increased alcohol craving. This result contradicted substantial evidence that larger doses of morphine in the reward area reduce craving for
alcohol. The probable explanation is that small amounts of morphine increase
craving for alcohol; larger amounts reduce it.

2. G. Spinosa, E. Perlanski, F. H. H. Leenen, R. B. Stewart, and L. A.
Grupp, Angiotensin converting enzyme inhibitors: animal experiments suggest
a new pharmacological treatment for alcohol abuse in humans, *Alcoholism:
Clinical and Experimental Research,* 12 (1988): 65–70.

The idea of using anti-enkephalinase chemicals as anti-craving agents was
intriguing. If enkephalinase could be prevented from destroying enkephalin,
perhaps the craving for alcohol could be reduced. To test that hypothesis,
Larry Grupp and associates at the University of Toronto used captopril and
enalapril on rats, and found that these anti-hypertensive drugs significantly
reduced their alcohol intake.

Both of the drugs, called "angiotensin converting enzyme inhibitors," were
developed to control blood pressure, but they also inhibit the enkephalin-destroying enzyme enkephalinase. Grupp commented:

> The experiments . . . suggest that [these drugs] may provide a promising
> new pharmacological treatment for human alcohol abuse and merit a clinical
> trial . . . to assess this possibility. In view of the well-documented finding
> that a significant number of alcoholics and heavy drinkers are hypertensive
> and use anti-hypertensive medication, the intriguing possibility arises that
> one and the same medication might be useful in treating both the drinking
> problem and the hypertensive state.

3. V. A. Russel, M. C. L. Lamm, and J. J. F. Taljaard, Effect of ethanol
on [3H] dopamine release in rat nucleus accumbens and striatal slices, *Neurochemical Research* 13 (1988): 487, 492. An experiment by V. A. Russel and associates
at the University of Stellenbosch in the Republic of South Africa threw new
light on the ability of alcohol to produce an initial and temporary enhancement
of pleasure. The group found that alcohol can cause a release of dopamine
directly in the nucleus accumbens. This is in contrast to the earlier view that
alcohol causes dopamine release in this area indirectly; for example, by offsetting
the inhibitory action of GABA in the reward area, thereby releasing dopamine.
The finding does not invalidate the theory of the alcohol/GABA interaction;
it merely shows that other direct effects of alcohol also take place.

4. The following facts provided the impetus for the experiment by Banks and Kastin:

- Alcohol and its metabolic by-products act on opiate receptors to interfere with brain enkephalins.
- Alcoholics have lower concentrations of opioid peptides in their cerebral spinal fluid than normal individuals.
- Alcohol intake, or a genetic predisposition to drinking, is associated with low concentrations of enkephalins in the brain.
- Increasing of the enkephalin supply by direct administration of enkephalins reduces voluntary alcohol intake in alcohol-preferring animals.
- Protecting enkephalin supplies by preventing their destruction by enkephalinase reduces voluntary alcohol intake in alcohol-preferring animals.

5. W. A. Banks and A. J. Kastin, Inhibition of the brain-to-blood transport system for enkephalins and Tyr-MIF-1 in mice addicted or genetically predisposed to drinking ethanol, *Alcohol* 6 (1989): 53–57. Into the mouse brains the investigators injected a radioactive substance called Tyr-MIF-1, a natural peptide which uses the same transport carrier systems as enkephalins. Whatever happened to this substance at the blood/brain barrier presumably would happen to enkephalins as well. At intervals after the injection they measured the radioactivity remaining in the brains. The decline in the readings showed the amount of radioactive material that had been transported out of the brain into the blood. Tyr-MIF-1 was transported out of the brains of the alcohol-hating DBA mice faster than it was from the brains of the two alcohol-loving types.

6. On the morning of the tenth day, half of the alcohol-drinking mice were switched to sucrose to elicit a withdrawal response; the other half remained on alcohol. Nine hours later the enkephalin transport rate was determined in all three groups. The findings were:

- In the mice that had received sucrose, half of the radioactive Tyr-MIF-1 was transported from the brain to the blood in 11.8 minutes.
- In the withdrawal group, half of the material was transported in 11.0 minutes.
- In the group that remained on alcohol, half of the material was transported in 18 minutes.

7. W. A. Banks and A. J. Kastin, Effect of neurotransmitters on the system that transports Tyr-MIF-1 and the enkephalins across the blood-brain barrier: a dominant role for serotonin, *Psychopharmacology* 98 (1989): 380–85.

8. L. Lucchi, R. M. Maresco, S. Govoni, and M. Trabucchi, Effect of chronic ethanol treatment on dopamine receptor subtypes in rat striatum, *Brain Research* 449 (1988): 347–51. In the experiment, they forced one group of rats to drink a 6 percent ethanol solution as their only fluid for 25 days. A control group was forced to drink a sucrose solution that had similar amounts of calories. At the end of the 25-day period, both groups were sacrificed, and neuronal membranes were extracted from an area of the brain known to be rich in

dopamine D2 receptors. To each batch of material they then added a dopamine agonist and a radioactive dopamine antagonist. Using a scintillation counter for measurement, they found that fewer of the agonist molecules had bound to dopamine D2 receptors in the brain material derived from alcohol-drinking rats than in similar material from non-alcohol-drinking rats, which meant that fewer of these receptors were present.

9. Ivan Diamond's earlier experiment had shown that short-term alcohol exposure stimulates cyclic AMP activity, but as exposure continues the activity diminishes. Indeed, long-term exposure may lead to inhibition below normal levels. This stimulation of cyclic AMP was known to be due, in part, to the action of the dopamine D1 receptor. Lucci's results helped to explain Diamond's original findings, and further suggested that the reduction of dopamine D1 binding sites could be responsible for the virtual disappearance of alcohol's short-term stimulatory effect on cyclic AMP activity.

10. For a brief overview of second-messenger activity, let us first take a "walk through" the components of one cyclic AMP second-messenger system that is receptor-activated. The key components are:

- a neuroactive agent (adenosine)
- a receptor (dopamine 1 or dopamine 2)
- a nucleotide complex (a guanine nucleotide component)
- regulatory enzymes (catalytic units of adenylate cyclase, phosphodiesterase, protein kinase, phosphoprotein, and phosphatase)
- phosphylated nucleotides (GTP, GDP, ATP, cAMP, and AMP)
- calcium ion channels
- dephosphorylated proteins that shut off the calcium ion channels and bring the system to rest.

These components interact in complex patterns to carry out the work within the neuron and across the synapse at the adjacent dendrite.

For a scenario of one action sequence in one system:

- When the neuroactive agent adenosine stimulates a dopamine 1 receptor, the guanine nucleotide regulatory component called "guanine stimulatory" complex (GS) is activated. This activation leads to the removal by hydrolysis (water action) of a phosphate from the triphosphate GTP to leave the diphosphate GDP.
- When this occurs the enzyme adenylate cyclase is activated and it, in turn, causes the hydrolysis of another triphosphate, ATP, to cyclic AMP.
- Cyclic AMP activates the enzyme protein kinase until its action is brought to rest by the enzyme phosphodiesterase, which converts cyclic AMP to AMP.
- During its period of activity, protein kinase aids in phosphylating proteins that open calcium ion channels to increase calcium action in the neuron, leading to a biological response such as the release of a neurotransmitter from the axon bulb.

- These calcium ion channels can be closed by the action of an enzyme called phosphoprotein phosphatase which dephosphorylates the proteins.

D. Mochly-Rosen, F.-H. Chang, L. Cheever, M. Kim, I. Diamond, and A. S. Gordon, Chronic ethanol causes heterologous desensitization of receptors by reducing alpha messenger RNA, *Nature* 333 (1989): 848–50. In a key experiment that illustrates the effect of alcohol on second-messenger responses, Ivan Diamond and his group at the Ernest Gallo Clinic in San Francisco exposed neural culture cells to alcohol for 48 hours, then measured cyclic AMP and messenger RNA activity in a specific site in the neuron involved in the manufacture of cyclic AMP. The site chosen was the alpha subunit of the guanine nucleotide stimulatory protein Gs.

They found that alcohol had decreased the amount of this subunit by 29 percent. Furthermore, they found that alcohol had reduced the activity of the messenger RNA that *makes* the subunit by 30 percent.

The significance of these findings is that long-term alcohol abuse reduces the formation and activity of this protein, causing a reduction of activity in the cyclic AMP second-messenger system, resulting in reduced neural firing.

The findings also help to explain the fact that in the alcoholic there is a marked lowering of cyclic AMP activity in the lymphocytes as was earlier discovered by Diamond's group. This bears on the phenomenon of tolerance in which, over time, more and more alcohol must be drunk to feel the "high." In extreme cases, alcohol intake eventually leads to dysphoria, a condition in which drinking makes the alcoholic feel worse instead of better.

11. B. Tabakoff, P. L. Hoffman, J. N. Lee, T. Saito, D. Willard, and F. De Leon-Jones, Differences in platelet enzyme activity between alcoholics and non-alcoholics, *New England Journal of Medicine* 318 (1988): 134–39.

12. T. M. Worner and C. S. Lieber, Plasma glutamate dehydrogenase: a marker of alcoholic liver injury, *Pharmacology, Biochemistry, and Behavior* 13 (1980) Suppl. 1: 107–10; T. M. Worner and Charles S. Lieber demonstrated that the presence of high levels of the enzyme glutamate dehydrogenase in the blood indicated severe liver damage due to alcohol. The greater the liver damage, the higher the level of the enzyme.

A. Konttinen, G. Hartel, and A. Louhija, Multiple serum enzyme analyses in chronic alcoholics, *Acta Medica Scandinavica* 188 (1970): 257–64. The presence of high levels of the enzyme gamma glutamyl transpeptidase (GGTP) in the plasma was found by A. Konttinen and associates to be correlated with alcoholism.

H. Stibler and O. Sydow, Quantitative estimation of abnormal microheterogeneity of serum transferrin in alcoholics, *Pharmacology, Biochemistry and Behavior* 13 (1980) Suppl. 1: 47–51. Helena Stibler and her group found an abnormal form of transferrin in the cerebral spinal fluid of alcoholics. Later, they learned that this change in transferrin is brought about by alcohol, and suggested that the abnormality might be used as a marker to identify heavy drinkers.

13. K. Blum and H. Topel, Opioid peptides and alcoholism: genetic deficiency and chemical management, *Estratto da: New Trends in Funcitonal Neurology* 1 (1986): 71–83.

14. K. Matsubara, A. Akane, C. Maseda, S. Takahashi, and Y. Fuki, Salsolinol in the urine of non-alcoholic individuals after long-term moderate drinking, *Alcohol and Drug Research* 6 (1986): 281–88.

15. B. Sjoquist, S. Borg, and H. Kvande, Catecholamine derived compounds in urine and cerebral spinal fluid from alcoholics during and after long-standing intoxication, *Substance and Alcohol Actions/Misuse* 2 (1981): 63–72; B. Sjoquist, S. Borg, and H. Kvande, Salsolinol and methylated salsolinol in urine and cerebral spinal fluid in healthy volunteers, *Substance and Alcohol Actions/Misuse* 2 (1981): 73–77.

16. W. D. Myers, L. MacKenzie, K. T. Ng, G. Singer, G. A. Smythe, and M. W. Duncan, Salsolinol and dopamine in rat medial basal hypothalamus after chronic ethanol exposure, *Life Sciences* 36 (1985): 309–14.

17. W. D. Myers, K. T. Ng, G. Singer, G. A. Smythe, and M. W. Duncan, Dopamine and salsolinol levels in rat hypothalamus and striatum after schedule-induced self-injection (SISI) of ethanol and acetaldehyde, *Brain Research* 358 (1985): 122–28.

18. B. A. Faraj, V. M. Camp, D. C. Davis, J. D. Lenton, and M. Kutner, Elevation of plasma salsolinol sulfate in chronic alcoholics as compared to non-alcoholics, *Alcoholism: Clinical and Experimental Research* 13 (1989): 155–63.

19. A. L. von Knorring, M. Bohman, L. von Knorring, and L. Oreland, Platelet MAO activity in subgroups of alcoholism, *Acta Psychiatrica Scandinavica* 72 (1985): 51–58. This conclusion was borne out by an experiment carried out by A. L. von Knorring in Sweden. The data showed that Cloninger's Type II alcoholics—those with a high rate of heritability—have a low level of monoamine oxidase activity.

20. K. Blum, A commentary on neurotransmitter restoration as a common mode of treatment for alcohol, cocaine and opiate abuse, *Integrative Psychiatry* 6 (1989): 199–204; K. Blum and G. P. Kozlowski, Ethanol and neuromodulator interactions: a cascade model of reward, in H. Ollat, S. Parvez, and H. Parvez, eds., *Alcohol and Behavior,* vol. 2 (Utrecht, Netherlands: VSP Press, 1990), pp. 131–49.

21. W. J. McBride, et al., Regional differences in the density of serotonin 1A receptors between P and NP rats, *Alcoholism: Clinical and Experimental Research* 14 (1990): 316. F. C. Zhou, et al., Serotonergic immunostriatal terminal fibers are decreased in selected brain areas of alcohol-preferring P rats, *Alcoholism: Clinical and Experimental Research* 14 (1990): 555; H. Hwang, et al., Increased number of GABAergic terminals in the nucleus accumbens is associated with

alcohol-preferring P rats, *Alcoholism: Clinical and Experimental Research* (in press, 1990).

22. K. Blum, M. C. Trachtenberg, C. E. Elliot, M. L. Dingler, R. L. Sexton, A. I. Samuels, and L. Cataldie, Enkephalinase inhibition and precursor amino acid loading improved inpatient treatment of alcohol and polydrug abusers: double-blind placebo-controlled study of the nutritional adjunct SAAVE™, *Alcohol* 5 (1988): 481–93.

23. R. J. Brown, K. Blum, and M. C. Trachtenberg, Neurodynamics of relapse prevention: a neuronutrient approach to outpatient DUI offenders, *Journal of Psychoactive Drugs* 22 (1990): 173–87.

24. D. J. Clauw, D. J. Nashel, A. Umhau, and P. Katz, Trytophan associated eosinophilic connective-tissue disease: a new clinical category? *Journal of the American Medical Association* 263 (1990): 1502–6.

Chapter 13
Alcogenes

1. J. H. Mendelson, Alcohol abuse and alcohol-related illness, in P. B. Beeson and W. McDermott eds., *Textbook of Medicine,* 14th edition (Philadelphia: W. B. Saunders, 1975), p. 597.

2. L. Lumeng, T. D. Hawkins, and T.-K. Li, New strains of rats with alcohol preference and non-preference, in R. G. Thurman, J. R. Williamson, H. Drott, and B. Chance, eds. *Alcohol and Aldehyde Metabolizing Systems,* vol. 3 (Academic Press, New York, 1977), pp. 537–544.

3. M. B. Waller, W. J. McBride, G. J. Gatto, L. Lumeng, and T.-K. Li, Intragastric self-infusion of ethanol by ethanol-preferring and non-preferring rats, *Science* 225 (1984): 78–80.

4. M. A. Schuckit, D. W. Goodwin, and G. Winokur, A study of alcoholism in half-siblings, *American Journal of Psychiatry* 128 (1972): 1132–36.

5. D. W. Goodwin, F. Schulsinger, L. Hermansen, S. B. Guz, and G. Winokur, Alcohol problems in adoptees raised apart from alcoholic biological parents, *Archives of General Psychiatry* 28 (1973): 238–43.

6. M. Bohman, Some genetic aspects of alcoholism and criminality: a population of adoptees, *Archives of General Psychiatry* 35 (1978): 269–76. Bohman then made a detailed study of 192 individuals selected from the main sample. The ones chosen had parents with serious records of alcohol abuse: 50 men and 50 women had fathers who were alcoholic; 42 men and 50 women had mothers who were alcoholic. He found that male adoptees with severely alcoholic fathers had a 20 percent incidence of alcohol abuse, compared with 6 percent in those of nonalcoholic parents. Also:

N. S. Cotton, The familial incidence of alcoholism, *Journal of Studies in Alcoholism* 40 (1979): 89–96. Cotton reviewed 39 studies on the heredity of alcoholism that had been carried out since the late 1930s. The review data covered families of 6,251 alcoholics and 4,083 nonalcoholics. Cotton concluded from the studies that alcoholics were more likely than nonalcoholics to have an alcoholic father, mother, sibling, or distant relative. Almost one-third of any sample of alcoholics had at least one parent who was alcoholic.

7. C. R. Cloninger, M. Bohman, and S. Sigvardsson, Inheritance of alcohol abuse, *Archives of General Psychiatry* 38 (1981): 861–68.

8. M. Bohman, S. Sigvardsson, and C. R. Cloninger, Maternal inheritance of alcohol abuse: cross-fostering analysis of adopted women, *Archives of General Psychiatry* 38 (1981): 965–69.

9. C. R. Cloninger, Genetic and environmental factors in the development of alcoholism, *Journal of Psychiatric Treatment Evaluation* 5 (1983): 487–96.

10. M. Irwin, M. Schuckit, and T. L. Smith, Clinical importance of age at onset in Type I and Type II primary alcoholics, *Archives of General Psychiatry* 47 (1990): 320–23.

11. H. Begleiter, B. Porgesz, B. Bihari, and B. Kissin, Event-related brain potentials in boys at risk for alcoholism, *Science* 225 (1984): 1493–95.

R. Elmasian, H. Neville, D. Woods, M. Schuckit, and F. E. Bloom, Event-related brain potentials are different in individuals at high and low risk for developing alcoholism, *Proceedings of the National Academy of Sciences of the United States of America* 79 (1982): 7900–7903. An earlier experiment by Helen J. Neville and associates at the Salk Institute in San Diego, using a similar technique, also suggested a link between the P3 wave deficit and children at risk. They studied 30 young men, half of whom had alcoholic fathers, and half of whom had no family history of alcoholism. None was alcoholic. After alcohol or a placebo was administered, their P3 brain waves were recorded. Significant differences were found in the amplitude and shape of the P3 waves of the sons of alcoholics compared to those of the sons of nonalcoholics, regardless of whether alcohol was administered or not.

12. S. F. A. Elston, K. Blum, L. DeLallo, and A. H. Briggs, Ethanol intoxication as a function of genotype dependent responses in three inbred mice strains, *Pharmacology, Biochemistry and Behavior* 16 (1982): 13–15.

13. M. A. Schuckit, Subjective responses to alcohol in sons of alcoholics and control subjects, *Archives of General Psychiatry* 41 (1984): 879–84.

14. M. A. Schuckit, Ethanol-induced changes in body sway in men at high alcoholism risk, *Archives of General Psychology* 42 (1985): 375–79.

15. The alcoholic fathers of the subjects had abstained from drinking for a minimum of two years; none of the mothers was alcoholic, and their intake of alcohol during pregnancy had not exceeded two drinks per week. The average age of the boys was ten years, and none of them had drunk alcohol or used illicit drugs. There were no significant environmental differences among the members of the three groups in education, economics, and marital status.

The electroencephalograph detected changes called "event-related potentials" (ERP), and recorded them as an electroencephalogram. The two electrical tests were: (1) the ability to see a match between the two sets of stimuli; and (2) the magnitude of response to the stimuli. A third, behavioral, test evaluated visual perception and memory in the three groups.

16. S. C. Whipple, E. S. Parker, and E. P. Noble, An atypical neurocognitive profile in alcoholic fathers and their sons, *Journal of Studies in Alcoholism* 49 (1988): 240–44.

17. M. A. Schuckit, N. Butters, L. Lyn, and M. Irwin, Neuropsychologic deficits and the risk for alcoholism, *Neuropsychopharmacology* 1 (1987): 45–53. In this 1987 study of children of alcoholics, Marc Schuckit and his associates were unable to confirm the findings of neurocognitive behavioral differences between sons of alcoholics and sons of nonalcoholics. His experiment involved students in their late teens and early twenties who were attending medical school. Schuckit remarked:

> It is tempting to speculate on the reasons for differences between our and other reports in the literature which showed neurocognitive deficits. The population reported here was taken from students who had a relatively high level of functioning. This could mean that those children with the greatest level of cognitive impairment would have been excluded from testing. . . . However, it would seem unlikely that any specific array of neurocognitive or psychomotive test results will, in the near future, prove to be a clinically relative general marker of risk of alcoholism.

18. K. W. Schaeffer, O. A. Parsons, and A. Errico, Abstracting deficits in childhood conduct disorders as a function of familial alcoholism, *Alcohol: Clinical and Experimental Research* 12 (1988): 612–18.

19. M. A. Schuckit, E. Gold, and C. Risch, Serum prolactin levels in sons of alcoholics and control subjects, *American Journal of Psychiatry* 144 (1987): 854–59. In the experiment they tested prolactin response to alcohol in 30 healthy sons of alcoholics and, as a control, 30 matched sons who had no family history of psychiatric problems, or drug or alcohol abuse. None of the subjects indulged in more than social drinking. Each individual was tested three times, receiving in random order a placebo, a small dose of alcohol, and a larger dose.

20. K. Blum, E. P. Noble, P. J. Sheridan, A. Montgomery, T. Ritchie, P. Jagadeeswaran, H. Nogami, A. H. Briggs, and J. B. Cohn, Allelic association of human dopamine D2 receptor gene in alcoholism, *Journal of the American Medical Association* 263 (1990): 2055–67. The paper included the following caveats:

- The sample was small compared to typical molecular genetic studies using white blood cells from living individuals as a source of DNA.

- The results suggested that other genes as well as nongenetic factors may be involved in this form and other forms of alcoholism.
- Additional research is needed on living alcoholics and their relatives, using white blood cells, from large pedigrees, as well as from unrelated individuals of several different racial and ethnic groups.
- The findings do not imply that the dopamine D2 receptor gene probe is the only antecedent to alcoholism, and without further research cannot be used as a diagnostic tool for determining risk of alcoholism.
- The defect discovered may not be directly related to the dopamine D2 gene, but to some other mutation located nearby on the chromosome.

21. E. P. Noble, K. Blum, T. Ritchie, A. Montgomery, and P. J. Sheridan, Allelic association of the D2 dopamine receptor gene with receptor binding characteristics in alcoholism, unpublished paper.

J. A. Severson, P. K. Randall, and C. E. Finch, Genotypic influences on striatal dopamine regulation in mice, Brain Research 210 (1981): 201–15. These authors found that alcohol-loving C57 black mice had 50 percent fewer dopamine D2 receptors compared to alcohol-hating DBA mice.

E. R. Korpi, J. D. Sinclair, and O. Malminen, Dopamine D2 receptor binding in striatal membrane of rat lines selected for differences of alcohol-related behaviors, Pharmacology and Toxicology 61 (1987) 94–97. Korpi and associates in Finland showed that alcohol-preferring rats had significantly fewer dopamine D2 receptors than alcohol-hating rats.

Chapter 14
The Addictive Brain: Hope for a Cure

1. Supreme Court of the United States, Traynor v. Turnage, Administrator, Veterans Administration et al., and McKelvey v. Turnage, Administrator, Veterans Administration et al., 108 SCt 1372, 99 (1988).

2. G. A. Marlatt, The controlled-drinking controversy: a commentary, American Psychologist 38 (1983): 1097–1100.

3. D. L. Davies, Normal drinking in recovered alcohol addicts, Quartery Journal of Studies on Alcohol 23 (1962): 94–104.

4. G. Edwards, A later followup of a classic case series: D. L. Davies' 1962 report and its significance for the present, Journal of Studies on Alcohol 46 (1985): 181–90.

5. M. B. Sobell and L. C. Sobell, Alcoholics treated by individualized behavior therapy: one year treatment outcome, Behaviour Research and Therapy 11 (1973): 599–618. M. B. Sobell and L. C. Sobell, Second year treatment outcome of alcoholics treated by individualized behavior therapy: results, Behaviour Research and Therapy 14 (1976): 195–215.

6. H. Fingarette, *Heavy Drinking: The Myth of Alcoholism as a Disease* (Berkeley: University of California Press, 1988), p. 125.

7. M. L. Pendery, I. M. Maltzman, and J. L. West, Controlled drinking by alcoholics? New findings and a re-evaluation of a major affirmative study, *Science* 217 (1982): 169–75.

8. D. J. Armor, J. M. Polich, and H. B. Stambul, *Alcoholism and Treatment* (New York: John Wiley, 1978).

9. M. E. Chafetz, Alcoholism report draws overreaction, *Rochester Democrat and Chronicle*, Sunday, August 15, 1986;

10. E. P. Noble, Announcement on Rand Report, *HEW NEWS*, Washington, June 23, 1976.

11. J. Wallace, Waging the war for wellness, part 2, *Professional Counselor* 1 (1987): 21–27.

12. S. Peele, Ain't misbehavin': addiction has become an all-purpose excuse, *The Sciences* 29(4) (1989): 14–21.

13. J. Wallace, Addict and institution, *The Sciences* 30(1) (1990): 11–12.

14. E. P. Noble, Alcoholic fathers and their sons: neuropsychological, electro-psychological, personality and family correlates, in C. R. Cloninger and H. Begleiter eds., *Banbury Report 33: Molecular Genetics and Biology of Alcoholism* (Cold Spring Harbor, N.Y.: Cold Spring Harbor Laboratory Press, 1990).

Glossary

AA. Alcoholics Anonymous, *q.v.*

abusable substance. Any substance that can be misused or excessively used. Illegal and prescription drugs are abusable, as are inhalants and alcoholic beverages.

acetaldehyde. A colorless liquid that is an intermediate substance formed in the metabolism of alcohol.

acetaldehyde dehydrogenase. A natural enzyme in the body that aids in the conversion of dopamine aldehyde to dopamine acid, and of acetaldehyde to carbon dioxide and water.

acetylcholine. A neurotransmitter at synapses in the central and parasympathetic nervous systems. It causes the heart to slow and is involved in learning and memory.

acetyltransferase. An enzyme that transfers an acetyl group from one compound to another.

acquired immunodeficiency syndrome. See *AIDS.*

addiction. A physiological or psychological dependence upon a substance such as alcohol.

adenine. Along with guanine, one of the two purine bases, found in DNA and RNA.

adenosine monophosphate. A nucleotide involved in energy metabolism and nucleotide synthesis. Important in the "second-messenger" system of neuronal action. Also called cAMP, or cyclic AMP.

adenylate cyclase. An enzyme that hastens the conversion of adenosine triphosphate (ATP) to cyclic AMP and inorganic phosphates.

adjunct. An additional treatment, substance, or procedure, administered to facilitate the performance or increase the safety of the primary treatment.

adrenal gland. Either of two ductless glands, located on top of the kidneys, consisting of the cortex and the medulla. The cortex secretes cortisol and androgens, and is regulated by the pituitary gland. The medulla manufactures the catecholamines epinephrine and norepinephrine.

agonist. A substance that binds to a receptor and produces a physiological effect.

AIDS. Acquired immunodeficiency syndrome, a disease transmitted sexually or through the exchange of blood; for example, when IV drug abusers share needles. Not fatal of itself, it weakens the immune system and results in the contraction of other, often terminal, diseases. The causative agent is believed to be the retrovirus HTLV-3.

Al-Anon. An international self-help organization, founded in 1951, for the families and associates of alcoholics. It is based on the Twelve-Step Alcoholics Anonymous program, and offers help to its members through discussion and information services.

Alateen. An international self-help organization for the children of alcoholics.

alcogene. A specific gene that may lead to alcoholism.

alcohol dehydrogenase. An enzyme that converts alcohols to acetaldehydes.

alcoholic. A person suffering from alcoholism, *q.v.*

Alcoholics Anonymous. An international self-help group, founded in 1935, whose members are alcoholics who want to stop drinking. Their program emphasizes psychological and spiritual resources in overcoming alcoholism.

alcoholism. A severe dependence on excessive amounts of alcohol; a chronic illness with a slow onset that can occur at any age. It is a biogenetic disease in at least 50 percent of the alcoholic population.

aldehyde dehydrogenase. An enzyme that metabolizes aldehydes.

aldehyde reductase. An enzyme that metabolizes dopamine and norepinephrine to their acidic form.

alkaloid. An organic basic substance found in plants, or a synthetic substance with similar structure that has pharmacological uses. Includes caffeine, morphine, nicotine and TIQs.

allele. An alternate or abnormal form of a gene.

alpha-endorphin. An opiate-like peptide, existing naturally within the body, that has pain-relieving and behavioral effects. It is less potent than beta-endorphin and comprises the amino acid sequence 61 to 76 in the beta-lipotropin molecule.

alpha-methyl-para-tyrosine (Alpha-MpT). A substance that reduces norepinephrine in the brain by preventing its synthesis.

amino acid. An organic chemical compound that contains both an amine group and a carboxyl group; the unit of structure of proteins. They exist in both essential (not produced in the body in sufficient amounts) and nonessential (synthesized sufficiently in the body) varieties.

amino acid decarboxylase. The enzyme that facilitates the removal of carboxyl from an amino acid.

amino acid loading. A technique in which large amounts of amino acids, which function as synthetic precursors to natural neurotransmitters in the brain, are administered.

amino-peptidase. An inactivating enzyme that metabolizes enkephalins.

anal stage. In psychoanalytic theory, the second social and sexual stage of development, occurring between one and three years of age, in which the infant derives most of his or her pleasurable stimulation from its bowel movements.

Antabuse. Brand name for disulfiram, an antioxidant used in aversion therapy to create an aversion to alcohol. It builds up acetaldehyde, leading to severe nausea and potentially fatal side effects when alcohol is consumed.

antagonist. A substance that binds to a receptor, has no effect on the receptor itself, but prevents the bonding of an agonist to that receptor.

antibody. An immunoglobulin produced in response to an antigen, such as a bacteria or a virus, that inhibits the growth of or destroys the antigen.

arginine vasopressin. A pituitary neuropeptide involved in maintaining tolerance to alcohol and other addictive drugs such as morphine. It is also involved in maintaining water balance.

arrhythmias. Irregularities in heartbeat; can be lethal.

ascorbic acid. Vitamin C, a white crystalline vitamin essential to the formation of tissues in teeth, bone, cartilage, and skin. Beneficial in reducing the effects of withdrawal.

autonomic. Pertaining to that part of the nervous system that regulates vital involuntary functions. It has two divisions: sympathetic and parasympathetic.

aversion therapy. A form of behavior therapy, used in the treatment of conditions such as alcoholism, in which a painful or unpleasant stimulus is administered prior to the intake of alcohol in order to suppress craving.

aversive conditioning. See *aversion therapy.*

axon. A neuronal process that conducts impulses away from the cell body.

BALB. A strain of mice that has been bred to prefer alcohol to water until they are eight weeks old, at which time they change their preference to water.

barbiturate. A derivative of barbituric acid, used for sedative or hypnotic effect.

base. An aromatic, nitrogen-containing molecule, such as purine or pyrimidine. The purine bases include adenine and guanine; the pyrmidine bases include uracil, thymine and cytosine.

benzodiazepine. Any of a group of active central nervous system depressants, such as chlordiazepoxide and lorazepam, which are used as sedatives.

betacarboline. A natural brain substance that causes anxiety-like states.

beta-lipotropin. A polypeptide hormone containing 91 amino acids, chiefly serving as a prohormone for the endorphins and enkepahlins.

beta-endorphin. An opioid peptide secreted by the cells of the hypothalamus and pituitary gland. It acts as a pain reliever and has behavioral effects, and comprises the amino acid sequence 61 to 91 of the beta-lipotropin molecule.

bichloride. A compound in which two atoms of chlorine are combined with another group or element.

bind. In chemistry, to combine or unite molecules.

biochemical. Pertaining to the chemistry of living organisms and life processes.

biofeedback therapy. A process in which a person is provided with visual and auditory stimuli and learns, through trial and error, to control functions previously thought to be involuntary.

biogenetic. Related to biological and hereditary factors.

blackouts. Periods of unconsciousness that occur in moderate to severe alcoholics.

blood/brain barrier. Semipermeable walls of capillaries in the central nervous system that control the passage of substances from the blood into brain cells.

bonding. In chemistry, the combining of two or more elements or molecules to form a new molecule. Also, the joining of an agonist or antagonist to a receptor.

brain wave. Within the brain, a rhythmical fluctuation of electrical potential.

bromocriptine. An ergot alkaloid that inhibits lactation and stimulates ovulation. This substance stimulates dopamine receptors and can reduce drug hunger.

buffer fluid. A fluid that acts to control the hydrogen-ion concentration (pH) of a solution by absorbing hydrogen ions when a basic substance is added, or releasing them when an acid is added.

bulimia. An eating disorder characterized by binge eating followed by self-induced catharsis.

buprenorphine. A synthetic derivative of thebaine, used as a pain reliever and local anesthetic. It has mixed agonist/antagonist opiate-like effects.

buspirone. A tranquilizer and anti-anxiety drug.

C3H. A strain of mice divided in their preference for alcohol and water.

C57BL. A strain of black mice that has been bred to prefer alcohol over water.

CAI cluster cells. Groups of cells found in the hippocampus that respond to cocaine stimulation.

capillaries. Minute blood vessels that connect the arterioles to the venules.

carbohydrates. Sugars, starches and cellulose; organic compounds composed of carbon, hydrogen and oxygen.

carboxypeptidase. Enkephalinase, an enzyme that metabolizes enkephalin.

carboxypeptidase B. An enzyme that converts proenkephalin, a precursor, to enkephalin.

carrier system. A capillary component that assists in carrying amino acids or peptides across the blood/brain barrier.

catechol-O-methyltransferase. An enzyme that metabolizes dopamine and other biogenetic amines, or catecholamines.

catecholamines. Substances that contain the catechol function. Both dopamine and norepinephrine are catecholamines.

catheter. A tubular instrument for the passage of fluid from or into a body cavity.

caudate. Pertaining to the nucleus caudatus, one of the basal ganglia in the cerebral cortex, and part of the corpus striatum. This region contains very high amounts of dopamine and dopamine receptors.

cell body. That part of the neuron that manufactures messenger and control substances.

centrifuge. A machine that uses centrifugal force to separate particles in suspension in a fluid.

cerebellum. A dorsal portion of the brain that functions to coordinate skeletal muscular activity and voluntary muscular movement.

cerebral cortex. The gray, convoluted surface of the hemispheres of the brain.

cerebrospinal fluid. The fluid produced in the ventricles of the brain. It circulates through the central nervous system, maintains uniform osmotic pressure, and assists in the metabolic exchange of materials.

cesium fluoride. A chemical that prevents the metabolism of alcohol.

chemical messenger. A neurotransmitter substance involved in neuronal communication.

chloral hydrate. A crystalline substance used as a hypnotic.

chlordiazepoxide. An antianxiety agent.

chromatography. A type of analysis of mixtures in which a column of powder selectively absorbs parts of the solution passed through it, in sharply defined, colored bands.

chromium. Cr, element number 24, a lustrous metal. Traces of chromium are essential to higher animals. Chromium induces insulin secretion and increases tryptophan penetration into the brain.

chromosomes. Structures in the nucleus of animal cells containing linear threads of DNA that transmit genetic information.

circadian rhythms. Certain biological activities that occur in regular cycles of 24 hours.

cirrhosis. An inflammation that occurs in the interspaces of the tissues of the liver.

cloning. The process of asexually creating one or more cells or organisms from a single cell or organism. The resultant clone will be genetically identical to the parent.

co-factor. A heat-stable substance that allows enzymes to function properly.

cocagene. A specific gene that may lead to cocaine addiction.

CODA. A self-help organization similar to Al-Anon whose members generally are co-dependents of alcoholics.

codeine. A white, crystalline, bitter alkaloid; an opiate, used as a pain reliever, sedative, or hypnotic, or to inhibit coughing.

co-dependent. An individual who is as dependent on an alcoholic as the alcoholic is dependent on alcohol.

cognitive. Relating to mental processes and cognition, including thinking, perceiving, and remembering.

compulsive. Pertaining to a strong, often irresistible impulse to perform an act against one's will.

conductance. The ability to transmit a nerve impulse.

congenital. Present at birth.

convulsant. An agent that causes convulsions.

convulsion. An involuntary contraction of the voluntary muscles.

corpus striatum. A mass of gray and white tissue beneath the cerebral cortex, in front of and lateral to the thalamus in each hemisphere.

craving. A strong desire for something, including alcohol, drugs, food, or behavioral activities.

cross-tolerance. The phenomena that occur when one drug reduces the effects of a second drug.

cyclic AMP. Cyclic adenosine monophosphate, cAMP, a cyclic nucleotide involved in the action of many hormones.

cystic fibrosis. An autosomal recessive disorder that results in sterility, deafness, ocular damage, and chronic broncho-pneumonia.

cytosine. 4-amino-2-hydroxypyrimidine, one of the four bases found in DNA.

diazepam binding inhibitor. Known as DBI, this natural substance causes an anxiety-like state.

dipeptidylaminopeptidase. An enzyme involved in the breakdown of neuropeptides, including enkephalins.

disease concept. The theory that alcoholism is a chronic illness, the onset of which is influenced by biochemical sensitivities, and psychological and social factors.

DNA. Deoxyribonucleic acid, the substance in the chromosomes that carries the genetic code for the production of genes.

dopamine. A neurotransmitter in the central nervous system and an intermediate in the synthesis of norepinephrine. It is made from amino acids and sends messages that increase well-being, aggression, alertness, and sexual excitement.

dopamine acid. The final product of dopamine, after it is converted to dopamine aldehyde.

dopamine aldehyde. Formed in the brain from dopamine, it is an intermediate in the synthesis of dopamine acid.

dopamine beta-hydroxylase. The enzyme that aids in the conversion of dopamine to norepinephrine.

dopaminergic. Pertaining to the dopamine system.

double-blind study. Clinical methodology in which neither the patient nor the experimental administrator is aware of the contents of the administered substances being tested.

D-phenylalanine. An alternate form of an essential amino acid; inhibits enkephalinase.

dry drunk. Anxiety, irritability, or aggressiveness occurring in an alcoholic who has deliberately refrained from drinking for a long period.

duodenum. The first division in the small intestine, about 10–12 inches in length.

dynorphin. A class of neuropeptides that are made from pro-dynorphin peptides. They are opioid peptides that regulate the immune response, raise the pain threshold, stimulate feelings of well-being, regulate sexual and mental activity, and reduce compulsive behavior.

dynorphin convertase. The enzyme that converts the precursor protein to dynorphin.

dysphoria. A feeling of discomfort or unpleasantness.

efficacy. Relating to a drug or treatment, the maximum ability of a drug or treatment to produce a result, regardless of dosage. Compare potency.

electroencephalograph. A device that records the electric potentials of the brain. It consists of electrodes that are attached to the skull, an amplifier, and a write-out device.

electrolyte. A substance that dissociates into ions in solution, thus becoming capable of conducting electricity.

electron paramagnetic resonance. A condition of a molecule in which the electrons could occupy several orbitals. Electrons move between these orbitals, making the structural formula of the molecule the average of the possible structures.

electrophoresis. A technique used to separate and identify serum proteins and other physiological substances.

electrophoretic. Relating to the movement of particles in an electric field toward one pole or another.

electrophysiological. Relating to electrical phenomena associated with the physiological process, such as that which occurs in neurons.

emetine. A substance that causes vomiting.

enabler. A person who, often unwittingly, supports an alcoholic's drinking habit.

end bulb. A structure located at the end of the axon. Its outer surface constitutes one wall of the synapse.

endocrine. Pertaining to an organ, gland, or structure that secretes a substance, such as a hormone, into the gland or lymph, producing a specific effect on another organ or part.

endogenous. Produced within or caused by factors within the organism.

endo-oligopeptidase A. An enzyme that destroys natural peptides.

endopeptidase. A peptidase enzyme capable of acting on any peptide linkage in a peptide chain.

endoplasmic recticulum. An extensive network of membrane-enclosed tubules in the cytoplasm of cells that functions in the synthesis of proteins and lipids and in the transport of these metabolites within the cell.

endorphin. Any of a group of endogenous neuropeptide brain substances that bind to opiate receptors in various areas of the brain. They are involved in craving behavior, pain, sexual function, and other brain and systemic functions.

endorphin convertase. The activating enzyme of endorphin.

endorphinergic. Pertaining to the endorphin system.

enkephalin. Either of two naturally occurring pentapeptides (methionine or leucine) in the brain, that have potent opiate-like effects and serve as neurotransmitters.

enkephalin convertase. An enzyme that converts enkephalin to an active state.

enkephalinase. Carboxypeptidase A, an enzyme that destroys enkephalins.

enzyme. A protein that acts as a catalyst to speed up certain chemical changes in the body, yet itself remains unchanged.

ephedrine. A drug used as a central nervous system stimulant.

epinephrine. A hormone that stimualtes the nervous system and increases blood pressure and cardiac output. It also increases metabolic activities, such as glucose release. Also called adrenaline.

esophagus. A tube connecting the mouth with the stomach. Part of the digestive system.

estrogen. One of a group of hormonal steroid compounds that promote the development of female secondary sex characteristics.

ethanol. Alcohol.

fallopian tube. One of the tubes leading from either side of the uterus to the ovary.

feedback loop. The process whereby the effects of a circulating hormone regulate the release of a target hormone.

fetal alcohol syndrome. The mental retardation or physical deformity of a fetus due to alcohol consumption by the mother during pregnancy.

fetus. The unborn young. For humans, it represents the product of conception from the end of the eighth week to the moment of birth.

firing rate. The speed or rate at which a neuron discharges to cause an effect.

fluidity. The quality of changing readily, shifting, not being fixed or rigid.

folic acid. An orange-yellow crystalline compound, found in green leaves, mushrooms, yeast, and some animal tissues. It is part of the vitamin-B complex and also known as vitamin B_{12}.

formaldehyde. A gas used as an antiseptic or disinfectant or as a fixative for slides. An aldehyde, it can combine with biogenic amines to form TIQs.

GABA transaminase. The enzyme that metabolizes GABA.

gamma aminobutyric acid. Known as GABA, an inhibitory neurotransmitter that reduces anxiety and induces an increased heart rate, increased blood pressure, tremors, and convulsions, especially during withdrawal. It is made from glutamic acid.

gastritis. An inflammation of the stomach.

gastroenterologist. A physician who specializes in diseases of the stomach and intestine.

gel. A jelly or the semisolid form of a colloidal solution. Also, the act of forming a gel.

gene. The unit of heredity responsible for transmission of a characteristic to the offspring. It occupies a specific place on the chromosome.

genetic. Pertaining to heredity, rather than being environmentally caused.

genetic predisposition. An inheritable characteristic; for example, the risk of acquiring a disease such as alcoholism.

germicidal. Refers to an agent destructive to germs or microbes.

glucogene. A specific gene which may lead to carbohydrate bingeing.

glucose. Sugar, the principal source of energy for man and many other animals.

glutamate dehydrogenase. An enzyme believed to be responsible for both the biosynthesis and the catabolism, or breakdown, of glutamate.

glutamic acid. The building block of GABA. One of the amino acids, it also is responsible for aiding in digestion.

glutamic acid decarboxylase. The activating enzyme of GABA.

glutamine. A substance derived from the combination of glutamic acid and ammonia. It is present in proteins in blood and other tissues, is a source of urinary ammonia, and can also increase GABA in the brain.

glycine. A nonessential amino acid which functions as an inhibitory neurotransmitter in the central nervous system. It is used as a gastric antacid and dietary supplement.

grand mal. A severe epileptic seizure marked by a sudden loss of consciousness immediately followed by generalized convulsions.

guanine. Along with adenine, one of the two purine bases, found in DNA and RNA.

hallucination. A sense perception (sight, touch, sound, smell, or taste) that has no basis in external stimuli.

hallucinosis. A mental disorder marked by hallucinations.

haloperidol. A major tranquilizer used especially in the management of mental disorders. It blocks dopamine receptors.

hepatitis. An inflammation of the liver.

hepatosis. Any functional disorder of the liver.

heroin. An alkaloid prepared from morphine. It is prohibited in the United States due to its addictive nature.

hippocampus. An important functional component of the limbic system.

histamine. An amine produced by the decomposition of histidine and released in allergic reactions that dilate blood vessels and reduce blood pressure, stimulate gastric sensations, and cause contraction of the uterus.

hormone. The chemical produced by an endocrine gland that affects the functions of specifically receptive organs or tissues when transported to them by the bodily fluids. Examples include insulin and endorphins.

Huntington's disease. An autosomal dominant disorder, beginning between ages 30 and 50, causing involuntary, spasmodic movement of the face and extremities and a gradual loss of mental faculties.

hydrocinnamic acid. A breakdown product of D-phenylalanine. It inhibits the enzyme enkephalinase.

hydroxyl. A group consisting of one atom of oxygen and one of hydrogen. As an ion, it has a negative charge.

hypoglycemia. Deficiency of glucose concentration in the blood, which may lead to nervousness, hypothermia, headache, confusion, and sometimes convulsions and coma.

hypothalamus. Part of the limbic structure of the brain that is involved in ingestive behavior.

immune response. A defense function of the body that produces antibodies to destroy invading antigens and malignancies.

in vitro. A biological reaction occurring in a laboratory apparatus.

in vivo. A biological reaction occurring in a living organism.

inhibitory. Tending to stop or slow a process. A substance that suppresses a nerve impulse is inhibitory.

insulin. A naturally occurring hormone that acts to regulate the metabolism of glucose. It lowers blood glucose levels and promotes transport and entry of glucose into muscle cells and other tissues. Inadequate insulin results in hyperglycemia and other conditions.

ion. An atom or molecule that has gained or lost one or more electrons and acquired a positive or negative charge.

kelatorphin. A potent inhibitor of the enzymes that destroy or break down enkephalins.

Korsakoff's psychosis. A form of amnesia often seen in chronic alcoholics, characterized by a loss of short-term memory and an inability to learn new skills. Often accompanied by Wernicke's syndrome.

lactic acid. A syrupy, odorless, and colorless liquid obtained by the action of the lactic acid bacillus on milk sugar; a caustic in concentrated form, used internally to prevent gastrointestinal fermentation.

lateral ventricle. The cavity in the cerebral hemisphere that contains cerebrospinal fluid.

L-dopa. 3,4-Dihydroxyphenylalanine, an amino acid that is the precursor to dopamine.

leucine. A white, crystalline amino acid needed for optimal growth in infants and nitrogen equilibrium in adults. It cannot be synthesized by the body and is obtained by the hydrolysis of protein during pancreatic digestion.

leucine-enkephalin. A potent natural opioid peptide of the enkephalin type that reacts at opiate receptors, specifically the delta type.

leucocytes. White blood cells.

Levorphanol. A pain reliever similar in action to morphine.

Librium. A drug that is known to reduce anxiety. It acts on the benzodiazepine receptor site.

limbic system. A group of structures within the rhinencephalon, that part of the brain once thought to be devoted to smell, which is associated with various emotions such as anger, fear, sexual arousal, pleasure, and sadness. The structures of the limbic system are the cingulate gyrus, the isthmus, the hippocampal gyrus, the uncas, and the hippocampus.

locus ceruleus. A shallow depression in the floor of the fourth ventricle of the brain.

longitudinal studies. Studies that deal with the growth or change in individuals or groups over a period of time.

L-phenylalanine. The precursor to L-dopa.

LSD. Lysergic acid diethylamide, a serotonin antagonist that may produce visual hallucinations and precipitate psychoses. It is occasionally used in the treatment of chronic alcoholism.

lymphocytes. White blood cells that contain dense chromatin in a sharply defined nuclear membrane, and comprise 22 to 28 percent of a normal adult's leukocytes.

male-limited alcoholism. Classified as Type II alcoholism, it comprises 25 percent of all male alcoholics. It is a genetically determined, antisocial personality disorder. Associated with criminality, it is considered a severe form of alcoholism with an early age of onset.

marker. A fingerprint, either electrophysiological, biochemical, or genetic, of a particular disease state.

melatonin. A hormone secreted in the bloodstream by the pineal gland. It inhibits numerous endocrine functions, and reduces alcohol-craving behavior.

membrane. A thin layer of tissue that covers a surface, lines a cavity, or divides a space; for example, neuronal walls.

mescaline. A substance that is related chemically to epinephrine and causes heart palpitations, pupillary dilation, and anxiety. Taken orally, it produces visual hallucinations. It is derived from a plant called peyote.

metabolite. A substance produced by metabolic action, or one necessary for a metabolic process.

metabolize. The chemical process that takes place in living organisms, resulting in the generation of energy, growth, the elimination of wastes, and other daily functions as they relate to the distribution of nutrients in the blood after digestion.

methadone. An oral narcotic and opiate used to reduce pain and as a heroin substitute in addicted individuals.

methionine. A naturally occurring amino acid that is a necessary component of the diet, furnishing both methyl groups and sulfur necessary for normal metabolism.

methionine-enkephalin. A potent natural opioid peptide that interacts with opiate receptors, specifically of the delta type.

methyl-pyrazole. A substance that inhibits the activity of the enzyme alcohol dehydrogenase and prevents the conversion of alcohol into aldehyde.

methyl salsolinol. A metabolite of the TIQ salsolinol.

microsomes. Fragments of endoplasmic reticulum formed after disruption and centrifugation of cells.

microtubules. Slender, tubular structures, found in the cytoplasmic ground substance of nearly all cells. They are responsible for maintaining cell shape and form the spindle fibers of mitosis. In the neuron, the tubules are involved in the transport of neurotransmitters to the end bulb vesicles for storage and later release across the synapse.

milieu-limited alcoholism. Classified as Type I alcoholism, this is the major form of alcoholism, with a later age of onset than Type II male-limited alcoholism. It involves both females and males; environment and genetics both play a role. A mild form of alcoholism, it has a low association with criminality.

mitochondrion. A part of the cell that contains its own DNA and ribosomes, replicated independently, and synthesizes some of its own proteins. It is the principal source of cellular energy.

monoamine oxidase. An enzyme involved in the metabolism of neurotransmitters such as serotonin and catecholamines.

monoamine oxidase inhibitor. These drugs inhibit monoamine oxidase and exert an anti-anxiety effect, especially serving to counter anxiety related to phobias.

monoamines. Amines containing one amine group derived from food and carried by the blood into the brain. Compare *neuropeptides.*

morphine. The principal and most active alkaloid of opium, used as a narcotic pain reliever.

morphinomimetic. Refers to a substance or chemical entity that acts like morphine.

morphogene. A specific gene assumed to cause morphine craving.

mutation. A change in genetic material that is permanent and transmissible.

nalorphine. An antagonist to morphine and related narcotics used in the diagnosis of narcotic addiction.

naloxone. A narcotic antagonist; also used as an antidote to narcotic overdosage.

naltrexone. A narcotic antagonist, having the trade name Trexane, used in the long-term detoxification of opiate addicts. It acts to block the readministration of heroin. It is an adjunct to relapse prevention.

nanomoles. Near-dimensionless units of one billionth of a mole, equal to one billionth of the number of carbon atoms in 12 grams of pure carbon, or 602,205,000,000,000. Nanomoles are used to measure the amount of molecules of a substance. One nanomole consists of 1,000 picamoles.

neurobiologist. A specialist in the biology of the nervous system.

neurochemistry. The branch of neurology dealing with the chemistry of the nervous system.

neurocognitive. Pertaining to cognitive or neural functions.

neuron. A nerve cell.

neuronal system. Linked nerve cells that send messages to each other and receive messages from each other. The interaction of neurons determines mental and emotional conditions.

neuropeptides. Neurotransmitters made from giant linked amino acids called peptides. They are inactive in this giant form, but are broken down into smaller active neuropeptides in the endoplasmic reticulum.

neurophysiological. Of or pertaining to the function of the nervous system.

neurotransmission. The process by which a substance is released from the axon terminal of a presynaptic neuron on excitation, diffusing across the synaptic gap to either excite or inhibit the target cell.

neurotransmitter-receptor complex. An entity which consists of a particular neurotransmitter molecule bound to a specific receptor system. GABA and one of its receptors would be an example.

nonalcoholics. Those who are not addicted to alcohol, and are not at risk for the future.

norepinephrine. A neurotransmitter, made from dopamine, that increases feelings of well-being and decreases compulsive behavior. An excess amount may cause anxiety or, in withdrawal patients, tremors.

nucleic acids. Substances of high molecular weight, found in the chromosomes, nuclei, mitochondria, and cytoplasm of all cells. DNA and RNA are nucleic acids.

nucleotide. A component of DNA or RNA, composed of a sugar, a nitrogenous base, and a phosphate group.

nucleus. The rounded mass of protoplasm within the cytoplasm of a cell, containing the chromosomes.

nucleus accumbens. An area in the brain that is the major site of reward. Dopamine released in this area leads to a feeling of well-being.

nutritional deficiency. In the nervous system, a state of imbalance of amino acids or other substances necessary for normal functioning. One result of a nutritional deficiency of amino acids in the brain, for example, may be a lack of essential chemical messengers.

O-methylation. A type of chemical reaction that results in the destruction of biological amines, such as dopamine or norepinephrine.

omnipotentiality. The quality of being all-powerful, of having infinite capacity.

opiate. A narcotic drug that contains opium, its derivatives, or any of several semisynthetic or synthetic drugs with opium-like activity. Opiates cause sleep, the relief of pain, and other pharmacological responses.

opioid peptides. Any substance that contains more than one linked amino acid, possessing the ability to interact with one or more neural opiate receptors. These substances are usually found in the brain and act as hormones.

oral stage. In psychoanalytic theory, the first social and sexual stage of an infant's development, when the mouth is the focus of the libido. Eating, sexual, and aggressive drives are satisfied by chewing, sucking, and biting.

orotic acid. 6-Carboxuracil, a pyrimidine synthesized in the cell.

P300 wave. A specific wave form that is characteristic of an individual's response to visual stimuli. When reduced, it indicates risk of alcoholism.

para-chlorophenylalanine. A chemical that prevents the manufacture of the neurotransmitter serotonin and, to a lesser degree, norepinephrine.

parasympathetic nervous system. A division of the autonomic nervous system.

pargyline. An antihypertensive substance that prevents the activity of the enzyme monoamine oxidase which is involved in the breakdown of neurotransmitters.

Parkinson's disease. A slowly progressive, degenerative neurological disease characterized by resting tremor, shuffling gait, forward flexion of the trunk, and muscle rigidity and weakness.

pentapeptide. A peptide having five linked amino acids, such as enkephalin.

peptides. A compound composed of two or more amino acids joined by peptide bonds.

Ph factor. The negative log of the percentage of hydrogen in a solution. It represents the relative activity of a solution. Seven is neutral, while a lower value is acidic and a higher one is basic.

phallic stage. In psychoanalytic theory, the third social and sexual stage in a young child's development, after the oral and anal stages. Interest in the child's own sex organs, and in those of others, replaces the earlier focusing on oral or anal pleasure.

phenobarbital. An anticonvulsant, sedative, and hypnotic.

phenylalanine. A naturally occurring amino acid essential for optimal growth in infants and for nitrogen equilibrium in human adults.

phenylalanine hydroxylase. An enzyme that converts the amino acid phenylamine to tyrosine, a precursor to the neurotransmitter dopamine.

physical dependence. A condition in which the body requires a particular agent for normal operation, following chronic abuse of that agent, or a similar one.

pilocarpine. A cholinergic alkaline that is used to contract the pupil.

pineal gland. A small, somewhat flattened, cone-shaped structure, suspended by a stalk in the epithalamus, that secretes the hormone melatonin.

pituitary gland. A gland, located in the brain, that secretes numerous hormones, including arginine vasopressin, prolactin, and beta-endorphin.

placebo. An inactive substance or treatment without therapeutic value, given to satisfy a patient's need for treatment. A placebo is also used in the control group of studies which test medicinal or other treatments.

placenta. A highly vascular fetal organ through which the fetus absorbs oxygen, nutrients, and other substances, and secretes carbon dioxide and other wastes.

poppy plant. One of numerous large-flowered herbs. Opium is derived from one type of poppy plant.

postsynaptic. Distal to or occurring beyond the synapse. Compare *presynaptic.*

precursor. In biological processs, a substance from which another substance, usually more active or mature, is formed.

presynaptic. Situated or occurring proximal to a synapse. Compare *postsynaptic.*

prohibition. In reference to alcohol, a period from 1920 to 1933 in which the manufacture, sale, and distribution of alcohol was illegal in the U.S.

prohormone. The precursor of a hormone, such as a steroid, that is later converted into a hormone by peripheral metabolism.

prolactin. A hormone secreted by the pituitary gland that prepares for and sustains lactation.

propiomelanocortin. A protein, the precursor of endorphin.

proteins. Any of a group of complex organic substances containing carbon, hydrogen, oxygen, nitrogen, and sulfur. They consist of alpha-amino acids connected by peptide links, and serve as enzymes and hormones, among other things, and are involved in oxygen transport and electron transport.

psychoactive drug. A pharmacologic agent that can change mood, behavior, cognitive processes, or mental tension.

psychoanalytic theory. The theory of psychology and mental development established by Sigmund Freud. See *anal stage, oedipal theory, oral stage,* and *phallic stage.*

psychomotor. Pertaining to motor effects of cerebral or psychic activity.

psychosocial. Pertaining to or involving both psychic and social aspects.

pyridoxal-5-phosphate. Vitamin B_6, a co-factor in the production of neurotransmitters.

pyrogallol. 1,2,3-Trihydroxybenzene, an easily oxidized substance formed by heating gallic acid. Its alkaline solutions are used to remove oxygen from air. This substance inhibits the breakdown of neurotransmitters such as dopamine.

receptors. Molecules on the surface of cells that recognize and bond with specific molecules, producing some particular effect.

reserpine. An alkaloid used as an antihypertensive and a tranquilizer.

restriction fragment length polymorphism (AFLP). A genetic technique that is used to detect genes responsible for genetic diseases.

RNA. Ribonucleic acid, a nucleic acid of high molecular weight that synthesizes proteins and acts in cell replication.

satiety. The condition of being satiated, filled to capacity.

scintillation spectrometry. The process of determining the frequency distribution of mass or energy spectra in a scintillation spectrometer.

scopolamine. An anticholinergic alkaloid used as a truth serum.

serotonin. 5-Hydroxytryptophan, an important hormone and neurotransmitter found in many tissues, including the central nervous system.

serum. The clear portion of any liquid, separated from its solid elements.

shakes, the. Delirium tremens, an acute form of abnormal behavior that occurs during alcohol withdrawal, characterized by sweating, anxiety, tremor, confusion, and often by hallucinations.

sodium amytol. A barbiturate drug.

sodium pentothal. A barbiturate drug that induces sleep.

somatopsychic syndrome. Organic brain pathology that induces changes in one's behavior.

spectrophotometer. A device for measuring the amount of colored matter in a substance by the measurement of transmitted light.

spirits. Chemically, the essence of a distilled or extracted substance. In common usage, beverages containing alcohol.

stereospecific. Describes a substance that exhibits structural specificity in interacting with a substrate.

stress. Biological reactions to any adverse physical, emotional, or mental stimulus, internal or external.

striatum. See *corpus striatum*.

substantia nigra region. A broad layer of nerve-containing grey matter found bilaterally throughout the mesencephalon, or upper brain stem. It is believed to synthesize dopamine.

sucrose. A sugar that occurs naturally in most land plants.

sympathetic nervous system. A division of the autonomic nervous system.

synapse. The junction between the processes of two neurons, or between a neuron and an effector organ, across which electrochemical messages are transmitted.

synaptic gap. The area through which neural impulses cross.

temperance movement. A political movement that sought to ban alcohol consumption, and gained strength in the United States prior to World War I, eventually winning a political victory when Prohibition was enacted.

testosterone. The principal male hormone, produced by the testes and modulated by the pituitary gland.

thiamine. Vitamin B_1, a part of the vitamin B-complex, present in the free state in blood plasma.

THP. Abbreviation of tetrahydropapaveroline.

thymine. 2,9-Hydroxy-5-methylpyrimidine, a base in DNA. In RNA, it is replaced by uracil.

TIQ. Abbreviation for tetrahydroisoquinoline.

tolerance. The lessening of the effect of a drug following repeated administration.

transferrin. A protein involved in iron transport, also involved in the activity of dopamine receptors, a marker in alcoholism.

trypsin. An enzyme formed in the intestine; an endopeptidase that acts on peptide linkages containing lysine or arginine.

trypsin-like-endopeptidase. A digestive enzyme that breaks down peptides.

tryptophan. A naturally occurring amino acid that is necessary for human metabolism and is found in proteins.

tryptophan hydroxylase. The enzyme central to the production of serotonin.

Twelve-Step program. The principles set forth by Alcoholics Anonymous to aid members in their personal recovery.

Twelve Traditions. The founding principles of Alcoholics Anonymous.

tyrosine hydroxylase. An enzyme involved in the production of dopamine.

uric acid. A colorless dibasic acid of slight solubility, found in human and animal urine.

vagus nerve. Either of the tenth pair of cranial nerves. Branches extend to the lungs, heart, and stomach.

vas deferens. The duct that conveys semen from the testicles to the seminal vesicles. These tissues contain large numbers of opiate receptors.

Wernicke's syndrome. A manifestation of vitamin B_1 deficiency, that occurs often in alcoholics, causing ocular damage. It is often accompanied by Korsakoff's psychosis.

withdrawal. The process of abstaining from a certain agent to which one is addicted. Also, the symptoms caused by such abstention.

withdrawal syndrome. A behavioral syndrome in alcoholics initiated by cessation of alcohol intake. Symptoms include severe craving, facial and hand tremors, nausea, weakness, and sometimes delirium tremens (see *shakes, the*).

zimelidine. A substance that blocks released serotonin from going back to the neuron for further destruction, and reduces alcohol intake.

Index